HMH | into **Reading**™
Texas

my Book 1

Authors and Advisors

Alma Flor Ada • Kylene Beers • F. Isabel Campoy

Joyce Armstrong Carroll • Nathan Clemens

Anne Cunningham • Martha C. Hougen

Elena Izquierdo • Carol Jago • Erik Palmer

Robert E. Probst • Shane Templeton • Julie Washington

Contributing Consultants

David Dockterman • Mindset Works®

Jill Eggleton

Printed in the U.S.A.

ISBN   978-1-328-76046-3

3 4 5 6 7 8 9 10   0029   27 26 25 24 23 22 21 20 19

4500751308   B C D E F G

HMH

into Reading™
Texas

my **Book** 1

Welcome to myBook!

Do you like to read different kinds of texts for all kinds of reasons? Do you have a favorite genre or author? What can you learn from a video? Do you think carefully about what you read and view?

Here are some tips to get the MOST out of what you read and view:

Set a Purpose. What is the title? What is the genre? What do you want to learn from this text or video? What about it looks interesting to you?

Read and Annotate. As you read, underline and highlight important words and ideas. Make notes about things you want to figure out or remember. What questions do you have? What are your favorite parts? Write them down!

Make Connections. How does the text or video connect to what you already know? To other texts or videos? To your own life or community? Talk to others about your ideas. Listen to their ideas, too.

Wrap It Up! Look back at your questions and annotations. What did you like best? What did you learn? What do you still want to know? How will you find out?

As you read the texts and watch the videos in this book, make sure you get the MOST out of them by using the tips above.

But, don't stop there… Decide what makes you curious, find out more about it, have fun, and never stop learning!

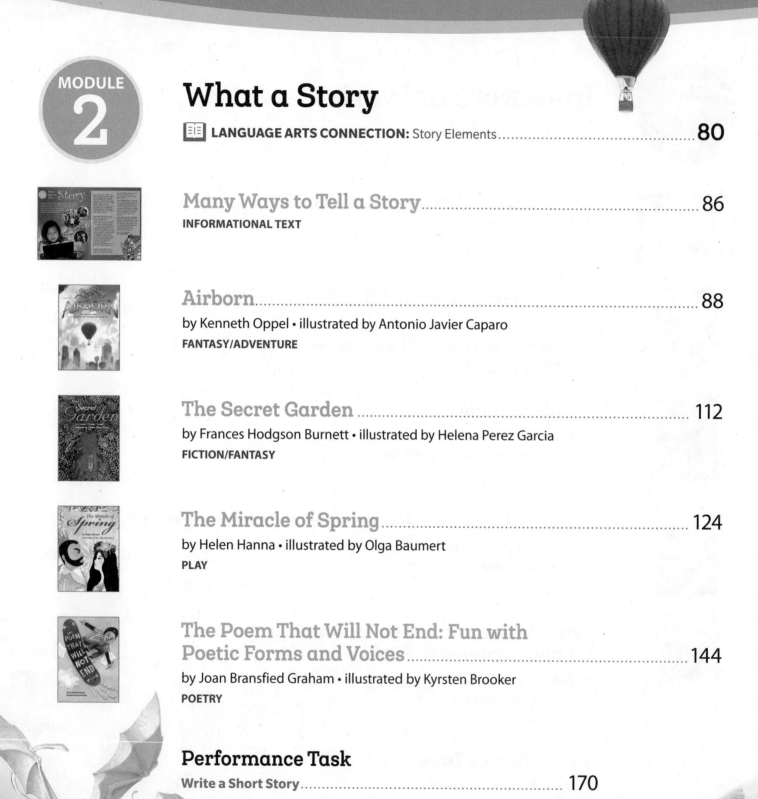

MODULE 2

What a Story

MODULE 5

Project Earth

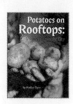

Inventors at Work

"I will not follow where the path may lead, but I will go where there is no path, and I will leave a trail."

—Muriel Strode

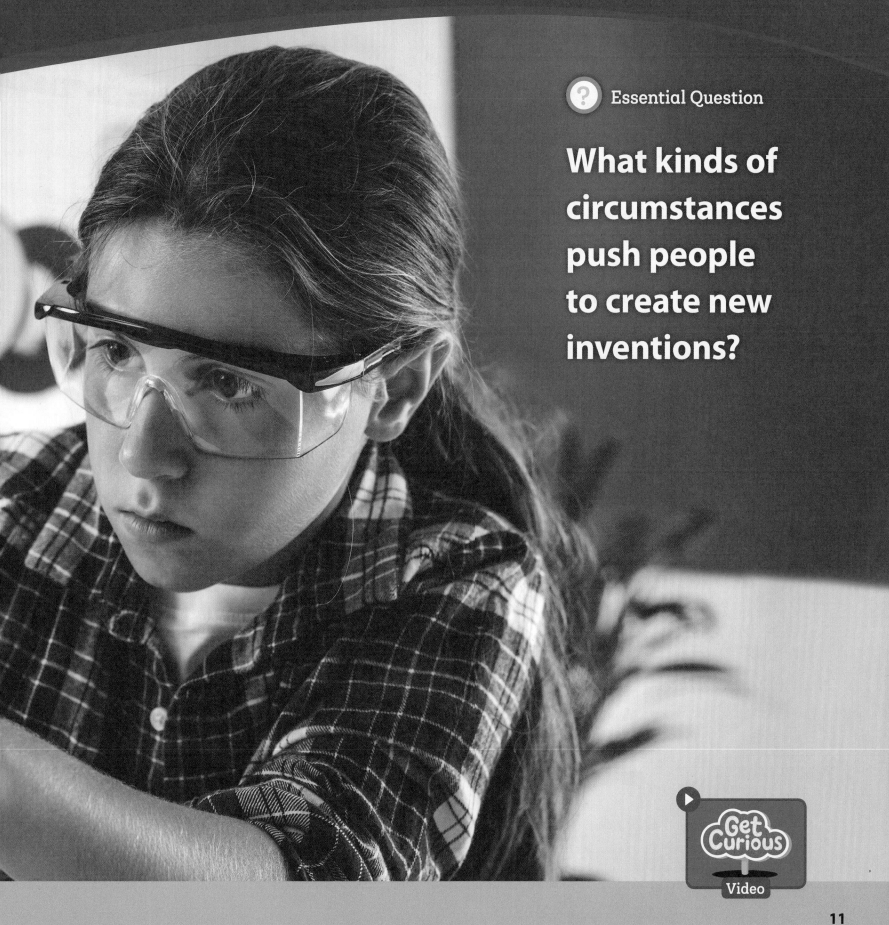

What kinds of circumstances push people to create new inventions?

Get Curious

Video

Words About Inventors

The words in the chart will help you talk and write about the selections in this module. Which words about inventors have you seen before? Which words are new to you?

Add to the Vocabulary Network on page 13 by writing synonyms, antonyms, and related words and phrases for each word about inventors.

After you read each selection in this module, come back to the Vocabulary Network and keep building it. Add more boxes if you need to.

WORD	MEANING	CONTEXT SENTENCE
transcend (verb)	If you transcend a boundary, you go above or beyond it.	Astronauts must transcend limitations and challenges.
excel (verb)	To excel at something is to be very good at it.	Keep practicing and you will excel.
illustrious (adjective)	An illustrious person is famous for his or her achievements.	The illustrious inventor was known around the world.
revere (verb)	If you revere someone, you think very highly of that person.	I revere people whose inventions improve the world.

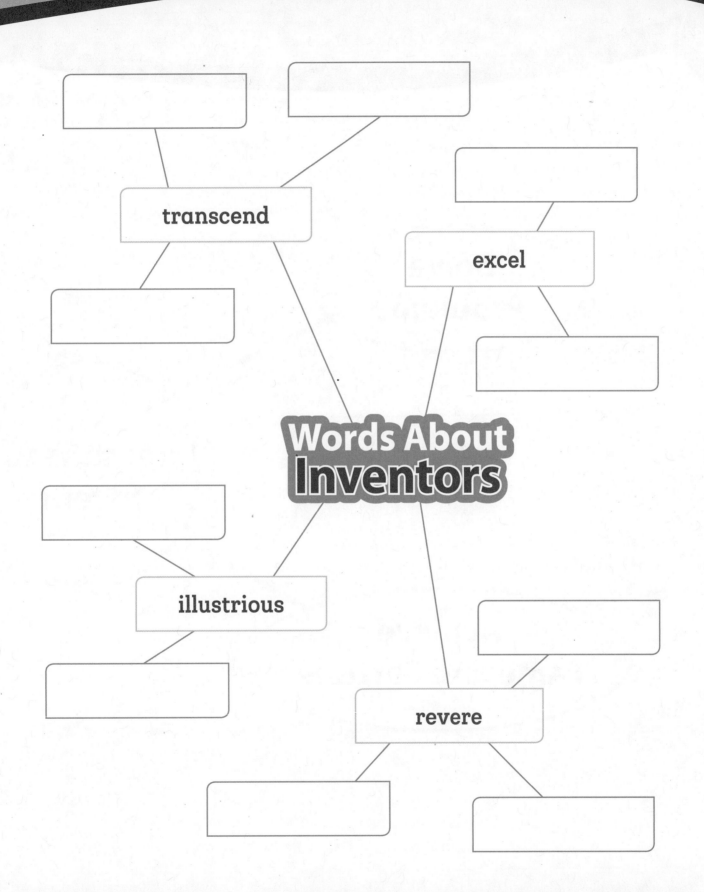

transcend

excel

Words About
Inventors

illustrious

revere

Solve Problems

Reasons to Invent

Achieve Fame and Fortune

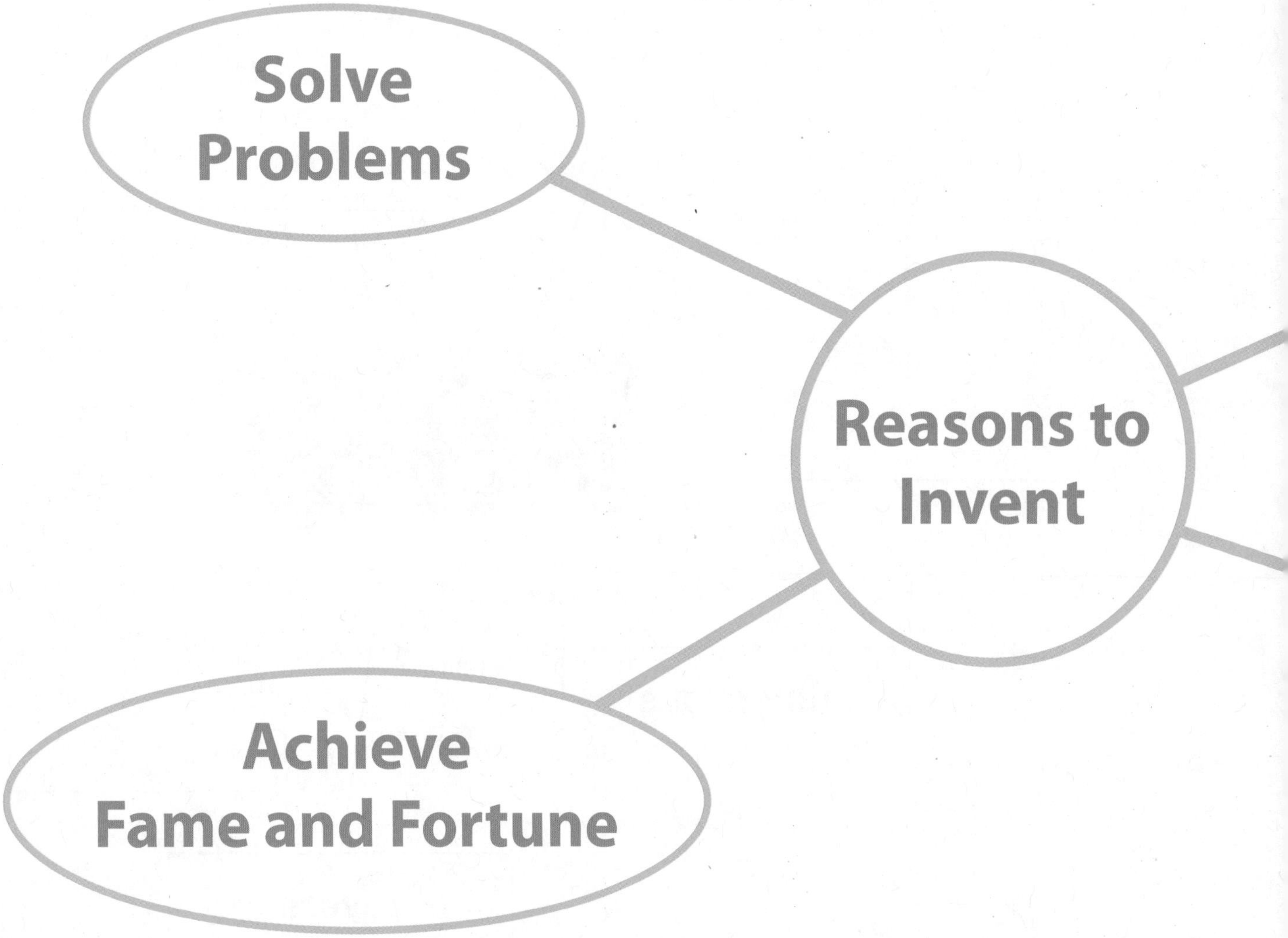

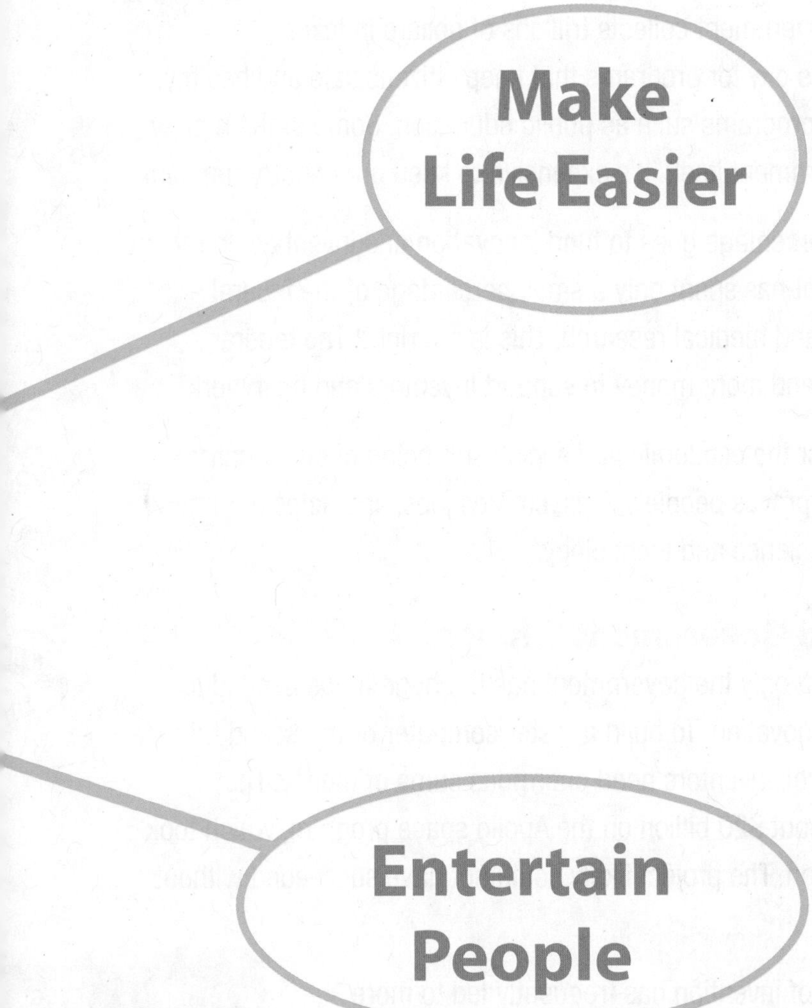

**Make
Life Easier**

**Entertain
People**

Government
Must Fund Inventors

1 Every year, our government collects trillions of dollars in taxes. Most of the funds pay for programs that keep citizens safe and healthy. Other amounts fund programs such as public education. Some of the money goes to run the government itself. It's expensive to keep our country running!

2 Sadly, just a small percentage goes to fund innovation and invention. In recent years, the government has spent only a small percentage of the federal budget on scientific and medical research. This is not right! The federal government must spend more money to support inventors and their work.

3 Invention is crucial for the economic and social well-being of our country. Funding inventors improves people's lives, creates jobs, and helps our nation excel as a leader in science and technology.

Inventors Need Government Support

4 It's often the case that only the government has the huge funds needed to support truly great innovation. To build a faster computer or transcend the barriers of space travel, inventors need enormous sums of money. The government spent about $20 billion on the Apollo space program, which took astronauts to the moon. The project likely could not have succeeded without government help.

5 Government support of invention has frequently led to more innovation. A simple example is memory foam. This "space age" material first helped protect astronauts from collisions. Consequently, many people today now sleep on mattresses made of this squishy, comfortable material. It's even used to add cushion in shoes! Other innovations include devices that help the deaf hear, probes that help doctors look inside arteries, and scratch-resistant eyeglasses.

Inventors Change Our Lives for the Better

6 Government support of innovation has always benefited society. Specifically, government funds have contributed to inventions such as cell phones, electric cars, and the Internet.

7 It's the government's job to improve the lives of its citizens. Inventors do this all the time. Think about the contributions of inventors like the illustrious Thomas Edison. Who can doubt that his light bulb made life easier? Think of computer giants like Bill Gates and Steve Jobs, whom many revere for how they changed the world. The government should be doing all it can to help new inventors follow in their footsteps.

Even Failures Help Inventors Learn

8 Now, some people might feel that invention is too risky a business for the government to be involved in. Yes, most inventors do fail—at first. But failure is a central part of the process. It is how great ideas become great products.

9 In 1967, for example, an Apollo spacecraft caught fire on the launch pad. Three astronauts died. Inventors learned from this terrible accident. They made improvements to the spacecraft. The improvements helped astronauts land on the moon.

Let's Be World Leaders!

10 Innovation in technology and science helps our country maintain its place as a world leader. Each year, thousands of students travel here from other lands. They come to study at our schools and universities.

11 Inventors improve the lives of everyone. Inventors help make our country strong and prosperous. Our government must continue to invest in inventors and their innovations.

Notice & Note
Contrasts and Contradictions

Prepare to Read

GENRE STUDY **Narrative nonfiction** gives factual information and tells true events in a way that reads like a story.

- Narrative nonfiction presents events in sequential, or chronological, order. Ordering events this way helps readers understand what happened and when.

- Texts about events that happened in the past include real people and may include quotations from them, or details about their thoughts and feelings.

- Narrative nonfiction can include visuals, such as illustrations, maps, and diagrams.

SET A PURPOSE **Think about** the title and genre of this text. What do you know about these inventors and their work? What do you want to learn? Write your ideas below.

CRITICAL VOCABULARY

locomotives

chugged

gadgets

phonograph

sputtered

flop

incandescent

cylinder

patents

Meet the Author and Illustrator:
Suzanne Slade and
Jennifer Black Reinhardt

The Inventor's Secret

What Thomas Edison Told Henry Ford

by Suzanne Slade

illustrated by Jennifer Black Reinhardt

1   **Not so long ago** the world was a little slower. A little simpler. And a whole lot quieter.

2   No airplanes roaring overhead. No cars rumbling down roads. No phones ringing in pockets.

3   Then things began to change because of two curious boys, Thomas and Henry.

4   And one secret.

5   Young Thomas got into trouble. A lot.

6   It always started with an "experiment." He just had to see how things worked.

7   Thomas was curious about chemistry. He mixed up colorful potions in his basement, but explosions shook the house night and day.

8   Thomas was curious about locomotives. He got a job as a newsboy, selling papers on a train, but one of his experiments set the baggage car on fire.

9   Most of all, Thomas was curious about electricity, invisible energy that flowed and stopped, sizzled and popped. He tied wires to his cats' tails and rubbed their fur. Sparks flew that day!

locomotives   Locomotives are the engines that make a train go forward.

10   Henry was born sixteen years after Thomas. He got in a heap of trouble, too. He was always doing experiments instead of his chores because he just had to see how things worked.

11   Henry was curious about windup toys. He took his sister's toys apart, but couldn't always get them back together.

12   Henry was curious about the rushing river. He built a dam and waterwheel to catch its energy, but flooded the neighbor's field instead.

13   Most of all, Henry was curious about engines—machines that chugged and purred, hiccupped and whirred. He built a steam engine from a ten-gallon can, tin blades, and a pipe, but it exploded and set the school fence on fire!

chugged   If a machine chugged along, it moved slowly and noisily.

14   As Thomas grew older he dreamed of creating his own inventions, electric gadgets to make life easier. He designed an electric pen so people could rest their weary hands. His sharp pen cut a stencil that made copies. In just one day people could print a pile of copies that would've taken weeks to write by hand.

gadgets Gadgets are small, specialized machines or electronic devices.

15 As Henry grew older he dreamed of creating his own inventions, too: powerful engines to make life easier. When he was twelve he spied something amazing: an engine-powered buggy. He'd never seen a vehicle that wasn't pulled by a horse.

16 Henry sprinted up to the buggy, his mind filled with questions. What powered the engine? How fast did it go? What could it do?

17 The driver boasted the vehicle ran on coal and steam and went about twelve miles an hour. Its engine powered farm equipment and huge saws.

18   The mighty machine got Henry's mind spinning. An engine didn't eat or rest like a horse. It could carry people, mail, and news. Fast!

19   From then on, Henry thought about one thing: making his own vehicle. A car hardworking families could afford. Then folks could go to town anytime, not just the weekly Saturday trip. They could visit faraway places they'd only heard about.

20   But Henry couldn't even repair his broken watch! How would he ever build a car?

21   Then he heard about Thomas's electric pen.

22   What's his secret? Henry wondered. How did he make such a marvelous machine?

23   Later, Thomas created an invention that recorded and played back sounds. When Thomas talked into his new phonograph: "Mary had a little lamb," it talked right back: "Mary had a little lamb." His phonograph could also play music.

phonograph   A phonograph is a machine that plays recorded music or sound.

24   Henry was still dreaming about cars. Everywhere he went, his pockets rattled with metal parts. When he was seventeen he took a job at a machine shop to learn more about engines and machinery. Then, two years later, a farmer hired Henry to operate a new steam engine.

25   Soon Henry began tinkering on a steam engine of his own. He strapped the homemade engine to an old mowing machine. His contraption sputtered along for forty feet, then collapsed.

26   Henry's design was a flop!

27   But everyone was buzzing about Thomas's talking phonograph.

28   *What's his secret?* Henry wondered.

> **sputtered**   If something sputtered, it worked in a rough or uneven way and made popping noises.
>
> **flop**   Something that is a flop is a complete failure.

29   Meanwhile, Thomas was working on an electric light so people could read past dark. After changing his design many times, he created an incandescent light bulb that burned all night!

30   Henry was determined to make his vehicle work, so he took a job at a company that made engines. One day he repaired a fancy engine from England. It had a four-stroke cylinder that burned gas to create power. Fascinated, he built a model of the engine to see how it worked.

31   After that, Henry spent long nights, and Saturdays, working on his car. Friends and coworkers helped, too. When he finally rolled his creation out of his workshop, it had two cylinders for double the power, a three-gallon tank for gas, and four bicycle tires for wheels.

32   Henry's Quadricycle could go up to twenty miles per hour—but it cost a fortune to make. Most people thought his rattling gas buggy was a joke.

---

incandescent   Something that is incandescent gives off a lot of light.

cylinder   A cylinder has circular ends and straight sides. In an engine, a cylinder takes in gas to make other parts move.

33   "Get a horse!" people shouted at Henry.

34   But the whole country was crazy about Thomas's electric light.

35   Henry scratched his head. What's his secret?

36   Still, Henry believed in his dream. Although he knew that other people were working on gas cars, he was determined to make the best. One that was easy to drive. Big enough for families. And most important—a car everyone could afford.

37   While Henry was working on his design, Thomas earned **patents** for over one hundred new inventions.

38   Henry couldn't stand it any longer.

39   He had to find out Thomas's secret!

> **patents**   Patents are legal documents. If you get a patent for an invention, no one else is allowed to make or sell it.

40   So Henry hopped a train in Detroit and chugged six hundred miles to New York City. That's where important businessmen, including Thomas, were gathering for a meeting.

41   Henry did some fast talking and got invited to a big dinner with Thomas as the guest of honor.

42   During dinner, everyone kept talking to Thomas.

43   Henry peered down the large table at the famous inventor.

44   He waited. And waited. And waited.

45   Finally Henry gathered his courage. He moved right next to Thomas and told him he was building a gas car.

46   "Is it a four-cycle engine?" Thomas asked.

47   Henry lit up brighter than any light bulb. He grabbed a menu and started sketching his engine.

48   Thomas fired off question after question.

49   Henry happily answered each one.

50   And that's when it happened.

51   Blue eyes sparkling, Thomas leaned in close to Henry.

52   He banged his fist on the table. "Keep at it!" he shouted.

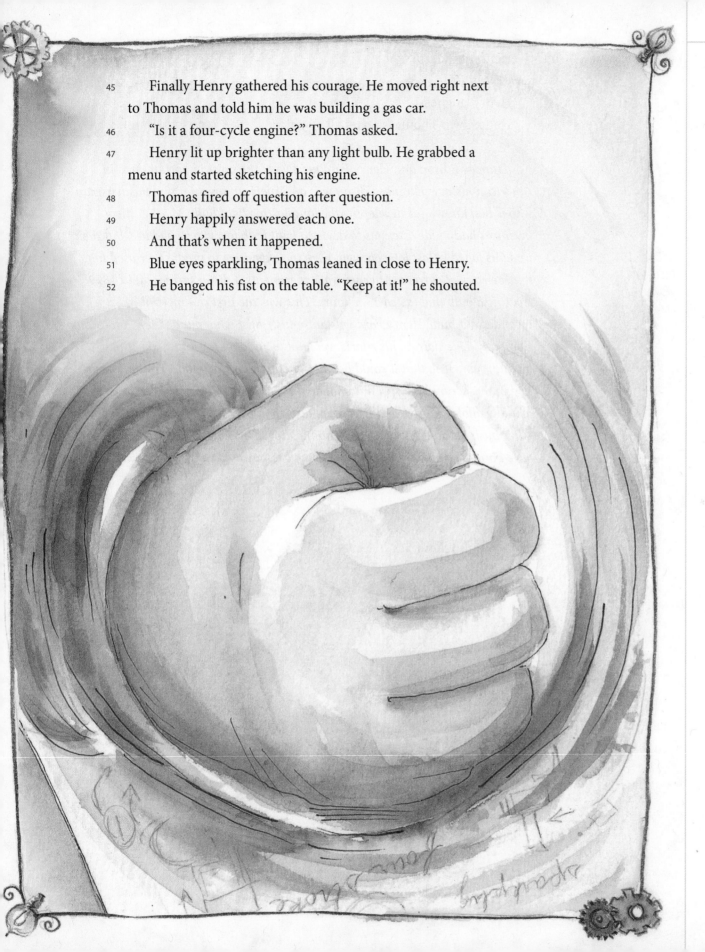

53   Henry smiled.

54   *Keep at it?*

55   Henry laughed.

56   He'd known Thomas's secret all along!

57   *Thomas Edison and Henry Ford are two of the most important men in American history. Thomas Edison was an American inventor and businessman who is best known for developing the long-lasting light bulb. Many earlier inventors had made attempts to devise a light bulb for widespread use, but their versions failed to last long enough, were too expensive to produce, or used too much electrical current. After several experiments, Edison succeeded, in 1879, in creating a bulb that lasted 13.5 hours. This was the first commercial incandescent bulb. Henry Ford was an industrialist who founded the Ford Motor Company. Like Edison, his efforts were not focused on inventing something, but on improving it so that it could be manufactured for the public. Ford developed and manufactured the first automobile that many middle-class Americans could actually afford. Edison and Ford were also good friends who often gave each other business advice and even vacationed together. Edison was the person who gave Ford the confidence to build his own gas-powered car.*

Collaborative Discussion

Look back at what you wrote on page 18. Tell a partner two things you learned during reading. Then work with a group to discuss the questions below. Find details in *The Inventor's Secret* to support your thoughts. In your discussion, respond to others by asking questions and making comments that build on their ideas.

1 Reread pages 20–25. What words and actions in the text show how Thomas and Henry are alike?

2 How does the author reveal Henry's feelings about Thomas?

3 Explain what the author means in this sentence on page 32: "He'd known Thomas's secret all along!"

Listening Tip

Listen carefully to the responses of others. What questions do you have about their ideas?

Speaking Tip

Ask questions to encourage a speaker to tell more about the topic. Add comments of your own to build upon the speaker's ideas.

Write a Personal Account

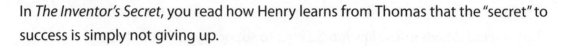

In *The Inventor's Secret*, you read how Henry learns from Thomas that the "secret" to success is simply not giving up.

Imagine that your class is creating a collection of personal stories about their paths to success. Think about a time when you had to "keep at it" in order to succeed. Write a two-paragraph personal account telling about a challenge you faced and what it took to overcome that challenge. Use evidence from *The Inventor's Secret* in your personal account. Don't forget to use some of the Critical Vocabulary words in your writing.

PLAN ....

Make notes about the central ideas and important details related to overcoming a challenge. Then use a two-column chart to compare and contrast a challenge you faced with one that is faced by someone in the text.

WRITE

Now write your personal account about a challenge you faced.

Make sure your personal account
☐ introduces the challenge that you faced.
☐ describes how the challenge was overcome.
☐ compares and contrasts with the text.
☐ uses sensory details to describe the experience.
☐ provides a conclusion.

Notice & Note
Contrasts and
Contradictions

Prepare to Read

GENRE STUDY **Magazine articles** give information about a topic, person, or event.

- Magazine articles often tell events in sequential—or chronological—order to help readers understand what happened and when.

- Magazine articles usually include visuals, such as photographs with captions.

- Magazine articles may include words that are specific to the topic or idea being discussed.

SET A PURPOSE **Think about** the title and genre of this text. What do you know about wind power? What do you want to learn? Write your ideas below.

CRITICAL VOCABULARY

irrigate

inspector

photographed

prestigious

auditorium

impoverished

**Build Background:
Alternative Power**

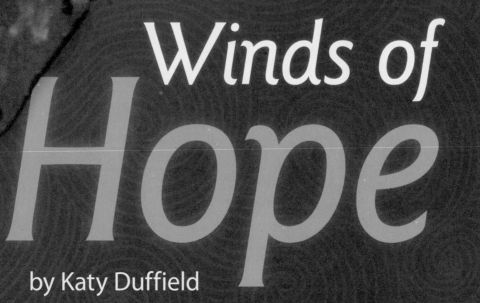

Winds of Hope

by Katy Duffield

1   *Parched red dust* swirled on the wind as William Kamkwamba (kam-KWAHM-bah) stooped between rows of *chimanga*, or maize, near his family's mud-brick thatched home in Malawi, Africa. As the searing sun scorched his back, the fourteen-year-old wrapped his hand around a withered stalk. Instead of being plump and green, the maize was dry and brittle. It had grown barely knee-high. The maize should have been up to his father's chest by that time, but the rains had not come to nourish it.

William Kamkwamba

2   The drought of 2001 dragged on and on. For many months, William's family had only enough maize for one meal each day. And then, for just a small handful at night; and finally, for only four mouthfuls. As they grew thinner and thinner, William feared they all would die of starvation.

3   The following spring, William and his father knew that all they could do was begin again. They planted a new maize crop. This time, the rains came. The maize grew—ankle-high, knee-high, chest-high.

4   William hoped that life could now return to normal. He'd worked hard to pass the exams to enter high school. When the term began, however, William's father explained that, because of the drought, there was no money to pay his school fees. It appeared that William's education would end at eighth grade.

5   Though he could not attend school, William still wanted to learn. He was curious about many things. He took apart radios, trying to discover how they made music. One day, turning a bicycle upside down and cranking the pedals by hand, he figured out that the dynamo that generated electricity for the headlight could be wired to power a radio instead.

6   Some days, William visited the village library. It had only three shelves, but William found books that interested him—science books about how things worked. One day, while looking for a dictionary on the bottom shelf, he found a book he hadn't seen before pushed behind the others. It was an American school textbook called *Using Energy*. On the book's cover was a picture of a row of windmills, tall steel towers with blades spinning like giant fans.

7   From this book William learned that wind—something of which Malawi had plenty—could produce electricity. William was delighted! Only two percent of the houses in Malawi have electricity. If William could build a windmill, his family could have lights in their home. And a windmill could be used to pump water to irrigate the family's maize fields. If another drought came, the windmill could provide the water for life.

8   William could picture in his mind the windmill he wanted to build, but collecting the parts and tools he needed would take months. In a junkyard across from the high school, William dug through piles of twisted metal, rusted cars, and worn-out tractors, searching for anything that might help him construct his machine. He took a ring of ball bearings from an old peanut grinder and the cooling fan from a tractor engine. Cracking open a shock absorber, he removed the steel piston inside. He made four-foot-long blades from plastic pipe, which he melted over a fire, flattened out, and stiffened with bamboo poles.

9   Earning some money loading logs into a truck, he paid a welder to attach the piston to the pedal sprocket of an old bicycle frame. This would be the axle of the windmill. When the wind blew, the rotating blades would turn the bicycle wheel, like someone pedaling, and spin a small dynamo. Although he had no money for a dynamo, a friend came to the rescue and bought one from a man in the road, right off his bike.

10 When he had collected all the parts, William took them out of the corner of his bedroom, laid them outside in the shade of an acacia tree, and began putting them together. Since he did not have a drill to make bolt holes, he shoved a nail through a maize cob, heated it in the fire, then pushed its point through the plastic blades. He bolted the blades to the tractor fan, using washers he'd made from bottle caps. Next he pushed the fan onto the piston welded to the bicycle frame. With the help of his two best friends, William built a 16-foot-tall tower from trunks of blue gum trees and hoisted the ninety-pound windmill to the top.

11 Shoppers, farmers, and traders could see William's tower from the local market. They came in a long line to find out what the boy was up to.

irrigate   To irrigate crops is to supply them with water through a system of pipes, sprinklers, or streams.

knew this was his moment—his
how everyone he wasn't crazy, to
is experiment would work. He
wo wires from the dynamo to a light
made from a reed and that held a
As the wind whipped around him, he
e bent spoke he'd jammed into the
ck it. Then he held his breath . . .
ades began to turn, slowly at first, then
faster. The light bulb flickered, then
life. The crowd cheered from below.
nth later William found enough wire to
m the windmill into his house. His
owded around to marvel as the small
p in William's room. Reading *Explaining*
y its light, he stayed up long after others
e to bed.

William's cousin climbs one of the
windmills on the Kamkwamba farm.

William's parents stand outside
their home. William's windmill towers
in the background.

15 **In 2006,** a school inspector saw the windmill and informed his head office. William's machine now powered four lights and two radios in his house. He'd added a storage battery with homemade switches and a circuit breaker. He also recharged village cell phones.

16 Soon William was being interviewed on the radio and photographed for the newspapers. The story of the boy with only an eighth grade education who'd built "electric wind" spread across the Internet.

17 In 2007, the nineteen-year-old who had not attended school for five years was flown to Tanzania to speak at the prestigious TED conference, featuring innovators from around the world in Technology, Education, and Design. Nervously struggling with his English, William received a rousing ovation from the auditorium of inventors and scientists when he modestly described what he had done.

18 William attended Dartmouth College in the United States, where he studied environmental science and engineering. He graduated in 2014. William is dedicated to bringing wind- and solar-powered electricity and water pumps to impoverished villages in rural Africa.

inspector An inspector reviews or examines something carefully.

photographed If someone or something was photographed, its photo was recorded on film or as a computer file.

prestigious Something prestigious is impressive and important.

auditorium An auditorium is a large room where an audience gathers for a presentation or performance.

impoverished To be impoverished is to be poor.

Collaborative Discussion

Winds of **Hope** by Katy Duffield

Look back at what you wrote on page 36. Tell a partner two things you learned from the text. Then work with a group to discuss the questions below. Support your answers with details from *Winds of Hope*. Before your discussion begins, choose a leader who will make sure everyone in the group has a chance to share ideas.

1. Reread page 38. What details in the text show how the drought affected William and his family?

2. Review pages 40–41. What does William do to find the parts he needs to build a windmill? What kinds of problem-solving skills does he demonstrate while he's working?

3. What details in the text show how William feels about helping others?

Listening Tip

Listen carefully to others in your group. Wait until your group leader calls on you to add your ideas.

Speaking Tip

Look at other group members as you speak. Speak loudly enough for everyone to hear you. When you're finished, ask if anyone has questions for you.

Write a News Article

PROMPT

In *Winds of Hope*, you read how William becomes known around the world after local newspapers write about his windmill. Reporters must prepare for conducting interviews so that they are able to record the most important facts and details related to the article.

Imagine that you are a reporter and your newspaper has sent you to interview William. Write a news article about William and his windmill. Begin by writing interview questions. Using the 5 Ws and H (*who, what, when, where, why*, and *how*) will help you create questions that include the most important information. Then use information from the text to answer your questions as you think William would answer. Don't forget to use some of the Critical Vocabulary words in your writing.

PLAN

Use the 5 Ws and H to prepare interview questions that focus on the central ideas and important details from the text. Then use the text to answer the questions as William would answer them.

WRITE

Now write your news article about William and his windmill from *Winds of Hope*.

Winds of **Hope**
by Katy Duffield

Make sure your news article

- ☐ introduces William and his invention.

- ☐ asks and answers questions using the 5Ws and H.

- ☐ develops the topic with facts and other examples from the text.

- ☐ uses informative words and language that show understanding.

- ☐ ends with a concluding statement.

Notice & Note
Contrasts and Contradictions

Prepare to Read

GENRE STUDY **Informational texts** give facts and examples about a topic.

- Authors of informational texts may organize their ideas using headings and subheadings, by grouping main ideas and key details, or by explaining causes and effects.
- Science texts also include words that are specific to the topic.
- Informational texts often include visuals, such as charts, diagrams, graphs, timelines, and maps.

SET A PURPOSE **Think about** the title and genre of this text. What do you know about wheelchair sports and how they affect the lives of people who are not able to walk? What do you want to learn? Write your ideas below.

CRITICAL VOCABULARY

maneuver

specialized

elite

objective

traditional

Build Background:
Sports for the Physically Challenged

Wheelchair Sports:

Hang Glider to Wheeler-Dealer

by Simon Shapiro

art by Theo Krynauw and Warwick Goldswain

In her new wheelchair, Marilyn Hamilton excelled at tennis, winning the U.S. Open Women's Wheelchair Championship twice, both in singles and doubles. (Eventually she did get her yellow wheelchair.)

1 **B**efore you jump off a mountain, there are a few things you have to do. Usually, Marilyn Hamilton did them all, and had a great time soaring in California's Sierra mountain range under her hang glider. But one day in 1978, she forgot to clip her harness to the glider. She was lucky not to be killed, but the crash broke her back. At the age of 29, Hamilton's life changed forever—but the lives of millions of others would also be changed by that simple mistake.

2 Hamilton was never able to walk again. After a stay in the hospital and three weeks of therapy, she was given a wheelchair and encouraged to get on with her life. She was eager to do that but worried about the things she would never be able to do again, like running, biking, squash and racquetball, hiking, and hang gliding.

3 Still, Hamilton was determined to live a full and active life, and ready to try new things. Regular tennis was out, but a friend got her started on wheelchair tennis. It was frustratingly difficult, and she'd come home from the courts at the end of the day with badly blistered hands. She hated her wheelchair! Its steel frame made it heavy (close to 27 kilograms, or 60 pounds) and hard to maneuver. And it was ugly. Being imprisoned in that wheelchair was the exact opposite of being able to fly in a hang glider. One day, that difference gave her an idea.

maneuver To maneuver something is to move it.

4 Hamilton talked to two friends who made hang gliders. She persuaded them to build her a new wheelchair using hang-glider technology. An aluminum frame made it strong, but light; it was half the weight of her regular chair, and she could really move in it. It even looked good. In fact, the only thing that stopped it from being absolutely perfect was that it was blue; she would have preferred yellow.

5 Hamilton and her friends knew they were on to something. Hamilton couldn't be the only one out there looking for a lighter, speedier chair. They formed a company to make and sell "Quickie" wheelchairs and specialized in meeting the needs of athletes. The company was hugely successful.

> **specialized** If a company specialized in something, it provided a specific type of product.

Wheelchair Sports

Wheelchair sports can be very competitive and very demanding. Elite wheelchair athletes have an awesome level of fitness, skill, and upper body strength. Wheelchair basketball is very similar to stand-up basketball. Rules are adapted for wheelchairs. For example, only two pushes are allowed before a player must dribble the ball. Wheelchair rugby was developed by a group of Canadian athletes whose reduced arm and hand functions didn't allow them to compete equally in basketball. The objective is to carry the ball over the opponents' goal line.

> **elite** Elite members of a group are those who are the best or most skilled.
> **objective** An objective is a goal.

● Center of mass

A regular wheelchair tips over fairly easily. The vertical dotted black line shows that the center of mass is directly over the tipping point.

Why They're Better

6 The reasons why a lightweight wheelchair is better for athletes than a traditional wheelchair are pretty easy to understand. In fact, Sir Isaac Newton figured out the exact math formulas to explain this stuff back in 1687, but here are the basics:

- to move something heavy, you have to push harder;

- given the same push, something light will go faster than something heavy; and

- it's easier to slow down a lighter object than a heavier one.

7 So, it's obvious that a lighter wheelchair will let an athlete move faster, stop faster, and change direction easily. The only thing that *isn't* obvious is why no one built a light wheelchair for athletes sooner. It seems this invention had to wait for Marilyn Hamilton: not only did she understand the need, she also had the connection to hang-gliding technology that turned a dream into a reality.

8 The lightness of the Quickie was the biggest innovation. But Hamilton and her friends didn't stop there. They worked hard to figure out what else an athlete would need. In the end, the Quickie was made more stable by giving it a lower center of mass and a wider wheelbase than a traditional wheelchair. An object will tip over when the center of mass is directly over the point of tipping. The diagram above shows that with a lower center of mass and a wider wheelbase, the sports wheelchair must be pushed to a much greater angle before it tips.

---

traditional Something that is traditional has been made or done in a certain way for a very long time.

The wide wheelbase on a sports wheelchair makes it very stable and hard to tip over.

● Center of mass

9   With a wheelchair, the center of mass is made lower by setting the seat lower. The Quickie also lets athletes adjust the height themselves. The wheelbase is made wider by using negative cambered wheels. This means that the wheels aren't vertical. Instead, they're angled so that the tops of the wheels are closer together than the bottoms.

10   Another advantage of the negative cambered wheels is that the athlete can reach the wheel more easily. The top part of the wheel is close to the athlete's body, so the hands push almost in line with the athlete's shoulders and not out to the side. This lets you push harder. The diagram shows how this works. The shoulder is the fulcrum, and the muscles in the upper arm provide the effort. The output force is delivered through the hand. The farther away your hand is from your shoulder when you push, the less output force you have.

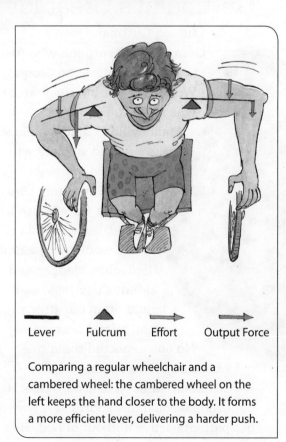

| Lever | Fulcrum | Effort | Output Force |

Comparing a regular wheelchair and a cambered wheel: the cambered wheel on the left keeps the hand closer to the body. It forms a more efficient lever, delivering a harder push.

51

Tipping Points and Center of Mass

If you want to feel how the center of mass/tipping point principle works, grab a can of vegetables from the kitchen cupboard. Now mark the middle of the label with a dot. The center of mass is in the middle of the can, right behind that mark. With the mark facing you, hold the can on its edge just where it's balanced but about to tip over. Notice where the dot is? Right above the edge of the can. Now do the same thing with a shorter can, like the kind tuna comes in. There's no doubt which is more stable.

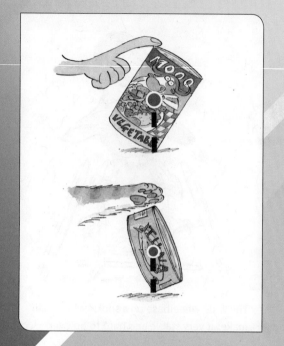

Guttmann's Great Idea

11   Dr. Ludwig Guttmann was a German brain surgeon who fled to England before the Second World War. During the war, he was in charge of Stoke Mandeville Hospital, a place that treated soldiers with spinal cord injuries.

Before Guttmann, these patients were left to lie in bed, doing nothing. They would get painful bedsores, bladder and kidney infections, and would often die after several miserable months. No one expected them to become active again.

12   Guttmann refused to accept this. He believed he could use sports as a way to get patients active and out of bed. He got a sergeant assigned to the hospital to play catch with patients in bed, using a heavy medicine ball. (They needed to build up enough arm strength to lift themselves into a wheelchair.) Then the games really began. Activity wasn't optional; it was prescribed medicine. Patients had archery and darts, pool and table tennis. They invented wheelchair polo and wheelchair basketball. Amazingly, patients were soon being discharged from the hospital to go home and live active lives.

13   In 1948, Guttmann held the first annual wheelchair competition at the hospital. In 1952, Dutch competitors made these games international. Eight years later, they were held parallel to the Olympics. The Paralympics are now held immediately following the Olympics, in the same cities. In 1960, Guttmann watched 300 athletes enter Rome's Olympic stadium for the first Paralympics Games. That number's now increased to over four thousand athletes.

Collaborative Discussion

Look back at what you wrote on page 46. Tell a partner two things you learned from the text. Then work with a group to discuss the questions below. Use details and examples from *Wheelchair Sports: Hang Glider to Wheeler-Dealer* to support your answers. Help keep your group's conversation focused on just one question at a time.

1. Reread pages 48–49. What led Marilyn Hamilton to invent a new kind of wheelchair?

Listening Tip

Listen carefully to what each person has to say. Try to add new thoughts or facts about the same question.

2. Review page 52. In what way was Dr. Guttmann's idea for helping his patients different from what had been done in the past?

Speaking Tip

Keep the conversation on track by speaking only about the topic your group is discussing at the moment.

3. What special features make sports wheelchairs better for athletes than traditional wheelchairs?

Write an Encyclopedia Entry

PROMPT ....

In *Wheelchair Sports: Hang Glider to Wheeler-Dealer,* you read how Marilyn Hamilton's own injury inspired her to design a new kind of wheelchair for athletes.

Imagine that you and your class are creating an encyclopedia of inventors. Write an entry that tells about Hamilton and her important invention. Begin your entry with a topic sentence that introduces your readers to the central idea and makes them want to know more. Use your understanding of the facts and details in the text to tell readers about Hamilton's life before she was injured, to describe her injury, to explain her invention, and to show how her invention has helped others. Don't forget to use some of the Critical Vocabulary words in your writing.

PLAN ....

Make notes about the central ideas and important details about Hamilton's life and her invention.

WRITE

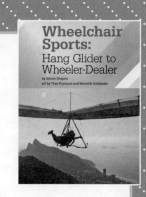

Now write your encyclopedia entry about Marilyn Hamilton's life and her invention.

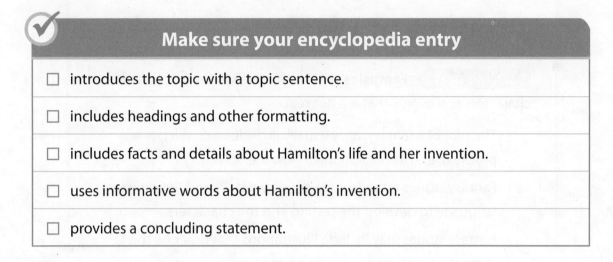

Make sure your encyclopedia entry
☐ introduces the topic with a topic sentence.
☐ includes headings and other formatting.
☐ includes facts and details about Hamilton's life and her invention.
☐ uses informative words about Hamilton's invention.
☐ provides a concluding statement.

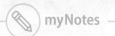

**Notice &
Note**
Again and Again

Prepare to Read

GENRE STUDY   **Fantasies** are imaginative stories that contain characters and events that are not real.

- The plot of a fantasy story usually includes a conflict, or a problem, and its resolution, or how it is solved.
- Fantasy stories often include sensory details and figurative language to develop the setting and the characters.
- Fantasy stories may include illustrations that describe the characters and setting or give clues about the plot.

SET A PURPOSE   **Think about** the title and genre of this text. As you read, pay attention to details in the text and illustrations that describe Captain Arsenio's inventions. What do you think Captain Arsenio wants to do? Write your ideas below.

CRITICAL VOCABULARY

passionate

impulse

contribution

distinguished

eccentric

circumstances

evidently

acceleration

prototype

conceived

**Meet the Author/Illustrator:
Pablo Bernasconi**

CAPTAIN ARSENIO

INVENTIONS AND (MIS)ADVENTURES IN FLIGHT

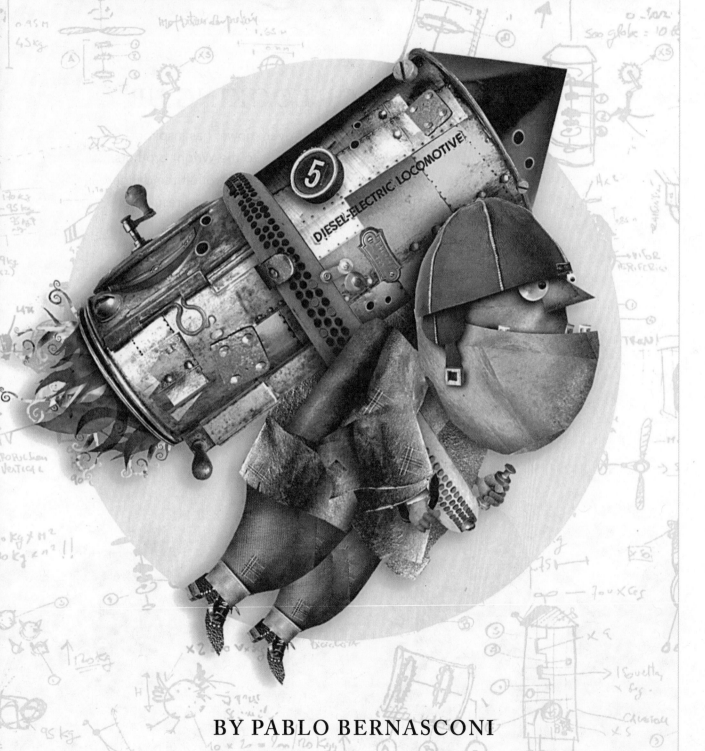

BY PABLO BERNASCONI

THE RESULT OF LOOKING UP

1 Flight, one of the most ancient wishes ever known, has inspired hundreds of fantastic creations. From Icarus to the Wright brothers, history has seen thousands of adventurers who have felt the dangerous urge to soar with the birds. This passionate impulse has resulted in many failures.

2 Scientists, philosophers, doctors, and even crazy people all have been pioneers of aviation, and each has made a different contribution —sometimes right, sometimes wrong—to the pursuit of flight. This is the story of one such man.

---

passionate   To have a passionate feeling is to have strong emotions about it.

impulse   An impulse is the desire to do something.

contribution   A person who helps to make something has made a contribution to that work.

THE END AND THE BEGINNING

3 Manuel J. Arsenio was a careless cheese master, blacksmith, scuba diver, and ship captain. Though he was given the easiest of missions in each of these careers, he still couldn't complete any of them successfully. This problem may be the reason he left those jobs behind to enter the distinguished pages of aviation history.

4 One day in 1782, Captain Arsenio decided to build the first in a long series of eccentric projects that would change his life. And although he had little knowledge of physics or mechanics and had access only to useless materials, he demonstrated great patience and determination throughout the course of his flight experiments.

5 " *My days of sailing and scuba-diving are over; I retire with grace to begin a new stage in my life that will undoubtedly go down in history. I'm going to achieve what has been humanity's desire for centuries: I will build a flying machine."*
—Captain Arsenio, May 1, 1782

THE DISCOVERY

6 How do we know about Captain Arsenio? His diary was found by chance just one year ago, under circumstances to be discussed later. In its ninety pages full of doodles, notes, and technical writings, Arsenio developed eighteen different designs for a flying machine, each one original, foolish, and fantastic. Here we explore three of the eighteen most influential projects that have contributed to modern aviation.

7 Captain Arsenio's diary is the oldest and most precious aviation manuscript ever known, second only to Leonardo da Vinci's. Fortunately, the text is still legible and Arsenio's notes, diagrams, and ideas take us back in time to reveal the hidden mystery of the inventor's thoughts.

8 *"Why can birds fly and we humans cannot? What cruel destiny stops all people from seeing the world from above, tasting the clouds, and undoing long distances by air?"*
—Captain Arsenio, June 7, 1783

---

distinguished A distinguished group is known and respected for its excellence.

eccentric Someone who is eccentric is odd.

circumstances The way an event happened or the causes of it are its circumstances.

PROJECT NUMBER 1: **MOTOCANARY**

9   The Motocanary was an ingenious experiment that demanded a lot of work. Evidently, it was harder for Captain Arsenio to find enough birds and tie them together with a rope than it was to achieve flight. Although the discovery was revolutionary, it took two days to get the captain down from the tree in which he was stuck.

10   *"Carts are dragged along by horses, sleighs by dogs, and plows by bulls. I think that if I concentrate enough birds together, the sustaining force will help me win the clouds. It cannot fail!"*

   —Captain Arsenio, February 18, 1784

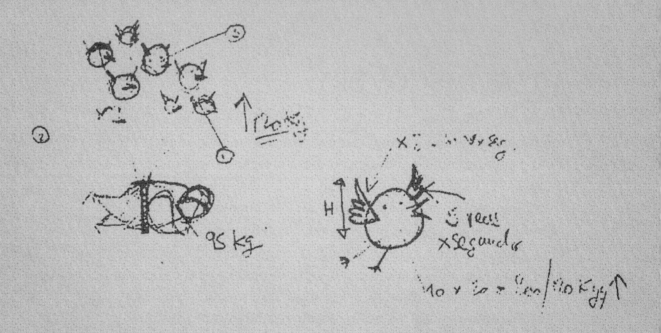

evidently   If something happened evidently, it happened for an obvious reason.

FLIGHT DIARY

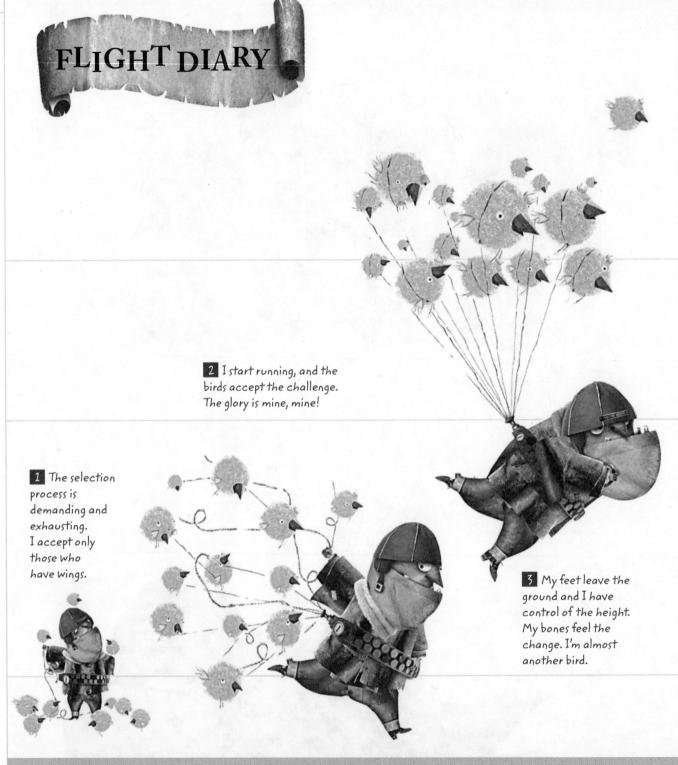

2 I start running, and the birds accept the challenge. The glory is mine, mine!

1 The selection process is demanding and exhausting. I accept only those who have wings.

3 My feet leave the ground and I have control of the height. My bones feel the change. I'm almost another bird.

Phase 1: 14 hrs   Phase 2: 10 min   Phase 3: 4.5 sec

NOTE: As improbable as it appears, this diary shows us that the Motocanary did fly for a few feet before crashing into a tree. Maybe the failure is due to Captain Arsenio's misplaced trust in the unreliable canaries.

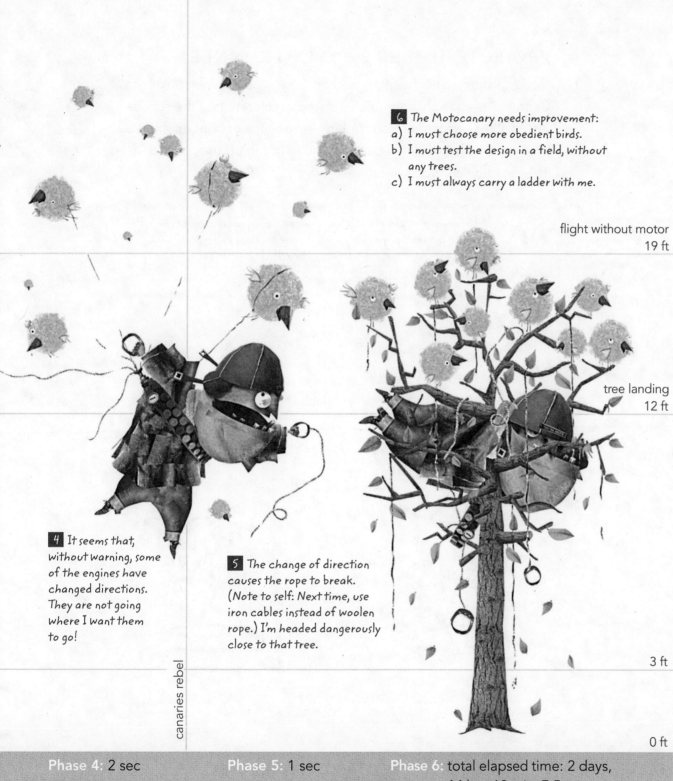

6 The Motocanary needs improvement:
a) I must choose more obedient birds.
b) I must test the design in a field, without any trees.
c) I must always carry a ladder with me.

flight without motor
19 ft

tree landing
12 ft

4 It seems that, without warning, some of the engines have changed directions. They are not going where I want them to go!

5 The change of direction causes the rope to break. (*Note to self: Next time, use iron cables instead of woolen rope.*) I'm headed dangerously close to that tree.

canaries rebel

3 ft

0 ft

Phase 4: 2 sec   **Phase 5:** 1 sec   **Phase 6:** total elapsed time: 2 days, 14 hrs, 10 min, 7.5 sec

PROJECT NUMBER 2: **FLYING RUNNER**

11   Good cardiovascular health would become a determining factor in Captain Arsenio's second ambition. The acceleration of the runner would allow—according to his plans—the wings to beat up and down in imitation of a bird's flight and lift the machine off the ground. The direction control is unknown.

12   *"I can leave the ground by the effort of an energetic run, transferred to the little wings and multiplied thirty times by the transfer pulleys.*
Running + wings = access to heaven. It cannot fail!"

—Captain Arsenio, March 23, 1785

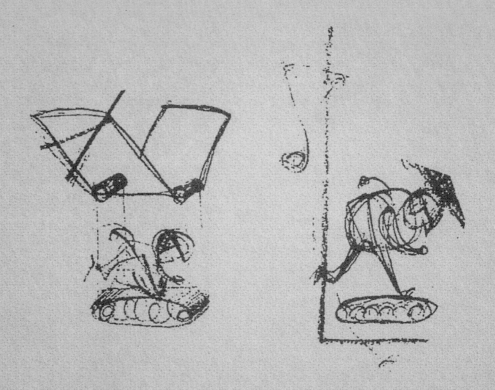

acceleration   Acceleration is the act of moving faster.

FLIGHT DIARY

4 All systems go, the balance is controlled —the prototype is a success . . . up until this point.

2 I start the acceleration, and the wings seem to be in working order. But I'm not elevating yet.

1 Countdown to zero. I'm preparing for the big run. I've got faith.

3 The machine starts to rise at maximum speed. I'm starting to get very tired.

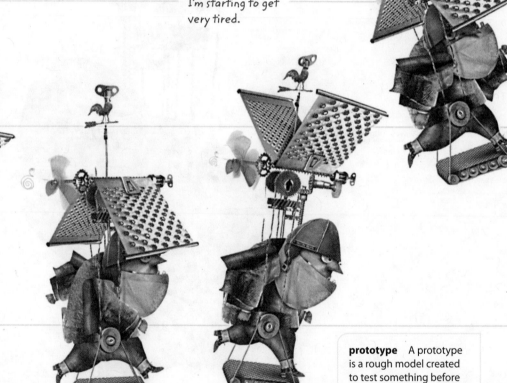

> **prototype** A prototype is a rough model created to test something before creating it in its final form.

Phase 1: at rest   Phase 2: 21 min   Phase 3: 47 sec   Phase 4: 1 min

NOTE: The reader may notice that there are significant differences between what is written and what actually happened. This may be due to Captain Arsenio's unflagging optimism (or the many bumps on the head that he suffered from his experiments).

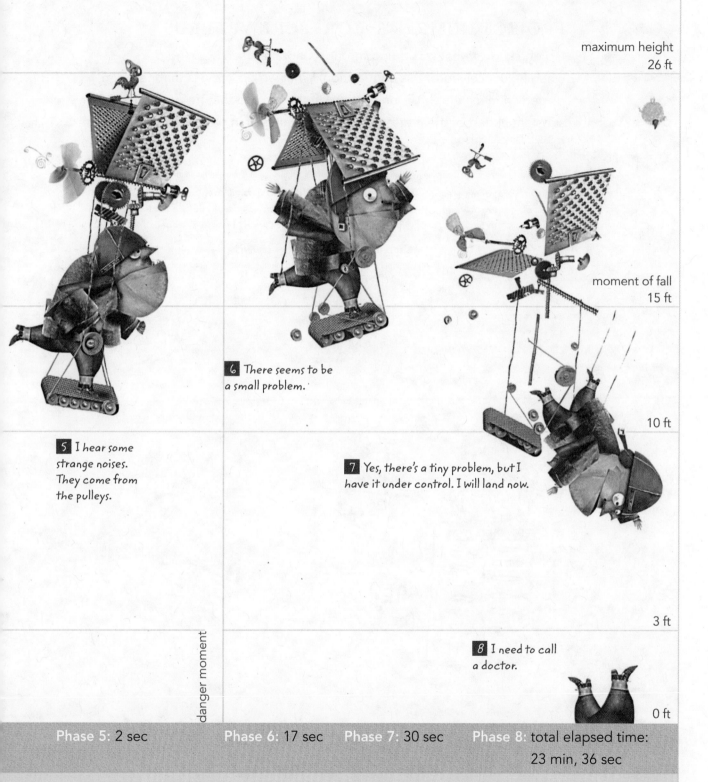

maximum height
26 ft

moment of fall
15 ft

6 There seems to be a small problem.

10 ft

5 I hear some strange noises. They come from the pulleys.

7 Yes, there's a tiny problem, but I have it under control. I will land now.

danger moment

3 ft

8 I need to call a doctor.

0 ft

Phase 5: 2 sec   Phase 6: 17 sec   Phase 7: 30 sec   Phase 8: total elapsed time: 23 min, 36 sec

PROJECT NUMBER 3: **CORKSCREWPTERUS**

13   No one knows what was going through Captain Arsenio's mind when he conceived of this contraption. What we do know is that he placed so much emphasis on getting off the ground that he forgot a substantial part of the matter: how to keep himself in the air. Obvious results.

14   *"All past propelling mechanisms were wrong. I need to find a way to beat gravity, despite my generous weight. The compression of two metal springs should do the trick; I anticipate a big leap. But I will put little wings on my back, just in case. It cannot fail!"*

—Captain Arsenio, November 15, 1785

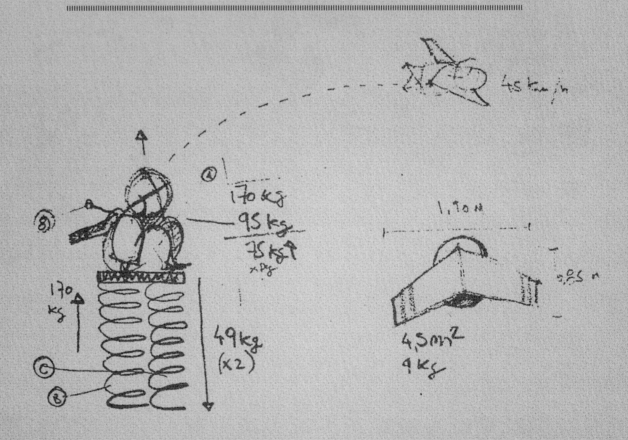

conceived   If you thought of the idea to create something, you conceived it.

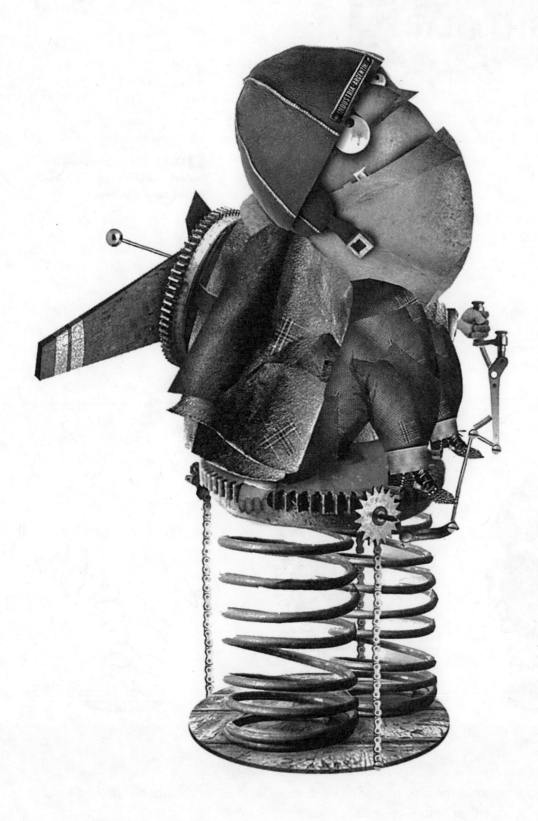

FLIGHT DIARY

3 Oh!!!! *The acceleration is violent, and I've conquered gravity without any problems.*

1 *Everything is ready for takeoff. The jump is possible.*

2 *I start the countdown: 10, 9, 8, 7, 6, 5, 4, 3, 2, 1.*

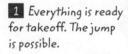

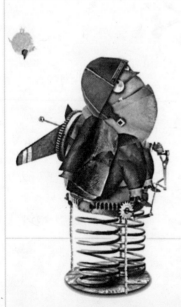

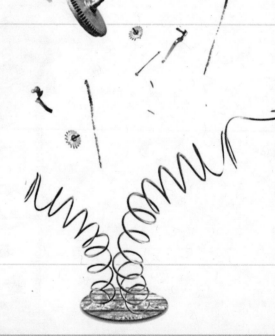

Phase 1: at rest   Phase 2: 10 sec   Phase 3: 3.5 sec

NOTE: This document is the only one of its kind; there is no other recorded data of a person surviving such a fall, either before or since.

4 I've already passed through the clouds; I start the controlled descent.

5 Now it is time for the wings.

maximum *measured* height
208 ft

99 ft

6 Descent is completely under control, although the wings do not respond as I had expected.

50 ft

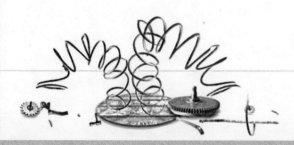

7 The doctor is not at home. I will call the veterinarian.

3 ft

panic point

0 ft

Phase 4: 1 min   **Phase 5:** 1 sec   **Phase 6:** 7.25 sec   **Phase 7:** total elapsed time: 1 min, 21.75 sec

GOODBYE FROM BELOW

15 As it happens with almost all legends, multiple versions contradict one another, proof disappears, and word of mouth constructs stories that differ greatly from the reality. No one knows for certain exactly what happened to Captain Arsenio and his flying machines; all that is left is his diary—ninety pages of consecutive failures—and one big question: Did he eventually succeed?

16 Some say that Arsenio's book was buried near Cairo, Egypt—7,508 miles away from where he lived in Patagonia, Argentina. Others disagree and tell us it was in a chest at the bottom of the sea, buried under a pile of rusty metal junk. But most people insist with determination that Captain Arsenio's diary was found on the surface of the moon on July 20, 1969.

〰〰〰

17 *"Many years have passed since that first Motocanary.*
Although I have failed many times, I have learned so much. And today, for the first time,
I am sure that this new machine I have developed is going to work.
I deserve a piece of heaven, and I am going for it!"

—Captain Arsenio, December 6, 1789

〰〰〰

Respond to the Text

Collaborative Discussion

Look back at what you wrote on page 56. Tell a partner two things you learned during reading. Then work with a group to discuss the questions below. Support your answers with details from *Captain Arsenio*. Connect your ideas to what other group members say.

1 Reread pages 58–59. How has the narrator come to know so much about Captain Arsenio? What does the author seem to think of him?

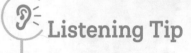

Listening Tip

Listen carefully to the speakers, noting how they use text evidence to support their thoughts.

2 What details might make readers think Captain Arsenio was a real person? What details show that he was not?

Speaking Tip

Restate a speaker's idea, and then share information that builds on that idea.

3 Review page 72. What hint does the narrator give that Captain Arsenio may have succeeded in his efforts to fly?

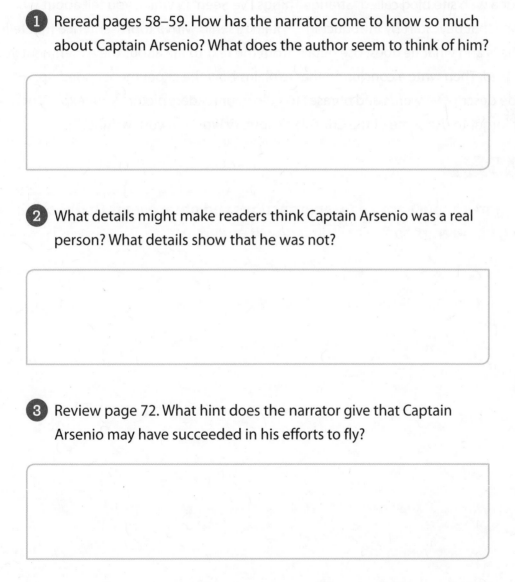

Write a Blog Post

PROMPT

In *Captain Arsenio*, you read the story of a man who created inventions that he believed would allow him to fly.

Imagine that you witnessed one of Captain Arsenio's attempts to fly. Write an account of it for a web site blog called "Strange Things I've Seen" in which you tell about what you saw that day. Start by introducing Captain Arsenio with a topic sentence that tells who he is and what he does. Use details from the text to tell about the experiment you witnessed. Then write a conclusion that explains how the experiment ended up. Include descriptive words and phrases to help your readers picture your experience. Don't forget to use some of the Critical Vocabulary words in your writing.

PLAN

Make notes about Captain Arsenio's actions and other events that took place during his attempt to fly, including how it ended.

Now write your blog post about Captain Arsenio's attempt to fly.

✓

Make sure your blog post
☐ includes a topic sentence that explains the situation.
☐ uses detailed evidence from the text.
☐ describes events in an order that makes sense.
☐ uses descriptive words.
☐ includes a conclusion.

(?) Essential Question

What kinds of circumstances push people to create new inventions?

Write a Personal Narrative

PROMPT Think about how each inventor in this module used curiosity and determination to solve a problem.

Imagine that your class is putting together a collection of personal narratives called *Class Inventors at Work*. Write a personal narrative about a time when you found a creative way to solve a problem. Use the inventors in the texts as inspiration.

I will write about the time when I _____.

✓ Make sure your personal narrative

☐ establishes that you are the narrator.

☐ draws inspiration from the selections in *Inventors at Work*.

☐ has an introduction that presents the setting and the problem.

☐ explains steps toward your solution in a clear sequence.

☐ uses concrete words and sensory details.

☐ has a conclusion that shows how the problem was solved.

Think about the problem you solved. What steps did you take? What challenges did you have to overcome? Look back at your notes and revisit the texts to help you brainstorm ideas for your narrative.

Use the story map below to plan your narrative. Identify your problem and the obstacles you faced. List in order the steps you took and how you overcame each obstacle. Then explain your solution and why it worked. Use Critical Vocabulary Words where appropriate.

My Topic: _____

Problem	Setting
Events/Steps	
Solution	

DRAFT ·· Write your narrative.

Write an **introduction** that clearly states your problem. Get readers interested in learning how you solved it!

⬇

Write **body paragraphs** that explain how you used creativity to solve your problem. Tell the steps in order and use a new paragraph for each one.

⬇

Write a satisfying **conclusion** that explains your solution.

REVISE AND EDIT · Review your draft.

Now it's time to review your draft and make changes to improve it. Read your narrative to a partner. Ask your partner for suggestions to make it clearer and more interesting. Use these questions to help you evaluate and improve your narrative.

✓	PURPOSE/ FOCUS	ORGANIZATION	EVIDENCE	LANGUAGE/ VOCABULARY	CONVENTIONS
	☐ Does my narrative show how I used creativity to solve a problem? ☐ Does every paragraph tell about how the problem was solved?	☐ Are the steps or events told in a clear sequence? ☐ Does the conclusion explain the solution to the problem?	☐ Did I include examples and inspiration from the texts I've read about inventors?	☐ Did I use concrete words and sensory details? ☐ Did I use transition words to connect my ideas?	☐ Have I spelled all words correctly? ☐ Have I used commas and other punctuation marks correctly?

PUBLISH · Share your work.

Create a Finished Copy. Make a final copy of your personal narrative. You can include a photo or drawing of your solution. Consider these options for sharing your narrative:

1. Bind your narrative together with those of your classmates to create a *Class Inventors at Work* collection.

2. Hold an inventors' conference at which you and other students read aloud your narratives and respond to questions from the audience.

3. Create an audio recording of your narrative. Read with expression to keep your listeners engaged. Make the recording available on a school website or media blog for others to listen and respond to.

What a Story

"They weren't true stories;
they were better than that."

—Alice Hoffman

? Essential Question

How does genre affect the way a story is told?

Get Curious
Video

Words About Stories

The words in the chart will help you talk and write about the selections in this module. Which words about stories have you seen before? Which words are new to you?

Add to the Vocabulary Network on page 83 by writing synonyms, antonyms, and related words and phrases for each word about stories.

After you read each selection in this module, come back to the Vocabulary Network and keep building it. Add more boxes if you need to.

WORD	MEANING	CONTEXT SENTENCE
climax (noun)	The climax of a story is its most important event and usually happens near the end.	At the exciting climax of the story, the hero ran into a burning building.
dialogue (noun)	The dialogue is the conversation among characters in a story.	The way this character speaks in his dialogue helps me understand more about him.
foreword (noun)	The introduction to a book is called its foreword.	You should read the book's foreword before you read the rest of the story.
prose (noun)	Unlike poetry, prose is "ordinary writing," in the form of sentences and paragraphs.	Most stories are written as prose, but some are written as poems.

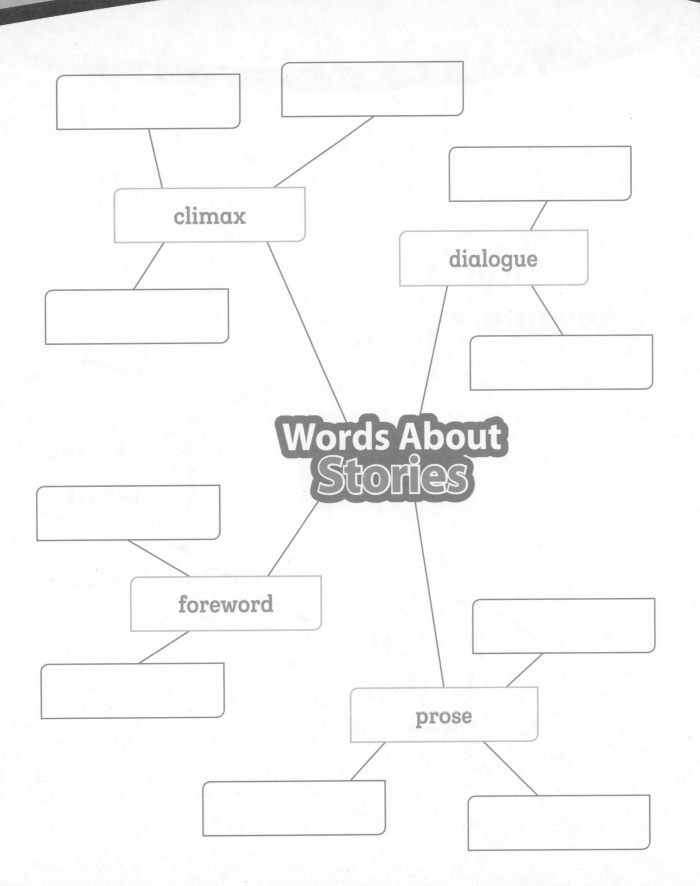

climax

dialogue

foreword

prose

Words About Stories

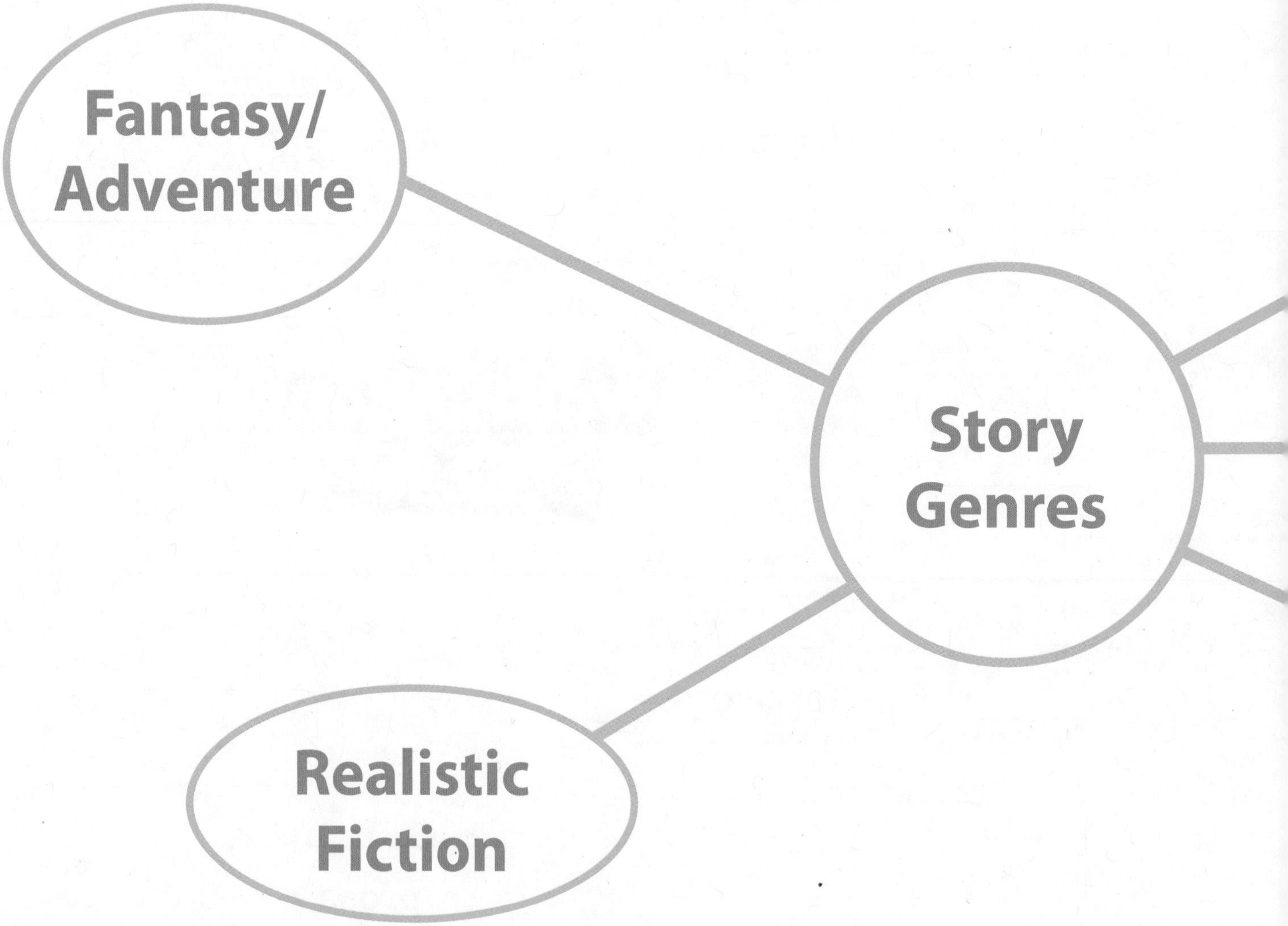

Fantasy/
Adventure

Story
Genres

Realistic
Fiction

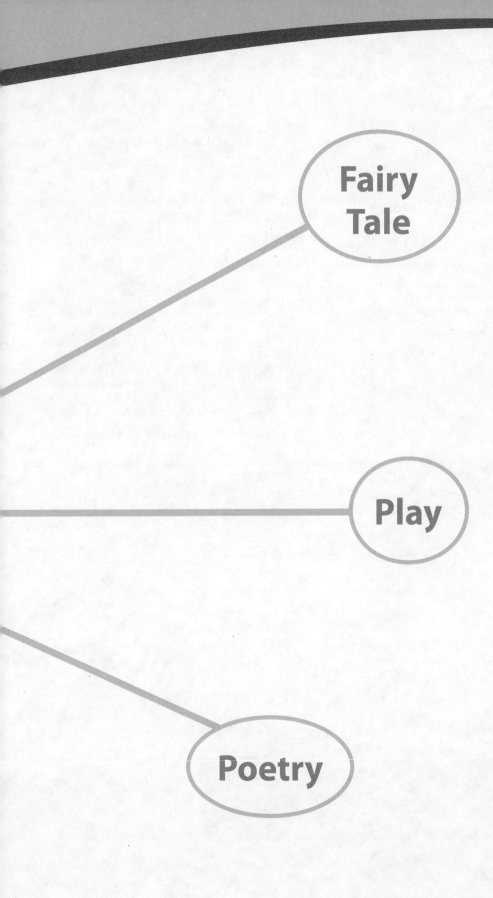

Many Ways to Tell a Story

1   Most of us think of books and **prose** when we think of stories, but a great story can come in many other forms, too—myths and fables, plays, movies, poems, and even songs. For a person who loves stories, they can be found nearly anywhere, and there are countless ways in which to enjoy them and share them with others!

Digital Formats

2 Have you ever read an "eBook" on a tablet computer or a story on a website? If so, you probably know that digital formats sometimes offer features you won't find in a printed book. You might be able to select a name or place and be taken to a website with extra information, pictures, or videos about it. Some eBooks even have multimedia embedded within them, like music the author wants readers to listen to during certain scenes or chapters.

Movies, Television, and Plays

3 People adore stories in the forms of movies, TV shows, and plays. These formats bring characters, dialogue, settings, and events to life. They often feature music that supports the mood of story scenes, especially the story's climax. But many people still prefer that special feeling of sitting down with a good printed book. Books allow readers to use their imaginations. They also allow authors to show more of what characters are thinking than a typical play or film would. There's almost unlimited room for the author to provide readers with descriptions and background information. Often, this kind of information is provided in a foreword at the beginning of the book, but in some books it can be found throughout.

Music and Other Art Forms

4 Is it hard to imagine telling a story through dance? Think about famous ballets, such as *The Nutcracker*. Like plays, many ballet productions feature characters and events. They use costumes, scenery, and music to help bring a story to life.

5 You can probably think of several songs that tell stories all on their own, too. Such a song might not include dialogue, but it will include characters and events. The music and the singer's voice help set the mood and convey meaning. A symphony called "Peter and the Wolf" tells a whole fairytale through music. The musicians' instruments play the roles of story characters.

6 Some paintings and other artworks tell stories, as well. The Bayeux (by-YOO) Tapestry is an embroidered cloth, created hundreds of years ago. It tells the story of a battle for control of England. Some native people of the Pacific Northwest carved totem poles that feature characters and events from their cultures' myths and legends.

7 What kind of storytelling form is *your* favorite?

Notice & Note

Aha Moment

Prepare to Read

GENRE STUDY   A **fantasy** is an imaginative story featuring characters and events that are not real. Some fantasies include elements of **adventure**, with a quest to solve a mystery.

- Authors of fantasy tell the story through the plot—the main events of the story. The plot includes a conflict, or problem, and the resolution, or how the problem is solved.
- Fantasy stories include sensory details and figurative language to develop the setting and the characters.
- The events and places in fantasies might defy time or logic.

SET A PURPOSE   **Think about** the title and genre of this text. As you read, pay attention to how characters react to one another and to real events. What do you think this text is about? Write your ideas below.

CRITICAL VOCABULARY

panic

favorable

porthole

densely

reasonable

delirious

projected

contents

deficiencies

**Meet the Author and Illustrator:
Kenneth Oppel and Antonio Javier Caparo**

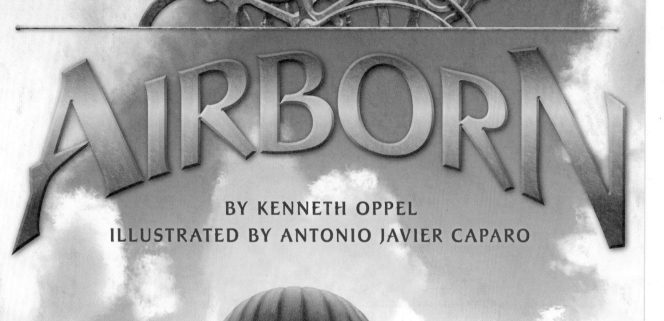

AIRBORN

BY KENNETH OPPEL

ILLUSTRATED BY ANTONIO JAVIER CAPARO

1 *Matt Cruse is a cabin boy aboard the airship* Aurora. *The* Aurora *stays afloat using a gas called "hydrium." One day Matt spots a damaged sky balloon with an old man named Benjamin Molloy inside. Molloy has fallen ill and is rambling on about beautiful creatures he saw in the sky. With Molloy unable to communicate clearly, Matt and Molloy's granddaughter, Kate, have only his journal entries to guide them on their mission to figure out whether these flying creatures are real or imagined.*

2 The journal's spine was cracked and flabby, and there was a hair ribbon round the book, holding it all together. Moths danced around in my stomach as I climbed up to my bunk and stretched out. My cabin mate, Baz, was on crow's nest duty until four. I turned on my reading lamp. I untied the ribbon and carefully turned back the cover. The pages were all scabby, as if the book had been soaked by rain then baked in the sun.

3 The pages were covered with small neat lines of ink: date, position, wind speed, altitude, observations. There was a little preface telling about how he, Benjamin Molloy, planned to do a complete west to east circumnavigation of the globe in his hot air balloon. I read quickly over these first pages, not because they weren't interesting but because I could see Kate's bookmark up ahead, and it made my stomach feel swirly, wondering what was written there. It was hard to concentrate on the stuff beforehand.

4 Kate's grandfather had started out in Cape Town to catch the jet stream and traveled quickly eastward over the Indian Ocean. But over Australia his luck ran out, and he got shunted off course to the northeast.

5 There was no sign of panic in his log. His days were busy with keeping the balloon shipshape, managing his supplies and provisions, taking weather readings and bearings. He described the countries and landscapes he was sailing over. Some days there were just coordinates and weather conditions, other days he had lots to write about: birds, the changing light, the landscape of the passing nations beneath him, the creatures below the ocean's surface. He seemed interested in everything.

6 I was keeping an eye on his coordinates and realized he was drifting along a flight path not too far off the *Aurora*'s route from Sydney to Lionsgate City. With every day his course veered more to the east, as he tried to catch favorable winds at different altitudes. Not for the first time I felt a sense of dread for him. I loved being aloft, but to be completely at the mercy of the winds, with no other means of power or steerage—it was a frightening thought. Obviously Kate's grandfather had a stouter heart than mine.

panic Panic is a feeling of strong fear that leaves someone unable to think clearly.
favorable Something that is favorable gives a benefit or contributes to success.

7   I lost track of how long I'd been reading, I was so caught up in the day to day journey. There weren't a lot of clues, but little bits of the man crept through, even in his log. He liked watching the weather; he hated the tinned baked beans but ate them because they were nutritious and portable; he enjoyed Shakespeare; he loved his granddaughter. He mentioned her often in his log. *Must remember to tell Kate*, he wrote. Or: *Will send Kate a postcard when I set down in Cape Town.*

8   With a start I realized that Kate's bookmark was just a page's turn away.

9   I put the journal down, climbed off my bunk, and went down the corridor to the bathroom. At the sink I splashed cold water on my face. Not that I was sleepy. It just seemed like the thing to do when you were up in the wee hours of the morning, reading the log of a strange, doomed voyage.

10   Back in the cabin, I slid down into the warm furrow of my bunk and took a glimpse at the stars outside my porthole. With a deep breath, I picked up the journal and turned the page.

September 2
15:23

11   *An island in the distance (171'43" west, 2'21" north) veiled in mist. Possibly volcanic given the cone-shaped silhouette it presents. It looks a tropical place, with a crescent-shaped beach behind a green lagoon, and densely forested.*

12   *Sighted two albatross foraging over the ocean, plucking fish and squid from the water's surface with their long hooked beaks.*

---

porthole   A porthole is a small round window on a ship.
densely   If something is covered densely, the covering is so thick that it is difficult to see through.

17:45

13   *Closer to island now. Huge flock of albatross in distance. Most unusual to see so many together. Perhaps island is nesting ground. Their coloring is odd, no dark coloration on their wingtips or bodies. Their plumage seems a misty white, so that against cloud and sky they are scarcely visible. Only when they are against the ocean or the island can I make them out with any clarity.*

18:02

14   *Not birds.*

15   It sent a tingle through me, those two words, and I had to look up from
the book. I imagined Benjamin Molloy peering through his spyglass, his
hand tightening around the gondola's rim. What was it he'd seen that told
him these creatures weren't birds?

16   *Their wings are not feathered. I was mistaken about their beaks; they*
have none. Considerably bigger than either magnificent frigate birds or
albatross. One of the creatures broke from the flock and made a slow circle of
the Endurance, quite high at first, than spiraling down closer to the gondola.
It seemed very curious. Its body is easily six feet in length and closely furred.
Its forelegs seem to turn into wings, like a bat's, with a single protruding claw
at the wing's leading edge. The span I would estimate as eight or nine feet
across. Its rear legs are stubby but with wickedly sharp curved claws. I feared
for the balloon, should he collide with it. How can such a creature stay aloft?
It looks too heavy. It is fiercely agile in the sky, dipping and spinning and
diving with ease, its wings infinitely versatile. It fairly seems to leap through
the air. Saw scarcely anything of its face. A gleam of sizable incisors on upper
and lower jaws. A flash of intelligent green-flecked eyes. Then it veered off,
hurtling back toward its fellows.

17   *An undiscovered species?*

18   I turned the page and there was a picture, a pencil sketch. Just looking
at it made my heart flutter, and I had to sit up and catch my breath. He'd
put the rim of the basket in the foreground, and the silhouette of the island
in the background to give a sense of scale. The creature's wingspan was
huge. He was a deft hand, the grandfather, that was certain. Couldn't have
had much time to get it down, but his lines were swift and assured. It was
the strangest-looking thing, half bird, half panther.

September 4
13:25

19   *I have dropped into a calmer stratum of air so I can hover over the island*
and observe them. They float. They face into the wind and scarcely need beat
their wings. I watched one move not a muscle for hours, sleeping maybe,
bedded down on the air itself. They cannot weigh much.

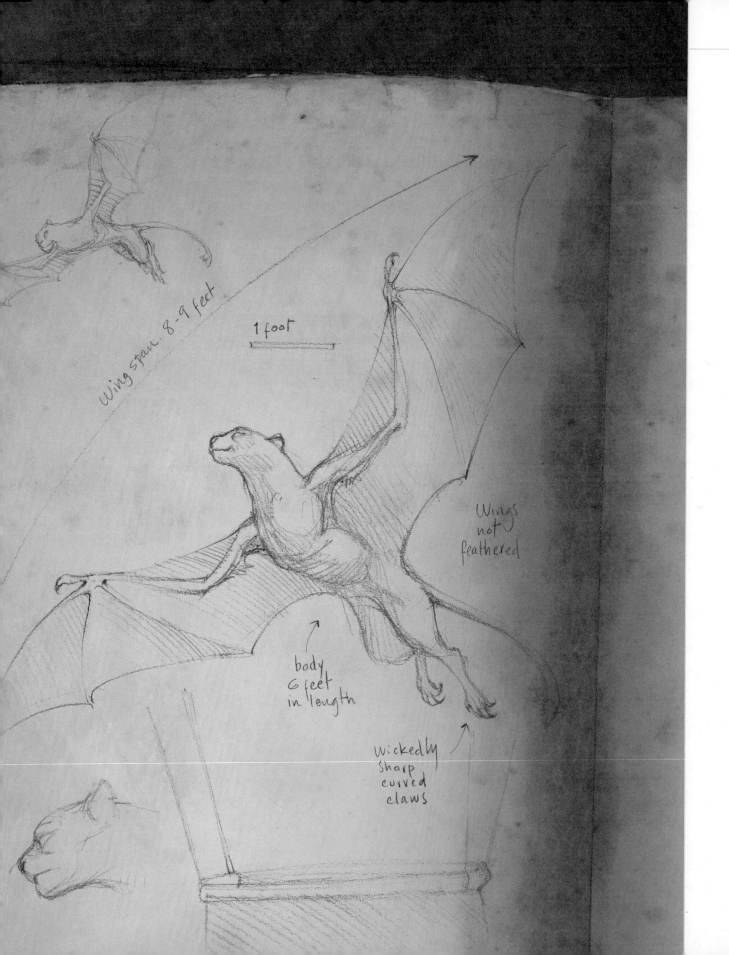

Wing span: 8-9 feet

1 foot

Wings not feathered

body 6 feet in length

Wickedly sharp curved claws

20   Across the next two pages were drawings of skeletons.

21   The first one was human, I saw that clearly enough, the rib cage, the hips, the skull atop the neck. Next to it was a skeleton that looked at first glance not so very much different. Except the hands. The bones of the fingers were all long and flared. It was freakish to look at, until I read Benjamin Molloy's caption underneath: *Bat*. Next to this was a third skeleton, and it seemed some sort of bizarre combination of the two. Shortened legs, like the bat, and instead of arms, the same weirdly flared finger bones of the bat. But the skull on this one was no bat's; nor was it human. The skull was flatter, with sharp teeth. Smaller, yes, but certainly no one would mistake this for a bat, and never for a bird. The drawings were made with scientific care, all shaded and with a length scale to the side. He was a clever man, Kate's grandpa, no questioning that. Seemed to know something about everything. Underneath were all sorts of Latin words.

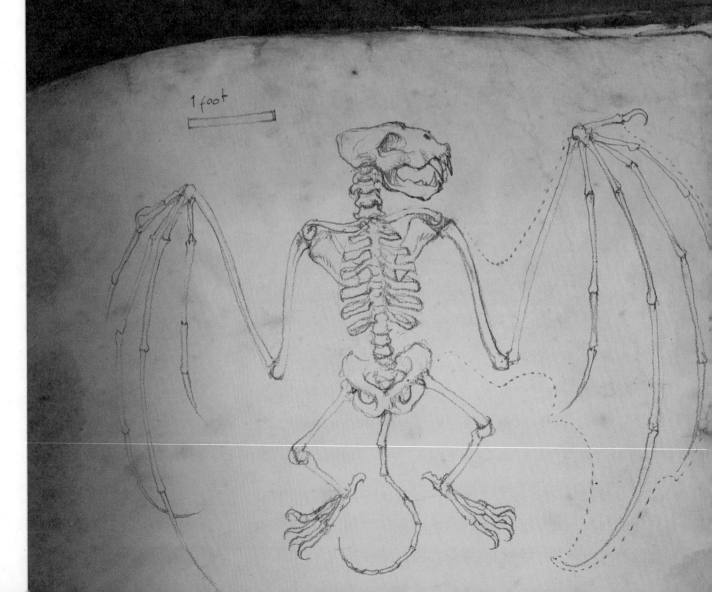

September 5

09:15

22 *Still playing the air currents around the island so I can watch them. They have a great curiosity for my balloon, circling high, but rarely drawing too close to the gondola. Difficult for me to see their bodies or faces more clearly. They seem wary of me; the sight of my spyglass makes them scatter in an instant. I wonder why?*

23 With a start I realized that these creatures could have been responsible for damaging his balloon. Had they tested the material with their sharp claws, torn enough little gashes to make it sink?

17:47

24 *They do not land. In all the time I've been observing, they haven't landed in the trees or on the water. They feed low over the island, preying on all manner of birds. They are voracious hunters. They also eat fish, strafing the water and plunging their rear claws into the sea as they brake. They come up with fish or small squid. They lift them high then flip them up to their mouths and take them whole. Sometimes they drop their prey and then dive down and snatch it into their mouths.*

September 6

11:17

25 *I have counted twenty-six of the creatures.*

26 *I wish Kate could see them, the way they gambol and swirl through the air. I've never seen an animal look so at home in its element. Like dolphins or porpoises or whales, they clearly love to play. Why has no one ever seen these before? Their natural camouflage is excellent, but with so many airships aloft now, surely someone else must have seen these creatures? Or are there very few? Are these the only ones in existence?*

27 On the next page was another sketch, of a great flock—or a herd, I wasn't sure what to call them—of these things circling over the coast of the island.

September 7
13:40

28　*They birth in the air.*

29　*One after another, one of the creatures—a female I now realize—
would soar to a great altitude, seven thousand feet or so. I increased my
lift so I could rise with them and keep watch. The female put her head to
the wind and angled her wings so she was hovering. Then something
dropped from her hindquarters. It happened so quickly all I was aware of
was a small dark bundle plunging away from her. At first I thought it was
merely her droppings. But I quickly realized it was too large. And the
female's behavior was most curious. Immediately she went into a dive too,
keeping pace with the falling object.*

30　*The object wobbled in the air and seemed to enlarge, even as it fell past
me. It was spreading its wings. It was no bigger than a kitten, but its
wings, as they unfurled, were many times the width of its body. Out went
the wings, instinctively angled so that the newborn's plunge began to slow
dramatically. After a moment or two I saw the wings lift and push
tentatively, then again, and again, each time with more force.*

31　*It was flying.*

32　*From the moment of birth, it knew how. How could such a thing be
possible? Incredible! But then, does not the newborn whale, born into the
element of water, know instantly how to swim? Why could it not be so
with this creature, then? Only air and not water was its element.*

33　*The mother flew close alongside its child, as if giving advice,
monitoring its progress.*

34　*I watched more females make the climb to the birthing altitude and
then release their newborns into the air.*

September 8th
12:51

35   *All are feeding today with a new kind of urgency. Are they on some kind of migration? I wonder where they're going? Where they come from? I suppose the sky is their home; they need no terrestrial haven. Perhaps they simply move from hemisphere to hemisphere looking for the warmest skies, and the birthing season coincides with the arrival in southern latitudes.*

19:35

36   *They're departing. Would like to follow, but they're too fast. With tailwinds, I would estimate eighty knots. Amazing creatures.*

37   *Gone now.*

38   *Weather changing.*

39   Maybe it was me, but I thought he sounded pretty dejected. When I turned the page I felt a bit queasy. Most of the handwriting was smeared, by torrential rain, I supposed, and I could make out only a few words. It seemed a tropical storm had overtaken him and kept him in its fist for some time. I think I saw the word *damage* in one entry, and a mention of a problem with the envelope. A hot flush swept my back. Was he leaking? Had the creatures torn his balloon, or was it just the storm?

40   Benjamin Molloy had stopped dating his entries, and his coordinates and weather observations seemed halfhearted now. His handwriting was all tilted, the letters slewing into one another. I remembered that we'd found him on September 13, so that left five days after his last dated entry. I wondered if he'd now fallen ill, too weak to repair his ship or keep his log properly. There were some more sketches of the creatures, and then, suddenly, the sketches became stranger, covering more and more of the pages.

41   Creatures with the faces of lions or eagles or women. Creatures with human faces, and furred bodies and wings that even not fully extended dwarfed their bodies. These were imaginings, surely, for they were so different from his earlier sketches, but drawn with such detail you'd have thought he'd had them right before his eyes.

42   There was only one more written entry in the log.

43   *Airship in the distance. Will signal for help.*

44   I looked for the date, but found none. It must have been the *Aurora* he'd sighted, but I'd certainly seen no signal from his gondola.

45   I stared at that last page for a while, the final words, the nothingness after it, and it got me feeling strange, so I had to close the book. I felt a keen disappointment. It was hard to know what to make of it all. At first the log had been so clear and reasonable, but by the end, especially with those pictures, it seemed he was dreaming. When did the real end, and the conjurings of a disturbed mind begin?

46   It was pushing two in the morning now, and I felt thoroughly ill at ease. I put the book on the shelf and eventually slept.

reasonable   If something is reasonable, it is logical and easy to understand.

47   I woke feeling as if I hadn't slept at all, head thrumming like a symphony. I sprang off the bunk, eager to get the journal back to Kate and talk to her. But it wasn't until lunch that I had a chance. At breakfast I was serving, and Kate's chaperone, Miss Simpkins, was at the table the whole time, and then she whisked Kate out before I could even hand her the journal. Then there was the clearing up and the preparing for lunch.

48   Around midday we were passing over the Hawaiis, and the captain slowed down and took us lower so the passengers could get a good look. On other trips we sometimes made stops, but this was a direct passage, so everyone had to content themselves with peering down at the lush foliage and hearing the shriek of macaws and spider monkeys and toucans and cockatoos; the heady scent of the islands' flowers reached us even at a hundred feet. We were close enough so people on the ground waved and cheered, and bathers on the beach shielded their eyes with tanned hands to look up at the great ship as it painted its massive shadow over the sand and water.

49   We were cruising over the outer islands when the captain entered the lounge, grinning.

50   "Ladies and gentlemen, a point of interest. Off the starboard side, we're passing Mount Mataurus, and, if I'm not mistaken, she is about to erupt."

51   Nearly everyone put down their forks and knives and rushed to the windows. In the distance was the island with its volcano, a great heap of stone, looking more like the devil's anvil than anything, despite the green hue of its lush vegetation. Great puffs of gray smoke were billowing up from its jaws, and getting darker by the second.

52   "Thar she blows!" shouted Baz.

53   Black bits of rock came shooting out from the cone, and the sound hit us a second later, a deep thunderous vibration that passed through the entire ship and rattled the windows. We were upwind of it, or we would have soon been choking on the ash and smoke it was venting high into the sky.

54   Soon the volcano was spitting out orange and red sparks, and then a glutinous tongue of black and orange lava oozed over the crater's rim and started a leisurely slide down the slope, incinerating everything in its path. Good thing this was an uninhabited island.

55   "Amazing, isn't it?"

56   I glanced over, and Kate was beside me. She was looking out the window, but I knew she wasn't talking about the volcano. There was no sign of Miss Simpkins, and there was no one else around us; everyone was watching the eruption, talking and pointing excitedly and snapping pictures.

57   "Incredible," I said and faltered, uncertain what to say next. I took the journal from my inside breast pocket and passed it to her. "Thank you."

58   "You don't believe it," she said coldly.

59   "I'm not saying that. It's just . . . I'm not altogether certain your grandpa really knew what he was seeing."

60 "How can you say that? He spent days watching them and taking down notes like a scientist. He couldn't have made up all these things. Not in such detail!"

61 It did seem an awful lot to imagine, even if he was delirious. I remembered his drawings. A weak, shaking hand couldn't have spun those lines.

62 "He always saw them from a distance," I pointed out.

63 "True, but think what he saw! The feeding, the birthing!"

64 "Those picture toward the end . . ." I had traversed the skies over Atlanticus and Pacificus and never had I seen such creatures. How to tell her that her grandpa had been ill and his fevered brain had projected these things on thin air for his failing eyes to see? I thought of all her camera equipment, her bottles of chemicals, and could not find it in my heart to speak the plain truth.

65 "You think like the others," she said, and there was a new hardness in her voice.

66 "I think your grandfather was unwell and saw things. Maybe," I added. All the friendly light in her eyes had frosted away, and it made me feel sick.

67 "No. He saw them. He'd been watching them for days."

68 She clenched the journal in both hands, knuckles white. "He was sick by then, I suppose," she said. "But maybe he didn't mean us to think those last drawings were real. He was just imagining."

69 "Your grandpa's not the first to see such things. They're called sky kelpies. You see them from time to time, reflections on the water mostly. All sorts of weird atmospheric things. Airshipmen used to report them all the time. It's like how sailors used to think there were mermaids. They were just porpoises and narwhals and such."

70 I could see she didn't like this much. I was insulting her. But what else could I say? I was just telling her the facts.

71 "Maybe you should talk to the captain about it," I suggested. "I'm sure he'd talk with you, miss."

72 Captain Walken surely must have read the journal last year when we took the gondola on board. I wondered that he'd never spoken of the strange things it contained—but of course he wouldn't have. He would never have divulged the contents of another captain's log to any but the relevant officers and authorities.

---

delirious When someone is delirious, he or she is confused due to fever or illness.
projected Something that is projected may appear to be real but is not.
contents The contents of a document are the topics or subjects it includes.

myNotes

73   "I don't need to talk to the captain about it. I expect I'd get much the same as what I've just heard from you."

74   "It's not that I haven't looked," I blurted out as she turned to leave. "I've looked, for all sorts of things, you can take my word on it. Every flicker in the sky." I shook my head. "I've never seen anything. But I'd love to. What your grandpa described is amazing. It sent shivers across my belly and then up into my armpits."

75   "Me too!" she said, nodding with a frown. "That tingly feeling. I get it every time I read it, and I've read it a hundred times now."

76   All the passengers in the lounge, including Miss Simpkins luckily, were still crowded around the windows, riveted by the eruption. The volcano was putting on quite a show. Half the island was aflame now, lava crackling and steaming as it poured into the water.

77   "Have you shown the journal to anyone else?" I asked her. "Your parents surely."

78   I saw her nostrils narrow as she sucked in an angry breath. "They're embarrassed by the whole business. Mother always thought he was odd. The traveling, the balloons. Just silly. They always thought he was a bit of a nutter. Hallucinations, that's what they said. 'Let's just forget the whole thing.' That's why I had to send the letter to the Zoological Society myself!"

79   I blinked.

80   "I couldn't let my parents stop this from getting out to the world! This is a major discovery—a new animal! I wrote them a letter describing more or less what my grandfather saw and asked them if they'd care to see a facsimile of his journal."

81   "Did they reply?"

82   "Oh, yes."

83   From her handbag she produced a letter. It was folded square, the creases so worn you could tell she'd folded and unfolded it many times. I could imagine her face when she read it, getting mad all over again. It wasn't a long letter, and I read it quickly:

84   Dear Miss de Vries,

85   Thank you for your letter. We appreciate your taking the time to tell us about your grandfather's observations on his balloon voyage, namely the sighting of "some kind of winged mammal."

86   We feel strongly that should such a creature exist it would surely have been sighted and documented long ago. Every year there are hundreds of unsubstantiated sightings of monstrous creatures in land, air, and sea and we feel it is our duty as men of science to gently remind you that your grandfather was not trained, and in his state of health, he may have suffered additional deficiencies of observation.

deficiencies   If someone has deficiencies, he or she has weaknesses or flaws.

87   "'Additional deficiencies of observation,'" Kate scoffed, reading over my shoulder. "They mean he was seeing things."

88   The rest of the letter was the usual "yours sincerely" and "thank you for your interest in the Zoological Society," etcetera, etcetera. It was signed Sir Hugh Snuffler. I saw him in my mind's eye. Short and balding with a big loud voice.

89   "As if they've explored every inch of the planet. As if anyone has! And what about you?" Kate fairly shouted.

90   "What about me?"

91   "You've flown for years, yes?"

92   "Well, three."

93   "And how much of the actual sky have you traversed?"

94   "Not much, when you put it that way."

95   "Exactly. Ships have their routes and, as you say, deviate from them only when necessary. That must leave millions and millions of miles of unexplored sky and sea!"

96   "I imagine you're right," I said, nodding.

97   "And how long have airships really been flying?"

98   "Fifty years or so now."

99   "Hardly any time at all, in other words. So how can we possibly know they don't exist?"

100   "Especially out here over the Pacificus," I said, surprising myself. "The skyways and sea lanes are much less well traveled, compared to the Atlanticus."

101   "Exactly," she said, beaming.

102   "Do your parents know you wrote to the Zoological Society?"

103   "Heavens, no! They would've locked me in my room without pen or paper! They'd have been mortified! Telling someone outside the family! Spreading his mad rantings!"

104   "Question is, is this all imagination or real?"

105   "The coordinates he wrote down, for the island. Do we pass over them?"

106   "I'd have to check, but I think not."

107   "Will you check, though?"

108   "Yes," I said.

109   "And if we don't pass over, will you tell me when we'll be nearest the spot?"

110   "I'll do that."

111   "Will you really?" She seemed amazed.

112   "Yes."

113   "Grandpa thought they were migrating, and this is the same time of year. We could see them."

114   I thought of her fancy camera.

115   "And what if you get a picture? What'll you do with it?"

116   "I'll send it directly to Sir Hugh Snufflynose at the Zoological Society. That'll set him straight."

117   I laughed. "I'm sure it will, miss."

118   "I wish you wouldn't call me 'miss.'"

119   "What should I call you?"

120   "Kate, of course."

121   "If I start calling you Kate now when it's just the two of us, I might slip up in public, and that'd be seen as impertinent."

122   "Silly rules."

123   "People like you invented them. Not me."

124   "Good point," she said appreciatively, a thoughtful crease in her brow. "Really good point."

125   "Here's what I'll do," I said. "When I get off duty, I'll check the charts and find out when we'll be closest."

126   "Thank you. I just hope it's during daylight."

127   "I hope you see them," I said. "I really do."

Collaborative Discussion

Look back at what you wrote on page 88 and talk with a partner about what you learned during reading. Then work with a group to discuss the questions below. Look for details in *Airborn* to support your answers. Think about ways to connect your ideas to what other group members say.

1. Reread pages 92–94. What do you learn about the narrator, Matt, based on his reactions to Benjamin Malloy's journal?

Listening Tip

Listen to the ideas and details each speaker shares. What new information can you add?

2. Review pages 94–96. What does Matt discover about the creatures from looking at Benjamin Malloy's drawings?

Speaking Tip

Think about how other speakers' ideas are related to your own. Ask questions to be sure you understand their ideas.

3. In what ways are the last entries in Benjamin Molloy's journal different from those at the beginning?

Write a Journal Entry

PROMPT

In *Airborn,* Matt and Kate have a journal, written by Kate's grandfather. The journal entries describe and illustrate mysterious flying creatures. At the end of the selection, Kate and Matt plan to search the area where her grandfather supposedly saw the creatures.

Imagine you are Kate or Matt, and you are writing a journal like the one Kate's grandfather kept. Write a journal entry telling about what happens when you look for the flying creatures. What do you see? How do you feel about your experiences? Be sure your journal entry tells the events of your experience in order and uses details from the text. You also can include an illustration with your entry, if you like. Don't forget to use some of the Critical Vocabulary words in your writing.

PLAN

Write a numbered list of the events you will describe in your entry. Make notes about each event.

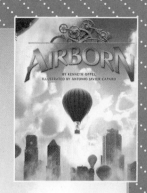

WRITE

Now write your journal entry describing your experience looking for the flying creatures.

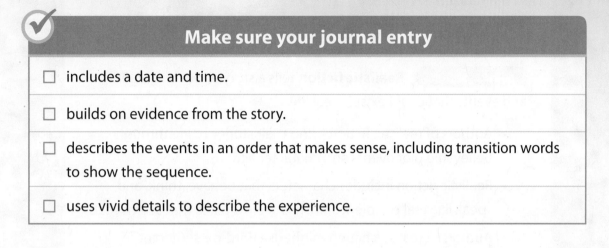

Make sure your journal entry

☐	includes a date and time.
☐	builds on evidence from the story.
☐	describes the events in an order that makes sense, including transition words to show the sequence.
☐	uses vivid details to describe the experience.

**Notice &
Note**
Contrasts and
Contradictions

Prepare to Read

> **GENRE STUDY**   **Realistic fiction** tells a story about characters
and events that could exist in real life.

- Authors of realistic fiction bring their stories to life through
  believable plot events and character actions.

- Realistic fiction includes characters that behave, think, and
  speak like real people would. It is set in a place that seems real.

- Authors of realistic fiction might use third-person point of
  view, where the story is told by an outside observer.

> **SET A PURPOSE**   **Think about** the title and genre of this text. As
you read, pay attention to descriptions that help you imagine the
characters and the setting. What do you think makes the garden
special? Write your ideas below.

CRITICAL VOCABULARY

mysterious

matted

tendrils

fastenings

awakening

**Meet the Author and Illustrator:
Frances Hodgson Burnett
and Helena Perez Garcia**

The Secret Garden

by Frances Hodgson Burnett

illustrated by Helena Perez Garcia

1 *Ten-year-old orphan Mary Lennox has recently moved from India to her uncle's mansion in England. Mary has made a few friends at the mansion, including the gardener, Ben Weatherstaff, and a friendly robin who often keeps Ben company. She's also discovered a mysterious, walled-off garden that's been abandoned for ten years. Mary would love to get inside this secret garden but hasn't been able to find an entrance. The day before, however, she found an old key, half buried in the dirt.*

2 The skipping-rope was a wonderful thing. She counted and skipped, and skipped and counted, until her cheeks were quite red, and she was more interested than she had ever been since she was born. The sun was shining and a little wind was blowing—not a rough wind, but one which came in delightful little gusts and brought a fresh scent of newly turned earth with it. She skipped round the fountain garden, and up one walk and down another. She skipped at last into the kitchen-garden and saw Ben Weatherstaff digging and talking to his robin, which was hopping about him. She skipped down the walk toward him. He lifted his head and looked at her with a curious expression. She had wondered if he would notice her. She really wanted him to see her skip.

3   Mary skipped round all the gardens and round the orchard, resting every few minutes. At length she went to her own special walk. She made up her mind to try to skip the whole length of it. It was a good long skip and she began slowly, but before she had gone halfway down the path she was so hot and breathless that she was obliged to stop. She did not mind much, because she had already counted up to thirty. She stopped with a little laugh of pleasure. There, lo and behold, was the robin swaying on a long branch of ivy. He had followed her and he greeted her with a chirp. As Mary had skipped toward him she felt something heavy in her pocket strike against her at each jump. When she saw the robin she laughed again.

4   "You showed me where the key was yesterday," she said. "You ought to show me the door today; but I don't believe you know!"

5   The robin flew from his swinging spray of ivy on to the top of the wall and he opened his beak and sang a loud, lovely trill, merely to show off. Nothing in the world is quite as adorably lovely as a robin when he shows off—and they are nearly always doing it.

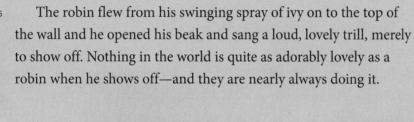

6   Mary Lennox had heard a great deal about Magic in stories, and she always said that what happened almost at that moment was Magic.

7   One of the nice little gusts of wind rushed down the walk, and it was a stronger one than the rest. It was strong enough to wave the branches of the trees. It was more than strong enough to sway the trailing sprays of untrimmed ivy hanging from the wall. Mary had stepped close to the robin, and suddenly the gust of wind swung aside some loose ivy trails. More suddenly still she jumped toward it and caught it in her hand. This she did because she had seen something under it—a round knob which had been covered by the leaves hanging over it. It was the knob of a door.

8   She put her hands under the leaves and began to pull and push them aside. Thick as the ivy hung, it nearly all was a loose and swinging curtain, though some had crept over wood and iron. Mary's heart began to thump and her hands to shake a little in her delight and excitement. The robin kept singing and twittering away and tilting his head on one side, as if he were as excited as she was. What was this under her hands which was square and made of iron and which her fingers found a hole in?

9   It was the lock of the door which had been closed ten years. She put her hand in her pocket, drew out the key and found it fitted the keyhole. She put the key in and turned it. It took two hands to do it, but it did turn.

10   And then she took a long breath and looked behind her up the long walk to see if any one was coming. No one was coming. No one ever did come, it seemed. She took another long breath, because she could not help it. She held back the swinging curtain of ivy and pushed back the door which opened slowly—slowly.

11   Then she slipped through it, and shut it behind her, and stood with her back against it, looking about her and breathing quite fast with excitement, and wonder, and delight.

12   She was standing *inside* the secret garden.

13   It was the sweetest, most mysterious-looking place any one could imagine. The high walls which shut it in were covered with the leafless stems of climbing roses which were so thick that they were matted together. Mary Lennox knew they were roses because she had seen a great many roses in India. All the ground was covered with grass of a wintry brown. Out of it grew clumps of bushes which were surely rose-bushes if they were alive. There were numbers of standard roses which had so spread their branches that they were like little trees.

14   There were other trees in the garden, and one of the things which made the place look strangest and loveliest was that climbing roses had run all over them and swung down long tendrils which made light swaying curtains. Here and there they had caught at each other or at a far-reaching branch and had crept from one tree to another and made lovely bridges of themselves. There were neither leaves nor roses on them now and Mary did not know whether they were dead or alive. But their thin gray or brown branches and sprays looked like a sort of hazy mantle spreading over everything, walls, and trees, and even brown grass, where they had fallen from their fastenings and run along the ground. It was this hazy tangle from tree to tree which made it all look so mysterious. Mary had thought it must be different from other gardens which had not been left all by themselves so long. Indeed it was different from any other place she had ever seen in her life.

15   "How still it is!" she whispered. "How still!"

16   Then she waited a moment and listened at the stillness. The robin, who had flown to his tree-top, was still as all the rest. He did not even flutter his wings; he sat without stirring, and looked at Mary.

---

mysterious   Something that is mysterious is not fully understood or explainable.

matted   Something that is matted is a tangled mess.

tendrils   Tendrils of plants are long, thin sections that often twist around an object or another plant.

fastenings   Fastenings attach objects to other things.

17   "No wonder it is still," she whispered again. "I am the first
person who has spoken in here for ten years."

18   She moved away from the door, stepping as softly as if she were
afraid of awakening someone. She was glad that there was grass
under her feet and that her steps made no sounds. She walked
under one of the fairy-like gray arches between the trees and looked
up at the sprays and tendrils which formed them.

19   "I wonder if they are all quite dead," she said. "Is it all a quite
dead garden? I wish it wasn't."

20   If she had been Ben Weatherstaff she could have told whether
the wood was alive by looking at it. But she could only see that there
were only gray or brown sprays and branches and none showed any
signs of even a tiny leaf-bud anywhere.

21   But she was *inside* the wonderful garden and she could come
through the door under the ivy any time and she felt as if she had
found a world all her own.

awakening   If you are awakening someone, you are waking him or her
from sleep.

120

Collaborative Discussion

Look back at what you wrote on page 112. Talk with a partner about what you learned about the garden. Then work with a group to discuss the questions below. Use details from *The Secret Garden* to back up your answers. In your discussion, build on what others say or add more details and examples.

1 Review pages 114–115. What words and phrases make Mary and what she is doing seem realistic?

Listening Tip

Listen closely to examples that other group members share. Add to or support their ideas using evidence from the text.

2 Reread pages 119–120. What details help you understand why Mary feels excited as she explores the garden?

Speaking Tip

Use linking words such as *also* or *another example* to show how your thoughts connect to what another speaker has said.

3 Why does the garden make Mary feel as if she has "found a world all her own"?

Write the Next Scene

PROMPT

In *The Secret Garden,* you read how Mary discovered a hidden, locked door and wondered what was on the other side. When she unlocked the door and saw the dead but wild-looking garden, she felt "as if she had found a world all her own."

Imagine what might take place next now that Mary has discovered this secret place. Write a scene to continue the story. Include a beginning, middle, and end for the scene, as well as details based on evidence from the story. Don't forget to use some of the Critical Vocabulary words in your writing.

PLAN

Make notes about events for your new scene, organized into "beginning," "middle," and "end." Include details gathered from text evidence.

WRITE

Now write the next scene in *The Secret Garden*.

Make sure your scene
☐ builds on previous information from the text.
☐ includes a clear beginning, middle, and end.
☐ explains events in an order that makes sense.
☐ uses strong, descriptive words to describe the characters, setting, and events.

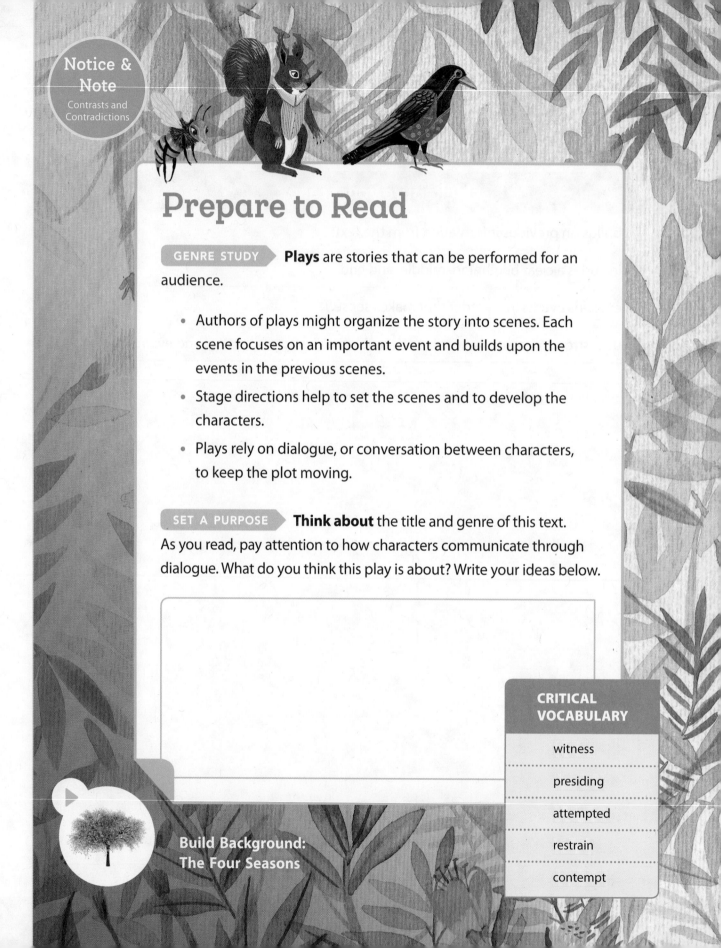

Notice & Note
Contrasts and
Contradictions

Prepare to Read

GENRE STUDY **Plays** are stories that can be performed for an audience.

- Authors of plays might organize the story into scenes. Each scene focuses on an important event and builds upon the events in the previous scenes.

- Stage directions help to set the scenes and to develop the characters.

- Plays rely on dialogue, or conversation between characters, to keep the plot moving.

SET A PURPOSE **Think about** the title and genre of this text. As you read, pay attention to how characters communicate through dialogue. What do you think this play is about? Write your ideas below.

Build Background:
The Four Seasons

CRITICAL VOCABULARY

witness

presiding

attempted

restrain

contempt

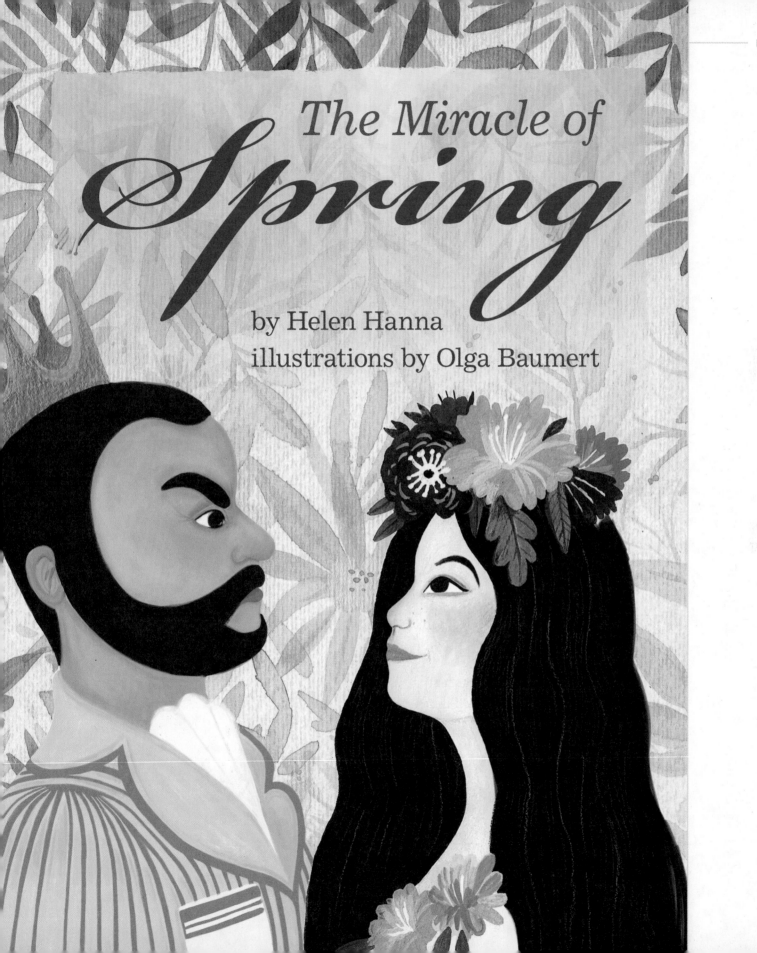

The Miracle of Spring

by Helen Hanna

illustrations by Olga Baumert

Characters

KING BARTHOLOMEW

KING'S VALET

PRIME MINISTER

DOOR GUARD

CAPTAIN OF THE GUARD

TWO GUARDS

SPRING

MOTHER NATURE'S COURT

JUDGE WISE OWL

THE CROW

EAGER BEAVER

MRS. APPLE TREE

MR. SQUIRREL

MS. WINTER WHEAT

MS. STRING BEAN

MS. BESSIE COW

MR. WOOLLY LAMB

MS. HONEYBEE

JURY

ANIMALS

BIRDS

INSECTS

TREES

FLOWERS

King Bartholomew bans Spring, only to realize that he has shown disrespect for Mother Nature, upset the cycles of the seasons, and destroyed the food supply.

Production Notes

CHARACTERS: 3 male, 6 female, 9 male or female; as many male and female as desired for jury. (Actors may also play more than one role with a change of costume.)

PLAYING TIME: 15 minutes

COSTUMES: The King wears pajamas, a small crown, and dressing gown at the end of the play. The members of his court wear the traditional costumes of fairy tale courts. Mother Nature's Court has headpieces suggesting their separate characterizations. Judge Wise Owl wears long black robe and glasses. Spring wears long white gown and a garland of flowers in her hair, and the word "Spring" on a sash across her chest.

PROPERTIES: Tray with spoon, dishes, medicine, Judge's bench, gavel, witness box, piece of paper for Prime Minister's report.

SETTING: King's bedroom. Down right is a door leading to castle interior. A large "French door" type window is at left. At center is a large bed with many pillows and quilts on it. Near the bed are a night table and a bell cord.

LIGHTING: Lights are dimmed for dream sequence and brought up full again as indicated in the text.

SOUND: Bell tolling six times.

---

witness   A witness is someone who appears in court to say what he or she knows about a crime.

Act 1

SETTING: *King Bartholomew's bedroom.*

AT RISE: *KING BARTHOLOMEW sits up in his bed, with a dinner tray on his lap. His VALET stands at his bedside. At the door stands DOOR GUARD.*

1   **KING** (*Making a grimace and replacing spoon in his plate*): Zounds! What is this tasteless pap?

2   **VALET:** Cook calls it Spring Pudding, Sire. It's on your diet!

3   **KING:** Bah! Take it away. It's not what I eat that makes my stomach ache. It's aggravation! That tour of the kingdom yesterday—that's what made me sick!

4   **VALET:** It was a beautiful day for a tour, Sire. Spring has warmed the air and budded the trees.

5   **KING** (*Extremely aggravated*): Indeed! And Spring has turned my hardworking subjects into daydreaming idlers, dozing in the sunshine. Everywhere I went—no one was working!

6   **VALET:** Just a touch of spring fever, Your Highness.

7   **KING:** Spring fever is just another name for laziness! And I won't have it! Has the Captain of the Guard reported yet?

8   **VALET:** No, Sire, but the Prime Minister is waiting to see you.

9   **KING:** Send him in. And find the Chancellor for me.

10   **VALET** (*To DOOR GUARD*): The King will see the Prime Minister. (*VALET exits.*)

11   **DOOR GUARD:** The Prime Minister to see the King. (*PRIME MINISTER enters and bows.*)

12   **PRIME MINISTER:** Your Majesty, good evening.

13   **KING:** Where is the report I ordered?

14   **PRIME MINISTER:** It's not quite finished yet, Sire. I came to ask a favor. I'd like to take the day off tomorrow, to take my kids fishing.

15   **KING** (*Exploding*): Fishing! Of all the ridiculous things! (*Doubles over in pain*) Out, out with you! (*As PRIME MINISTER hastily retreats, VALET enters.*)

16   **VALET:** The Chancellor has not yet returned from the tournament.

17   **KING** (*Exploding again*): Tournament! Then I'll talk to the Chamberlain.

18   **VALET:** He's taken his family on an outing, Sire.

19   **KING** (*Again in pain*): Outing! Give me my medicine. And get the Captain of the Guard, immediately!

20   **VALET** (*To DOOR GUARD*): Summon the Captain. (*GUARD exits.*)

21   **KING** (*Taking medicine which VALET hands him from night table*): Fishing! Tournaments! Outings! (*DOOR GUARD enters.*)

22   **DOOR GUARD:** The Captain of the Royal Guard! (*CAPTAIN enters.*)

23   **CAPTAIN:** At your command, Your Highness.

24   **KING:** Have you taken your prisoner yet?

25   **CAPTAIN:** Yes, Your Highness, the prisoner is outside.

26   **KING:** Then bring the criminal to me. (*CAPTAIN salutes and exits, returning immediately with TWO GUARDS, leading between them SPRING.*)

129

27   **VALET** (*Shocked*): 'Tis the maiden, Spring!

28   **KING:** You! You are the one who has turned my kingdom upside down with fishing tournaments and outings! I'll not have it, do you understand? I'll keep you under lock and key, so you can do no more mischief! (*SPRING remains silent.*) Take the prisoner to the dungeon, and see that every measure is taken to prevent her escape. (*KING falls back against pillows, exhausted, as GUARDS salute and lead SPRING away. KING turns weakly to VALET.*) You—stop staring like an idiot, and get out of here. I am exhausted. Wake me at six o'clock tomorrow morning.

29   **VALET:** As you wish, Your Highness. Pleasant dreams, Sire. (*VALET takes tray and exits.*)

30   **KING** (*To DOOR GUARD*): You, too, out!

31   **DOOR GUARD:** Good night, Your Majesty. (*Exits*)

(*KING closes his eyes. Lights dim.*)

Act 2

Scene 1

SETTING: *King's bedroom*

AT RISE: *KING is sleeping. Suddenly, the large, downstage window opens and CROW steps in. He looks around, then signals to the other members of Mother Nature's Court. All except JUDGE enter. They carry a bench and witness box, which they set up where it can be seen by KING. Jury sits together, either on the floor or on folding chairs which they carry with them. The witnesses remain together in another area.*

1   **CROW:** Caw! Caw! Hear ye! Hear ye! Mother Nature's Court is now in session. Judge Wise Owl presiding. All rise. (*All rise as JUDGE OWL enters, goes to bench and sits. KING awakens.*)

2   **JUDGE OWL** (*Pounding gavel*): What is the first case before the court?

3   **CROW:** Mother Nature vs. King Bartholomew, Your Honor.

4   **JUDGE:** Is the attorney for Mother Nature ready?

5   **EAGER BEAVER:** Ready, Your Honor. Your Honor, ladies and gentlemen of the jury, I, Eager Beaver, shall prove beyond a shadow of a doubt that King Bartholomew is guilty of attempted murder.

6   **KING** (*Sitting up in his bed*): Murder! I have never murdered anybody!

7   **JUDGE:** Quiet, please.

8   **BEAVER:** I said, "Attempted murder."

9   **KING:** I have never even "attempted" murder!

10   **JUDGE:** You will have to restrain yourself, Sire—or you will be held in contempt of court. You may proceed, Mr. Eager Beaver.

11   **BEAVER:** I speak of the attempt to murder by starvation.

12   **KING:** I have never starved anybody! Even the prisoners in our jail are given the finest peanut butter and jelly!

13   **JUDGE:** This is your last warning, Sire.

---

presiding   If you are presiding over an event, you are in charge of it.

attempted   If you attempted something, you tried to do it.

restrain   When you restrain yourself, you stop yourself from doing what you want to do.

contempt   When you show contempt, you show little or no respect for someone or something.

14   **BEAVER:** I call my first witness, Mrs. Apple Tree. (*APPLE TREE comes forward.*)

15   **CROW:** Raise your right hand. Do you swear to tell the truth, the whole truth, and nothing but the truth?

16   **APPLE TREE** (*Raising hand*): I do.

17   **BEAVER:** Mrs. Tree, will you tell the court, please, why you are all dressed in drab brown, instead of the bright green you usually wear this time of year?

18   **APPLE TREE:** Because there is no spring this year. King Bartholomew has forbidden spring to come to this kingdom.

19   **BEAVER:** And is that why you are not wearing your pretty bonnet, decked with blossoms?

20   **APPLE TREE:** Yes, and I miss it so, not only because every tree likes to look her prettiest, but also because it means I won't have any apples this year. The apples come from those spring blossoms.

21   **BEAVER:** And do you speak for the other fruit trees as well?

22   **APPLE TREE:** I do. There won't be any pears or peaches or cherries or plums. No spring—no blossoms—no fruit.

23 **BEAVER:** Thank you, Mrs. Tree. That will be all. We have now proved that the people of the kingdom will have no fruit to eat this year. Next witness, Mr. Squirrel. (*SQUIRREL steps forward and is sworn in by CROW.*) Now, Mr. Squirrel, you are not your usual cheery self these days. Why is that?

24 **SQUIRREL:** I'm worried. And so are all my brothers, sisters, cousins, and friends.

25 **BEAVER:** Will you tell the court why you are worried?

26 **SQUIRREL:** Because we are going to starve to death next winter. Last year's harvest of nuts is almost gone, and there won't be any nuts this year.

27 **BEAVER:** No nuts? How's that?

28 **SQUIRREL:** Because the nuts are the fruits of the nut trees, just as the apples and pears are the fruits of the trees in the orchard. No blossoms on the nut trees—no nuts!

29 **BEAVER:** Thank you, Mr. Squirrel. You may step down. (*SQUIRREL returns to his place.*) The court has now heard that we will have no fruit and no nuts in the kingdom this year. This will affect the lives of both the people and the animals. Next witness—Ms. Winter Wheat. (*WINTER WHEAT is sworn in by CROW.*) Will you tell the court, please, why you are known as "Winter Wheat."

30   **WINTER WHEAT:** Because the farmer sows my seeds very early in the winter, before the ground freezes. He does this because he wants an early wheat crop in the spring.

31   **BEAVER:** That is a wise farmer. Will he have an early wheat crop as a result?

32   **WHEAT:** No, he won't. Because the ground has to thaw and get warm before we can poke our green shoots through. Since there won't be any spring this year, there won't be any crop of winter wheat, or any other kind of wheat, for that matter!

33   **BEAVER:** What will that mean to the people?

34   **WHEAT:** No wheat, no alfalfa, or barley, or corn, or any other kind of grain. And that means no cereals, and no flour, no bread, or rolls, or cake, or pies.

35   **BEAVER:** Thank you, Ms. Wheat. You may step down. (*She does so.*) Well—no fruits. No nuts. No grains. No cereals. No flour. No baked goods to eat. Next witness, Ms. String Bean. (*STRING BEAN is sworn in by CROW.*) Ms. String Bean, your face looks especially long and thin this year. Why is that?

36   **STRING BEAN:** Because I'm so sorry for all the people who will be without me and all the other vegetables this year.

37   **BEAVER:** No vegetables this year? And why not, Ms. Bean?

38   **STRING BEAN:** Because the ground is hard and frozen, and the farmers cannot sow their seeds. And even the seeds that fell into the ground last year from Mother Nature's hand (*sobs*) cannot mature into plants without warm soil and sun. (*Sobs*)

39   **BEAVER:** There, there, Ms. Bean. I can see you're quite broken up. You are excused. (*She returns to her place.*) I think it's quite clear to the court why there will be no vegetables this year. Next witness, Ms. Bessie Cow. (*CROW swears in BESSIE COW.*) Bessie, I believe you have a story to tell the court.

40   **BESSIE:** A sad, sad story. I don't know how much longer there will be any milk, or cream, or cheese, or ice cream for the people of the kingdom.

41   **BEAVER:** Now, this sounds serious, indeed! Are you sure?

42   **BESSIE:** Cows can't give milk unless they have nice green grass to eat. Where are we going to find nice green grass in this winter landscape? And soon our winter supply of hay, alfalfa, oats, and corn will be all gone. No food—no milk!

43   **BEAVER:** Thank you, Bessie. (*BESSIE returns to place.*) No milk, no butter, no cream, no cheese, no ice cream. Next witness, Mr. Woolly Lamb. (*WOOLLY LAMB is sworn in by CROW.*) Mr. Lamb, you're extremely woolly for this time of year, aren't you?

44   **WOOLLY LAMB:** Shiver my timbers, yes. Usually the farmer's gone to work on me with his electric clippers by this time of year. But now— b-r-r-r-r! It's too cold for me to do without my overcoat.

45   **BEAVER:** What will this mean to the people of the kingdom?

46   **WOOLLY LAMB:** No wool for warm clothing and blankets, and if this winter weather continues, they will need more woolen clothing than ever before.

47   **BEAVER:** Thank you. (*LAMB returns to his place.*) Next witness, Ms. Honey Bee. (*HONEY BEE is sworn in by CROW.*) What are you buzzing about so furiously, Ms. Bee?

48   **HONEY BEE:** I'm so angry I could sting!

49   **BEAVER:** Why?

50   **BEE:** Because I'm the champion honey maker, that's why. Last year I won a blue ribbon at the county fair, and this year I won't be able to make a single drop of the delicious golden nectar.

51   **BEAVER:** No honey this year? That's terrible.

52   **BEE:** No one will be sorrier than King Bartholomew, because he just loves honey on his bread! A bee can't make honey without flowers, and you can't expect the gardeners to grow flowers when there isn't any spring. I tell you, I'm as angry as a bee can be.

53   **BEAVER:** Thank you, Ms. Bee. You may step down.

54   **BEE** (*Speaking angrily as she walks away from the witness box*): And the bears—they'll be simply wild without their honey!

55   **BEAVER** (*To jury*): We're all going to miss the flowers this year—and the birds—and the sunshine. But, most importantly (*Patting his stomach*) we're all going to miss our food! King Bartholomew is attempting to starve us! And I say he deserves to be found guilty and given the harshest punishment Judge Owl can deliver!

56   **JURY** (*Rising*): Yes! Guilty! Guilty! Guilty!

57   **KING** (*Jumping out of his bed*): Wait!

58   **JUDGE:** I warned you that the next outburst from you would be in contempt of court. See that he keeps quiet. (*CROW, witnesses, and jury advance menacingly toward KING, who hurriedly climbs back into bed and pulls covers over his head.*)

59   **JURY** (*Chanting in a low monotone*): Guilty. Guilty. Guilty. (*Suddenly, a bell tolls six times. All the characters of Mother Nature's Court quickly exit through the downstage window, taking their props with them.*)

137

Scene 2

SETTING: *King's bedroom*

AT RISE: *The lights come up full, and KING jumps out of bed, pulls bell cord. DOOR GUARD opens door, takes his customary stand.*

60 **DOOR GUARD:** Good morning, Your Highness. I trust you slept well.

61 **KING:** It was a terrible night, just terrible. What a dream! Where's my valet?

62 **DOOR GUARD:** He is coming now, Your Highness. (*VALET enters.*)

63 **VALET:** Good morning, Your Majesty.

64 **KING:** Get me my dressing gown. Hurry! (*VALET helps him into his dressing gown while he talks.*) Find the Captain of the Guard, immediately!

65 **VALET** (*To DOOR GUARD*): The Captain of the Guard, immediately!

66 **KING** (*Pacing*): I've done a very terrible thing. I only hope it's not too late.

67 **DOOR GUARD:** The Captain of the Guard! (*CAPTAIN enters.*)

68 **CAPTAIN** (*Trembling, and dropping to his knees*): It wasn't my fault. The chains were tight, and the door securely locked and barred.

69 **KING:** Stop your prattling. There's no time to lose. Go quickly and see to it that the chains are removed from the maiden, Spring, and bring her to me so that I may apologize to her.

70 **CAPTAIN:** That's what I'm trying to tell you. She isn't there. She's gone!

71 **KING:** Gone?

72 **SPRING** (*Stepping through downstage window*): Did you want to see me? (*She smiles at KING.*)

73 **KING** (*Dropping to his knees before her*): Can you forgive a foolish man the greatest mistake of his life?

74 **SPRING** (*Extending her hand to him and bidding him to rise*): A foolish man you have been—to think that you, or any other man or woman, could command the forces of nature at your will. Did you really believe that dungeon doors or iron chains could keep Spring from walking your land?

75 **KING** (*Contritely*): I was foolish. Now I know better.

76 **SPRING:** Spring is a yearly miracle of nature, as constant as the moon and the stars. Planting time and harvest time, summer and winter, day and night—these must always come.

77 **KING:** What can I do to earn your forgiveness?

78 **SPRING:** Open your eyes and heart to your environment. Now, if you don't mind, I must be on my way, my spring wonders to perform. (*SPRING takes KING's arm and they walk to window. SPRING steps through it, smiling, and disappears. KING remains at the window, watching her depart, waving. KING takes a deep breath and, smiling, turns back toward the room.*)

79 **DOOR GUARD:** The Prime Minister to see the King.

80 **KING:** Good. (*PRIME MINISTER enters with a paper in her hand.*) You're just the person I want to see.

81 **PRIME MINISTER:** Your report. I stayed up all night to finish it.

82 **KING:** Never mind that now. Tell me, is this the day you wished to take your kids fishing?

83 **PRIME MINISTER:** Forgive me, Sire. It was foolish of me.

84 **KING:** Not at all. You may have the day off—on one condition.

85 **PRIME MINISTER:** Condition?

86 **KING:** Yes—the condition that you take me with you!

87 **PRIME MINISTER** (*Astonished*): You? Fishing?

88 **KING:** Yes. I think it would be good for my stomachache. Besides, it
89 seems I have a touch of—spring fever! (*Curtain*)

The End

Collaborative Discussion

Look back at what you wrote on page 124. Tell a partner two things you learned during reading. Then work with a group to discuss the questions below. Support your answers with details from *The Miracle of Spring*. In your discussion, explain how your ideas connect to those of others in your group.

1　Review pages 128–129. Why is King Bartholomew so annoyed with his subjects?

Listening Tip

Look at each speaker while you're listening, to show you are paying attention.

2　Reread pages 132–136. Why will it be difficult to find food if spring is forbidden? How do the witnesses feel about this possibility?

Speaking Tip

Think about how discussion ideas are connected. Use other speakers' comments as a starting point for your own.

3　How does King Bartholomew change from the beginning of the play to the end? What causes this change?

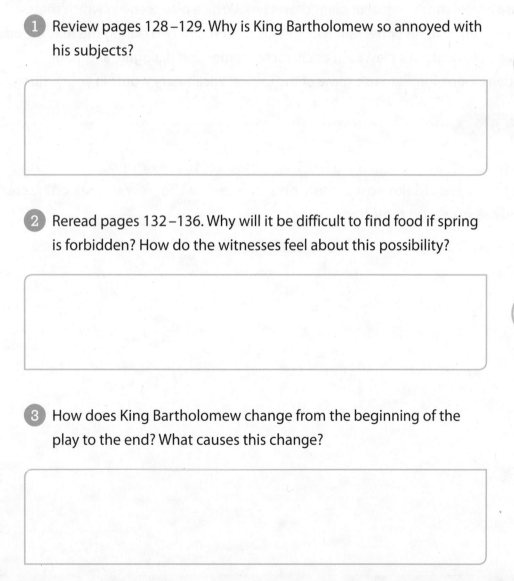

Write a Play Scene

PROMPT

In *The Miracle of Spring,* a king is angry because people are enjoying the arrival of Spring instead of working. So, he tries to lock Spring away. The king is then put on trial, and several animal and plant characters in the courtroom explain what would happen without Spring.

Choose one of those animal or plant characters. Write a play scene in which the character retells to his or her family or friends what happened during the trial. Include the basic elements of a play, such as character names and dialogue, and stage directions. Don't forget to use some of the Critical Vocabulary words in your writing.

PLAN

Take notes about events from the trial based on text evidence, in the order they happened. Make notes, too, about names for the new scene's characters and ideas for stage directions.

WRITE

Now write your play scene that retells what happened during the trial.

Make sure your play scene

- ☐ uses a play format, including character names and stage directions.
- ☐ has dialogue for the animal or plant character that is similar to how the character spoke in the story.
- ☐ retells events from the trial in sequence, based on evidence from the story.

Notice & Note
Contrasts and
Contradictions

Prepare to Read

GENRE STUDY **Poetry** uses the sounds and rhythms of words
to show images and express feelings.

- Poems include sound effects, such as rhyme, rhythm, and
  meter, to reinforce the meaning of the poem. Not all poems
  rhyme, but they all have a rhythm.

- Poems include word sounds, such as alliteration,
  onomatopoeia, repetition, and parallel structure, to
  emphasize particular words or ideas.

- Poems include figurative language to develop ideas.

- Poems might be organized into stanzas, or a series of lines
  grouped together. Each stanza builds upon what is described
  in the previous stanza.

SET A PURPOSE **Think about** the title and
genre of this text. As you read, pay attention to the
rhyme and rhythm in each poem. What do you
know about poetic forms? Write your ideas here.

CRITICAL VOCABULARY
seized
hesitate
watchful
scrawled
ditty
refrain
restless

Meet the Author and Illustrator:
Joan Bransfield Graham and
Kyrsten Brooker

THE POEM THAT WILL NOT END

FUN with POETIC FORMS and VOICES

by Joan Bransfield Graham

illustrated by Kyrsten Brooker

1 After most poems in this selection you'll see a label that identifies the poem's form. You'll learn more about these forms in "Ryan O'Brian's Guide to Poetic Forms" at the end of the selection.

2 **It started with a rhythm,
a rhythm and a rhyme.
It wouldn't let me stop,
it ate up all my time.**

Rhythm

3 I was seized by a rhythmical beat.
It was something I could not delete.
I went crazy with rhyme,
It just gobbled my time,
Had me clapping and tapping my feet.

LIMERICK

seized If you were seized by an idea or feeling, you were suddenly overwhelmed by it.

4 I tried to eat my breakfast
but didn't hesitate
to scribble on the napkins
and doodle cross my plate.

hesitate If you hesitate, you wait to speak or act because you're not sure what to say or do.

GOING BANANAS

5 Baby brother loves to smear
banana every place,
then squeeze it through his fingers
and wipe it on his face.

6 He blows banana bubbles
and makes banana goo—
oh yuck, ugh, ew, what a mess!
I'd like to do that, too.

QUATRAINS

7   It teased me as I walked to school—
I **scrawled** on Eddie's shirt.

Footprints

8   Smooth patch of white snow,
Stretched out before watchful eyes—
an invitation!

—Ryan O'Brian

HAIKU

scrawled   If you scrawled something, you wrote it quickly and sloppily.

watchful   If you are watchful, you pay attention to everything around you.

9 And, when we hit the playground,
I scratched words in the dirt.

THE BASEBALL GAME

10 The kids creamed the teachers,
listen to the score:
The third graders beat them—
twenty-five to four!

11 We got them out at second,
we caught their pop flies.
We got them out at home plate,
much to their surprise.

12 When we scored all the home runs,
we screamed and made a fuss.
We may get Ds in English,
but in baseball we're A+!

QUATRAINS

13 Then in the cafeteria—
with just two tasty tries—
between my lunch and Aimee's,
I wrote two lines with fries.

14 COUPLET FOR FRENCH FRIES
Two lines are not enough to express
How much I adore your potato-ness.

COUPLET

15　I ran outside at recess,
　　pulled out a piece of chalk,
　　didn't waste a minute—
　　dashed poems on the walk.

16　RECESS
Rambunctious
Excitement
Centering around
Excessive
Silly
Stuff

ACROSTIC

CAPTURED

17 I'm captured, won't you help me find a way,
to free me from this urgent need to write?
It follows me and hounds me night and day.
I'm captured, won't you help me find a way,
to toss aside this curse—I want to play!
You must admit . . . this is a scary sight.
I'm captured, won't you help me find a way,
to free me from this urgent need to write?

TRIOLET

18 I beg you, won't you help me?
Please help me, be a friend.
Rescue me, I'm captured—
this poem will not end!

19 The bell rang and I bolted,
wasn't running out of steam.
I wrote with mud out in the yard—
chased by the soccer team.

SOCCER BALL

20 Soccer ball,
you are the center,
sun of our universe.
We are planets orbiting
your supreme presence,
hoping to rocket you,
like a blazing comet,
into the galaxy of
our goal.

CONCRETE, FREE VERSE

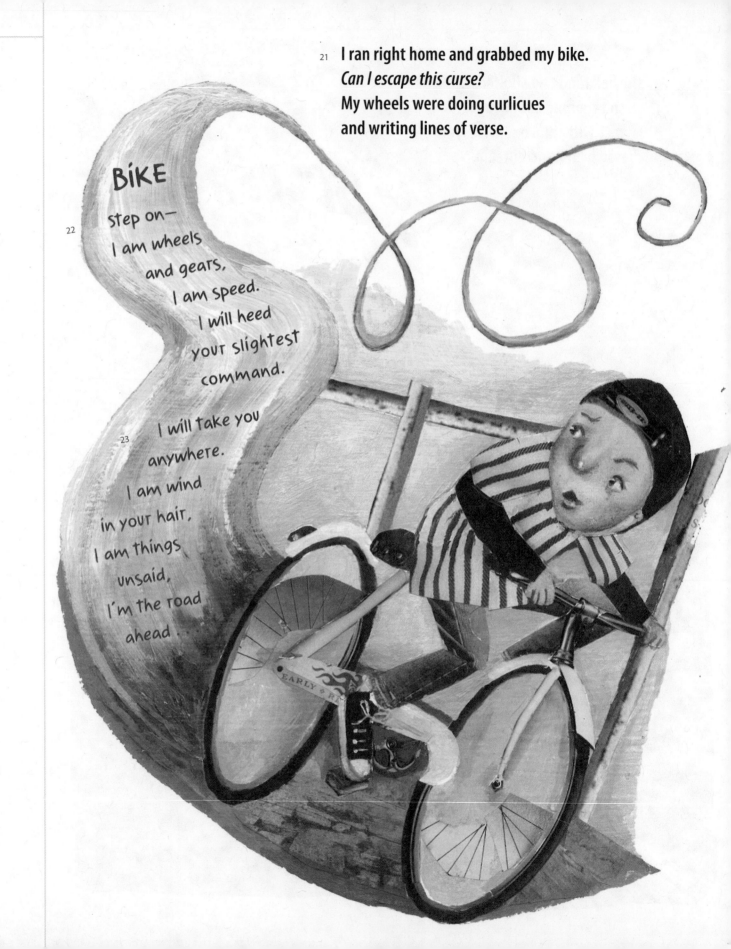

21 I ran right home and grabbed my bike.
Can I escape this curse?
My wheels were doing curlicues
and writing lines of verse.

BIKE

22 Step on—
I am wheels
and gears,
I am speed.
I will heed
your slightest
command.

23 I will take you
anywhere.
I am wind
in your hair,
I am things
unsaid,
I'm the road
ahead.

154

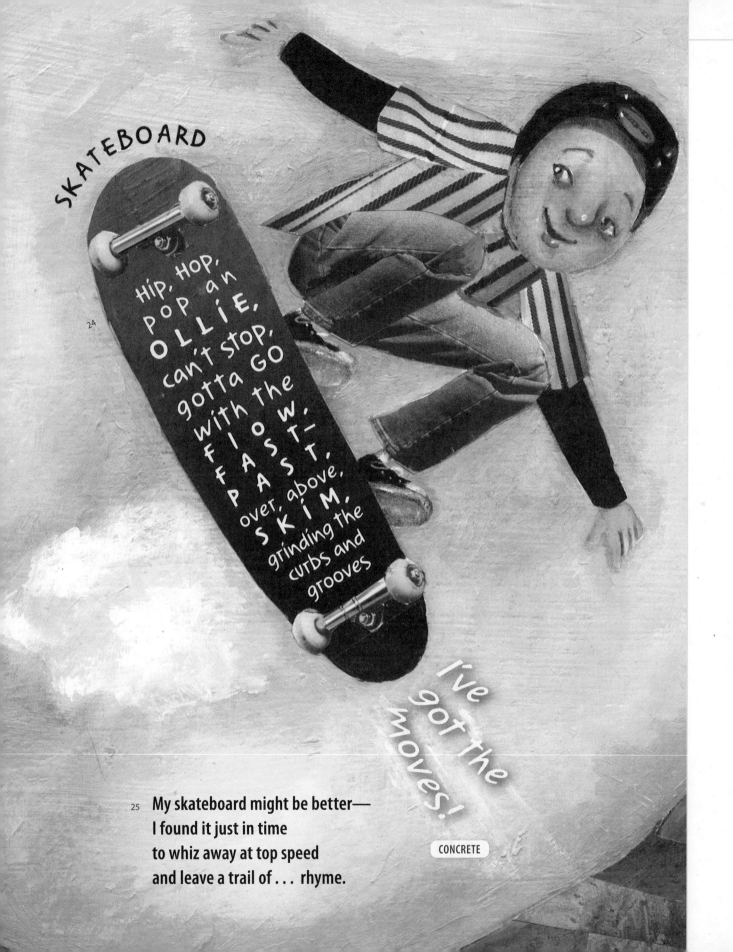

SKATEBOARD

24

Hip, Hop, an OLLIE, can't stop, gotta GO with the flow. FAST—FAST, over, above, SKIM, grinding the curbs and grooves

I've got the moves!

25 My skateboard might be better—
I found it just in time
to whiz away at top speed
and leave a trail of . . . rhyme.

CONCRETE

155

PEAS

26 My mouth is filled with peas,
No matter how I wheeze,
I can't hold back this S·N·E·E·Z·E!

27 Dinner was no different,
I had . . . I had to S-N-E-E-Z-E.
I looked up at the kitchen wall
and saw three lines in . . . peas.

TERCET

28 The ditty that I wrote that night
was delectable and meaty.
I inked with marker on my toes,
a new kind of gra-FEET-i.

FEET

29 My feet—
they can't stay still.
They are always moving
to some cool rhythm I hear
in my head.

CINQUAIN

ditty   A ditty is a song or poem that is short and cheerful.

156

30 **Used pick-up-sticks for limericks,**
wrote cinquain in the rain,
stacked sonnets up the staircase—
good grief, this is insane.

Conductor

31 In storms I can conduct a symphony:
   I stand in front of all those instruments,
   And, wow, I feel excited—what suspense—
   As all those sounds become a part of me.

32 I play the wind, the thunder, and the sea!
   I am in charge, this power is intense—
   A world of rhythm that is huge, immense,
   It swirls about me wild and mightily!

33 I get to choose the singer and the song.
   With my baton I tell them when to start.
   We work together great and I belong;

34 It's fun to be the leader, be a part
   Of all those sounds that sweep about so strong—
   That echo in the drumming of my heart.

SONNET

157

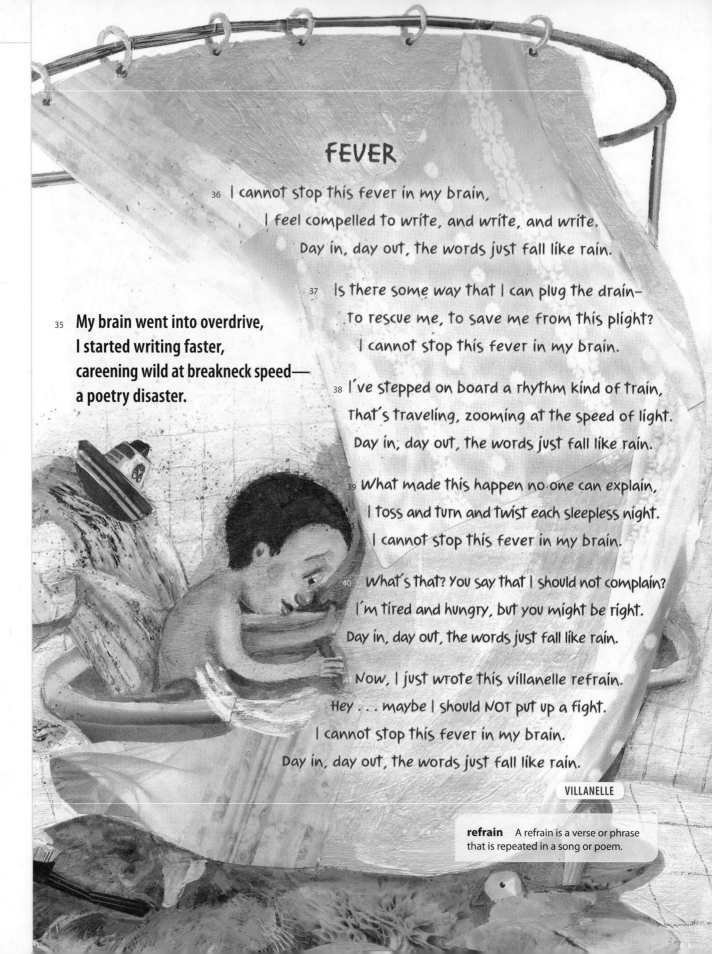

FEVER

35 My brain went into overdrive,
I started writing faster,
careening wild at breakneck speed—
a poetry disaster.

36 I cannot stop this fever in my brain,
I feel compelled to write, and write, and write.
Day in, day out, the words just fall like rain.

37 Is there some way that I can plug the drain—
To rescue me, to save me from this plight?
I cannot stop this fever in my brain.

38 I've stepped on board a rhythm kind of train,
That's traveling, zooming at the speed of light.
Day in, day out, the words just fall like rain.

39 What made this happen no one can explain,
I toss and turn and twist each sleepless night.
I cannot stop this fever in my brain.

40 What's that? You say that I should not complain?
I'm tired and hungry, but you might be right.
Day in, day out, the words just fall like rain.

41 Now, I just wrote this villanelle refrain.
Hey . . . maybe I should NOT put up a fight.
I cannot stop this fever in my brain.
Day in, day out, the words just fall like rain.

VILLANELLE

refrain A refrain is a verse or phrase that is repeated in a song or poem.

42 My mom called up, "Are you in bed?"
but I could hardly hear her.
I'd found a tube of toothpaste
and was writing in the mirror.

43 "You're handsome, smart, and wonderful;
you're special—like no other . . . ."

44 "Aw, you're just saying that . . .
you have to—you're my mother!"

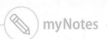
45 I spent a restless night and thought,
Whatever can I do?
When I woke up, I found my pillows
covered with . . . haiku!

restless If you are restless, you find it hard to relax or stay still.

SLEEP

46 Why is it I can
never remember the last
moment before sleep?

HAIKU

GOOSE DOWN PILLOW

47 My head sinks into
the feathered pillow; I think
I hear geese whisper.

HAIKU

FISHING

48 There are poems that swim in my head,
They take form as I lie in my bed.
With my pen for a hook,
I might quick have a look,
And then catch them on paper instead.

LIMERICK

TIRED

49 I am so tired
I'm part
of the bed—
a cover pressed
against the sheets,
dangling limply
down the sides.

FREE VERSE

50 I dragged into the classroom
as the bell began to ring.

51 My teacher's next assignment?

Write a poem about "spring."

Speechless

53 Sometimes when I am
asked to speak, my tongue shrivels,
dries, and disappears,
and then my mouth becomes a
hollow bell with no ringer.

TANKA

Blank Verse

54 I'm running out of steam—I've got to halt,
This inspiration spree has reached its end.
My fevered Brain Train screeches, brakes, and STOPS.
It pulls in, finds a track, where it can rest.

BLANK VERSE

52 My spring was sprung with this assault—
my brain came grinding to a halt.
My mind became a total blank,

55 and I have dear Ms. Frost to thank!

56 P.S. I asked Ms. Frost, "Instead of the poem about 'Spring,' can I turn in some of my 'recent work' if I write it on . . . paper?" She said, "Yes." Ms. Frost is so-o cool! I even got an A+. Life is good. To be more informed about poetic forms, I did some digging.

57 Here's what I discovered . . .

RYAN O'BRIAN'S GUIDE to POETIC FORMS

58 ACROSTIC: If you spell a word (it could be your name!) downward, you can use each of the letters as the beginning of a word or phrase. EXAMPLE: "RECESS"

59 BLANK VERSE: Blank verse is unrhymed iambic pentameter. To find out about that last part, keep reading.
EXAMPLE: "BLANK VERSE"

60 CINQUAIN: Say SIN-kane. The secret code for this poem is 2, 4, 6, 8, 2. (Two syllables/beats on the first line, four beats on the next, then six beats, eight, and back to two beats in the last line.) It's a building thought-wave that crashes and leaves some treasure. EXAMPLE: "FEET"

61 CONCRETE POEM: It's a picture poem that takes the shape of what it's about—word art, sculpting with words. Use simple shapes—make it easy to read. Experiment on your computer. Try out different fonts to see which works best. A major blast!
EXAMPLES: "SOCCER BALL,"
"SKATEBOARD"

62 COUPLET: Two lines that usually rhyme.
EXAMPLE: "COUPLET FOR FRENCH FRIES"

63 FOOT/FEET: Music has a beat, poetry has feet; each foot contains beats which are either stressed (´) or unstressed (˘). Iambs (˘ ´, "sur-PRISE") and anapests (˘ ˘ ´, "in my HEAD") have a *rising* rhythm; trochees (´ ˘, "LIGHT-ning") and dactyls (´ ˘ ˘, "RHYTH-mi-cal") have a *falling* rhythm. There are many other kinds of feet, but these are the most common.

64 FREE VERSE: A poem written without using a fixed, formal pattern of rhythm and rhyme.
EXAMPLES: "SOCCER BALL," "TIRED"

65 HAIKU: A Japanese form which, in only 17 syllables (5-7-5), can create a feeling or paint a scene; usually it's about nature and is written now, in present tense; makes you say "Ah ha! or "Oh, yeah!" EXAMPLES: "FOOTPRINTS," "SLEEP," and "GOOSE DOWN PILLOW"

66 LIMERICK: A funny five-line poem written in iambs and anapests; lines 1, 2, and 5 have three feet and rhyme, and lines 3 and 4 have two feet and rhyme. EXAMPLES: "RHYTHM," "FISHING"

67 PENTAMETER: Five feet to each line.
EXAMPLES: "CAPTURED," "CONDUCTOR," "FEVER," and "BLANK VERSE" are all written in iambic pentameter: "In storms I can conduct a symphony." ˘ ´ / ˘ ´ / ˘ ´ / ˘ ´ / ˘ ´

68 **QUATRAIN:** A four-line stanza or poem that usually rhymes; code—*abcb, abab, abba* (the letters tell which lines rhyme with each other). EXAMPLES: "GOING BANANAS" and "THE BASEBALL GAME." Both have *abcb* quatrains.

69 **RHYME:** A repetition of sounds at the ends of words and usually at the end of a line: score/four, flies/surprise, fuss/A+, "the kids creamed the teachers,/listen to the score:/the third graders beat them—/twenty-five to four!" No, a poem doesn't have to rhyme. Rhyme can boss you around—don't let it. And please, DO NOT throw in any dumb word just to rhyme. EXAMPLES: "GOING BANANAS," "THE BASEBALL GAME," "PEAS," and "HANDSOME," to mention a few.

70 **RHYTHM:** Arrangement, flow, measured motion, regular beat of words, meter—learning to move to the groove.

71 **SONNET:** (Was I channeling some 13th century Italian poet?) The code for this is *abbaabba, cdecde,* or *cdcdcd.* There is an octave (8 lines) and a sestet (6 lines). In the octave there are two envelope rhymes (that's the *bb* part) tucked into the middles. For a Shakespearean sonnet, the code is this: *abab, cdcd, efef, gg.* Both are 14 lines of iambic pentameter. EXAMPLE: "CONDUCTOR" is an Italian sonnet—*abbaabba cdcdcd.*

72 **STANZA:** A pattern or grouping of lines in a poem—couplet (2 lines), tercet (3), quatrain (4), quintet (5), sestet (6), septet (7), octave (8).

73 **TANKA:** A Japanese form, which includes a haiku and adds two more seven-syllable lines to extend or change the meaning: 5-7-5-7-7. EXAMPLE: "SPEECHLESS"

74 **TERCET:** A three-line, usually rhyming, poem or stanza. EXAMPLE: "PEAS"

75 **TRIOLET:** This eight-line form has one line that repeats three times. Lines 1, 4, and 7 are the same; lines 2 and 8 also match. The first two lines become the last two lines. Got it? Code: *abaaabab.* EXAMPLE: "CAPTURED"

76 **VILLANELLE:** Written in iambic pentameter ($\breve{~}$ ´/$\breve{~}$ ´/$\breve{~}$ ´/$\breve{~}$ ´/$\breve{~}$ ´), a French form, usually five stanzas of three lines each with a final stanza of four lines. There are two strong repeating lines. To see the pattern of how this puzzle fits together look at "Fever." If you get two good repeating lines and two sets of words that have lots of rhymes, *you can do this!* EXAMPLE: "FEVER"

165

VOICES

77 You know how you can make your voice scary or funny? Well, you can create different voices in poems, too.

78 **NARRATIVE:** A story-telling poem. EXAMPLES: "GOING BANANAS," "THE BASEBALL GAME"

79 **LYRICAL:** Explore the music of words and individual feelings. In fact, the words to songs are called *lyrics*. You are an important part of this poem, and often pronouns such as *me*, *my*, and *I* are used. EXAMPLES: "CONDUCTOR," "FEVER"

80 **MASK:** When you put on a mask, like at Halloween, and speak from the viewpoint of the object itself, you are using the mask or persona voice. EXAMPLE: "BIKE" (The bike gets to talk for itself!)

81 **APOSTROPHE (OR ADDRESS):** This is a poem where you address or speak to something or someone who doesn't answer. EXAMPLE: "SOCCER BALL" (I love talking to the soccer ball!)

82 **CONVERSATIONAL:** In this voice at least two people or things are speaking with each other in a conversation. EXAMPLE: "HANDSOME"

83 Lots of great books can help you learn more about all the forms, voices, and choices you can try when you write your own poems.

84 Have FUN! Happy reading! Happy writing!

85 P.P.S. From Ryan: If you show your teacher you wrote a villanelle or a sonnet, she is going to be so-o impressed. She might even faint or give you extra credit or both. You should definitely try it.

Collaborative Discussion

Look back at what you wrote on page 144 and talk with a partner about what you learned during reading. Then work with a group to discuss the questions below. Look for details in *The Poem That Will Not End* to support your ideas. Be sure to speak clearly and at a pace that's not too fast or too slow.

1 What are some of the places where Ryan writes his poems? What kinds of things seem to inspire him?

Listening Tip

Make eye contact with speakers to let them know you are paying attention to their ideas.

2 Review the poem and text on page 152. What has "captured" Ryan? Do you think he is serious about wanting to "escape" it? Why or why not?

Speaking Tip

Help listeners understand what you have to say. Share your ideas in a voice that is clear and easy to hear.

3 At the end of his notes about poetic forms, Ryan advises readers to "have fun" writing poetry. How do Ryan's poems show that he has had fun writing them?

Write a Poem

PROMPT ···

In *The Poem That Will Not End,* the narrator writes poems about things and events in his daily life, such as skateboards, soccer, and storms.

Imagine you are writing a poem for your school's online poetry magazine. The topic can be anything in your daily life: brushing your teeth, eating lunch, or studying for a test—you name it! Choose a poetic form, or type of poem, from *The Poem That Will Not End,* and use it as a model for your poem. It doesn't have to rhyme, but it does need to include specific, descriptive words and phrases to express your feelings and ideas. Think about your five senses as you develop these details. Don't forget to use some of the Critical Vocabulary words in your writing.

PLAN ···

Make a section for notes about the characteristics of your chosen poetic form. Then make another section of notes about ideas for your poem.

WRITE

Now write your poem about something from your daily life.

Make sure your poem
☐ uses one of the poem types used in the text.
☐ is about something from your daily life.
☐ includes sensory details and specific, descriptive words.

? **Essential Question**

How does genre affect the way a story is told?

Write a Short Story

PROMPT Consider all the different ways the stories in this module were told. How will you tell your own story?

Imagine that your school library is having a story-writing contest. The winning story will be printed, copied, and made available in the library for the whole school to read. Write a short story for the contest. Use the texts in this module as your models for good storytelling.

I will write a story about _____.

✓ Make sure your story

- ☐ begins by introducing the setting and the main character or narrator.

- ☐ includes dialogue and descriptions to show how characters respond to events.

- ☐ uses narrative techniques based on examples from the module's texts.

- ☐ uses transitional words to clarify the sequence of events.

- ☐ provides a satisfying ending that develops logically from the story events.

What kind of story will you write? Will it be realistic or a fantasy? Will it take place in the past, present, or future? Who will narrate your story? Look back at your notes and revisit the texts for ideas.

Use the story map below to plan your writing. Decide on a setting and characters. Think about what conflict or obstacle the characters face and how they respond. Use Critical Vocabulary words where appropriate.

My Topic: _____

Setting:	Characters:
Problem/Conflict:	
Events:	
Solution/Resolution:	

DRAFT .... Write your story.

Write a **beginning** that will get your readers thinking. Introduce your setting, main characters or narrator, and the conflict they will face.

Write the events that take place in the **middle** of your story. Use dialogue and descriptive details to make the events and your characters come alive for your readers. Be sure the events and characters' actions will help develop the story's conflict.

Write an **ending** that brings the story to a satisfying conclusion. Tell how your characters resolve their conflict.

REVISE AND EDIT · Review your draft.

Take a fresh look at your draft to see how you can improve it. Work with a small group of classmates to review each other's work and give helpful feedback. Use these questions to help you evaluate and improve your story.

PURPOSE/ FOCUS	ORGANIZATION	EVIDENCE	LANGUAGE/ VOCABULARY	CONVENTIONS
☐ Does my story clearly establish a setting and characters? ☐ Do the characters face and resolve a conflict? ☐ Does the ending make sense with the events that come before it?	☐ Is there a clear beginning, middle, and ending? ☐ Is the sequence of events easy to follow?	☐ Did I use dialogue and description like the texts in the module do?	☐ Did I use transition words to show how events are connected?	☐ Have I spelled all words correctly? ☐ Did I punctuate dialogue correctly?

PUBLISH · Share your work.

Create a Finished Copy. Use your best cursive handwriting to create a final copy of your work. You may want to include illustrations. Consider these options for sharing your story:

1. Bind your story together with those of your classmates to create a class literary magazine.

2. Turn your story into a readers' theater script. Perform it with a group of classmates.

3. Post a copy of your story on a school or class website. Invite readers to comment or share their own stories.

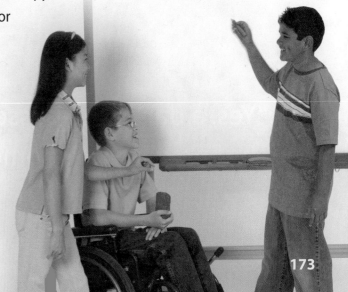

173

Natural Disasters

"Yes, a dark time passed over this land,
but now there is something like light."

—Dave Eggers

Essential Question

How can learning about natural disasters make us safer?

Get Curious

Video

Words About Natural Disasters

The words in the chart will help you talk and write about the selections in this module. Which words about natural disasters have you seen before? Which words are new to you?

Add to the Vocabulary Network on page 177 by writing synonyms, antonyms, and related words and phrases for each word about natural disasters.

After you read each selection in this module, come back to the Vocabulary Network and keep building it. Add more boxes if you need to.

WORD	MEANING	CONTEXT SENTENCE
notable (adjective)	If something is notable, it is worth noticing.	The scientist measured a notable increase in the hurricane's strength.
spontaneous (adjective)	A spontaneous action is one that happens naturally and isn't planned.	She made a spontaneous decision to jump into the lake.
tremor (noun)	A tremor is a small earthquake or uncontrolled shaking in a body part.	The tremor that shook the town was minor and did little damage.
hazard (noun)	A hazard is a danger.	Watch out for the storm surge; it is a major hazard.

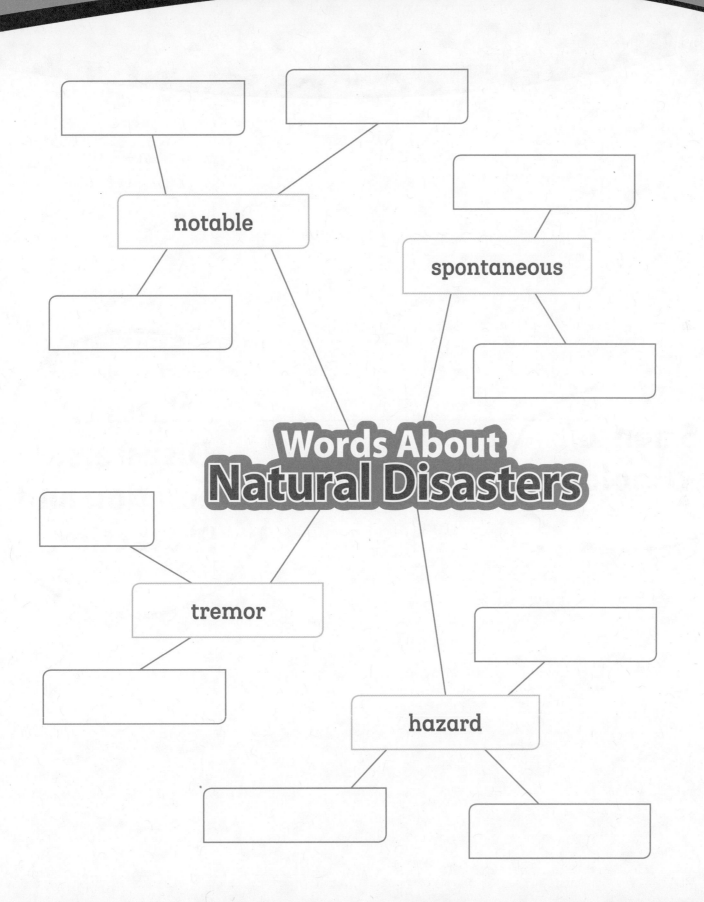

notable

spontaneous

Words About Natural Disasters

tremor

hazard

Science/ Technology

Natural Disasters: Prediction and Protection

Preparation

Short Read

WHO STUDIES NATURAL DISASTERS?

October 23, 2018

Dear Professor Melendez,

1   I'm writing to ask your advice about careers that involve studying natural disasters. My earth science (my favorite subject!) teacher told me you teach college classes on natural disasters and suggested I send you a letter.

2   Last year, my family explored Kilauea, a volcano in Hawaii. As part of the tour, we saw firsthand how a breathtaking natural occurrence can also lead to disaster. Our guide explained that a notable eruption in 2014 almost destroyed the nearby town of Pahoa.

3   The tour made me really interested in volcanoes. What processes inside the earth cause them? Why do they erupt? Most importantly, how can science and knowledge be used to keep people safe from them?

4   We experience earthquake tremors in California sometimes and have to practice safety drills for them. The spontaneous shaking of the earth has always left me feeling both fascinated and scared! I've been reading about other natural disasters, too. I think the swirling winds and drenching rains of hurricanes are as thrilling as earthquakes. They can also be just as dangerous, right?

5   I want to understand these kinds of events and maybe help other people understand them better someday, too. What careers would let me apply knowledge of natural disasters to help people?

6   I'd very much appreciate your advice on jobs I might consider. Thank you for your time and advice!

Sincerely,

Robin Thiersson

Robin Thiersson
267 Seismo Street
Tectonic, California 00000

November 1, 2018

Dear Robin,

7   Thanks so much for your letter. It's so encouraging to me to hear of your interest in science and natural disasters. The world needs budding scientists like you!

8   Your fascination with natural disasters could lead you to any number of exciting careers. For example, a volcanologist studies volcanoes. (You may have met one during your tour of Kilauea.) Volcanologists often work at the site of an erupting volcano. They also spend time in labs analyzing data about the eruptions.

9   You probably know that no one can predict earthquakes, but scientists called seismologists help us prepare for these natural hazards. These scientists also work both in labs and at sites of seismic activity such as fault lines.

10 If you'd prefer the high winds and ocean storm surges of hurricanes, you may want to be a meteorologist. These scientists forecast the weather or study the atmosphere and the world's climate. Their knowledge and direction is invaluable in helping people stay safe during these mighty ocean storms. Hurricanes can be every bit as dangerous as eruptions and earthquakes; you're absolutely right.

11 I gathered data for a seismologist for a number of years before I began teaching. I'd be happy to share my experiences with you and your classmates!

Sincerely,

Judy Melendez

Professor Judy Melendez
Tectonic University
University Avenue
Tectonic, California 00000

Seismograms such as this one help people study seismic activity.

Notice & Note
Numbers and Statistics

Prepare to Read

GENRE STUDY **Narrative nonfiction** gives factual information by telling a true story.

- Narrative nonfiction authors present events in sequential, or chronological, order. Doing so helps readers understand when events happened and how they're connected.

- Narrative nonfiction often includes visuals, such as photos. Captions help explain the photos and add details to the text.

- Texts written about events related to science or social studies may also include words that are specific to the topic.

SET A PURPOSE **Think about** the genre and title of this text. What do you know about volcanoes? What do you want to learn? Write your ideas below.

CRITICAL VOCABULARY

seismographs

evacuation

reservoir

conferring

consequences

widespread

alarming

victim

Meet the Author:
Elizabeth Rusch

ERUPTION!

Volcanoes and the Science of Saving Lives

by Elizabeth Rusch
photographs by Tom Uhlman

1   *When the Colombian volcano Nevado del Ruiz erupted in 1985, United States Geological Survey (USGS) scientist Andy Lockhart was horrified by the tragedy. A year later, he became one of the earliest members of a volcano crisis team, called the Volcano Disaster Assistance Program (VDAP). The VDAP's mission is to bring equipment and knowledge to areas threatened by volcanoes in order to predict eruptions and prevent catastrophes. Six years after the program started, Chris Newhall, another VDAP scientist, got a call about steam shooting from Mount Pinatubo (peen-uh-TOO-boh), a mountain in the Philippines. Until this happened, most people thought Mount Pinatubo was a huge jungle-covered mountain, not a volcano. Chris knew it was serious. He and the team had to do something. He and fellow VDAP scientists Andy Lockhart and Rick Hoblitt set out to try to predict Mount Pinatubo's next move. They worked from Clark Air Base, very close to the volcano.*

2   **On May 28,** Chris got a new gas reading from Mount Pinatubo. Sulfur dioxide (SO_2) had jumped tenfold, to 5,000 tons a day. The volcano was definitely ramping up.

3   A few days later, instruments recorded two unusual earthquakes. A shallow, continuous, rhythmic shaking known as a low-frequency earthquake meant magma was moving toward the surface and releasing more gas. Then the **seismographs** recorded the first earthquake directly under the vent.

4   Over the next few weeks, the volcano spat steam higher and higher into the sky. The plume changed color from white to gray. Then the volcano began shooting rock and ash. But the geologists tested the ash and found no sign of fresh lava. The steam explosions were just tossing up old material. Would the volcano erupt, or would it just spit steam until it slipped back into dormancy[1]?

---

1 dormancy: the period during which a volcano is temporarily inactive

---

seismographs   Seismographs are instruments that measure and record details about earthquakes, such as their strength and how long they last.

5   Then the sulfur dioxide plummeted, from 5,000 tons to 1,300 to 260 a day. That could mean the volcano was settling down.

6   Or . . . it could mean the volcano's vent was clogged, with pressure building.

7   Andy and the other scientists watched the seismograph around the clock. They saw bigger quakes, longer quakes, and a harmonic tremor, a constant humming earthquake that often means magma is rising and boiling away groundwater[2].

8   The Americans and Filipinos each had their own alert level systems. The VDAP scientists debated. Was it time to raise the alert level to three: high and increasing unrest; eruption possible in two weeks?

9   Ray, the head of the Filipino geologists, would need time to spread any warning to people scattered in villages all around Pinatubo. He raised his alert level to three: eruption possible in two weeks. About 10,000 members of the Aeta tribes[3] were moved to **evacuation** camps.

10   The quakes accelerated. Magma moving all along the conduit[4] was shaking the ground deep in the earth and quite near the surface. More and more steam and ash poured from cracks in the volcano, called fumaroles.

11   The volcanologists[5] estimated the size of the magma chamber (the **reservoir** of melted rock and gas under the volcano) and the potential size of the eruption. The eruption could be ten times larger than the 1980 eruption of Mount St. Helens, which was bigger than any living geologist had ever seen.

12   Military officers listened intently to the geologists' briefings. At the end of one, Major General William Studer asked: "What would you do?"

13   The scientists answered: "Move the dependents off the base."

14   The officers relocated pregnant women and the elderly. The air force newspaper and TV station began broadcasting details of an evacuation plan: what to bring and where to go.

2 **groundwater:** water found underground in the cracks in sand, soil, and rock
3 **Aeta tribes:** tribes of people native to the island of Luzon in the Philippines
4 **conduit:** a channel for moving some type of liquid
5 **volcanologists:** geologists who study active and inactive volcanoes

evacuation   An evacuation is the act of moving from a dangerous area to a safer one.
reservoir   A reservoir is a place where a supply of something is collected.

15   The earthquakes got even closer to the surface. A steam plume reached 28,000 feet (8,500 meters), the highest so far.

16   After **conferring** with VDAP scientists, Ray raised his alert to level four, enlarging the evacuation zone for the local population. Filipinos all around the volcano packed a few possessions and walked or rode carts down the mountain.

17   VDAP members debated: Should we move to level four? The air force had set VDAP's level four as a trigger for Clark to be evacuated. Evacuating 14,000 people and millions of dollars of equipment would be a huge challenge, and a huge burden to the military and their families.

18   Some VDAP members thought they should.

19   Then the earthquakes diminished.

20   "Volcanoes don't necessarily move from deep sleep to violent eruption in a straight, orderly progression," Andy said. "They ramp up and drop down, ramp up and drop down. The trend at Pinatubo was ramping higher and dropping down less. Any single episode of ramping up could lead to a full-blown eruption. But it could all just peter out to nothing." The scientists had to predict the unpredictable. The **consequences**—a costly false evacuation or tragic loss of life—weighed heavily on their minds and their hearts.

21   On June 8, a chopper lifted off to give scientists a closer view of the summit. The sky cleared. They could see that a big, ugly gray blob of rock had poked out of the east crater wall. It was a lava dome. Cold, hard, heavy rock could be clogging the vent. With magma moving up with nowhere to go and pressure building, this thing could blow—with deadly results.

22   The scientists told the air force commanders the new development and waited for them to take action.

23   Then, the next morning, June 9, when Andy and his colleague hopped into the helicopter, it took a detour—to the center of the base. General Studer and his second-in-command climbed aboard. The helicopter headed for the volcano.

24   Instead of billowing steam and ash, only a thin snake of yellow-gray plume drifted up from the summit.

25   "Geez, that's a lot of ash," the general commented.

---

conferring   If you are conferring with someone, you are discussing an idea or trying to make a decision.

consequences   Consequences are the outcomes or effects of events.

26   "That's nothing," the volcanologists said. They pointed out how underlying the jungle all around the mountain were signs of massive ancient pyroclastic flows[6]. "That's all ash from the last eruption." The helicopter turned, and the **widespread** devastation once wrought by this volcano became impossible to miss. The general stared silently out the window as the helicopter headed back to the base.

27   Finally, he turned to his second in command. "Do it tomorrow," he said.

6 pyroclastic flows: fast-moving flows of hot gas and rock

widespread   If something is widespread, it happens over a large area or among many people.

"Volcanoes don't necessarily move from deep sleep to violent eruption in a straight, orderly progression."

Mount Pinatubo steams behind an air force helicopter.

LOOKING FOR LUMPS

Changes in the surface of a volcano give clues about what is happening beneath. Imagine a mole tunneling under a lawn. When the mole moves, the grass bumps up. Magma moving underground does the same thing, actually lifting the ground above it. When magma is close to the surface, the bulge can grow hundreds of feet high and hundreds of feet wide.

Lava shoved out of an erupting volcano can also make a massive bulge or dome. Domes and bulges might plug a vent, causing pressure to build underground. Domes can also grow so large that they trigger landslides. So scientists have to track their growth, too.

How do scientists measure all these lumps and bulges? Digital elevation maps—compiled using photos and radar data—show the length, width, and height of every part of the volcano. Scientists compare DEMs compiled at different times to track how the shape of the volcano has changed. They can also makes these measurements using satellite radar images, GPS, meters that track how the ground tilts, or by careful surveying.

June 10, 1991

28   At 6 a.m., military television and radio echoed with the order to evacuate. The streets of Clark Air Base filled with cars, trucks, and buses that funneled downhill through the shantytowns[7] and toward a naval station an hour away. By noon, 14,500 people had evacuated.

29   The Filipinos extended their evacuation to twelve miles (20 kilometers), displacing 25,000 people. People with carts piled high with furniture and leading water buffalo shared the road with the long line of military trucks and the cars of people evacuating the base.

30   Left on the base were some officers, the Military Police (MPs), and engineers who could keep the lights on. The volcanologists moved their observatory to the farthest corner of the base. "We were just incredibly relieved that most everybody was out of the way," Andy said.

31   But the pressure still weighed on the scientists.

32   "I couldn't help second-guessing myself," said team member Dave Harlow. "All of us did. I was feeling as though the chances were pretty high that we would all be hauled in front of committees investigating the disastrous evacuation, its costs and impact to the Philippine economy and on the air force."

7 shantytowns: settlements on the outside of towns that consist of large numbers of run-down dwellings

People evacuating to avoid the dangers of the eruption.

"We were just incredibly relieved that most everybody was out of the way."

33   Would Mount Pinatubo really explode? The next few days would tell.

34   Andy woke up to a blue-sky morning on June 12. It was after 6 a.m., and the clouds had usually rolled in by then. But the sun shone brightly as he waited for geologist Rick Hoblitt, who was going to give Andy a lift to the observatory.

35   "LET'S GO!" Rick hollered from upstairs. *Geez,* Andy thought. *What's up with him?*

36   Rick raced down the stairs, taking two at a time, just as Andy opened the front door.

37   A huge black ash column pumped out of the volcano, filling the sky. The column rose up higher and higher. Rick and Andy jumped into their truck and raced off.

38   By the time they got to the observatory at the edge of the base, the ash column had hit the stratosphere. The cloud mushroomed out, reaching the sky right above them.

39   Then the cloud slowed, stopped, and started to dissipate.

40   "Wahoo! Whoa! Cool!" the MPs hollered. They started doing a victory dance, because they thought they'd just seen the eruption and survived.

41   But Andy and Rick didn't dance. They turned to their instruments. They knew that this could be just the beginning.

42   For the next few days Pinatubo shot steam, rumbled, and kept the scientists on edge. Several times, the volcano shot up columns as big as the one on June 12.

Military personnel and their families evacuate Clark Air Base.

43   But on June 14, the volcano stopped shooting steam and ash. Pinatubo shook as much as it had two days before, but nothing came out. *The volcano is all stopped up,* Andy thought.

44   He fell asleep late that night, restless and worried. Then on June 15, Andy and other scientists were jolted from sleep by a cry.

45   "GET UP! GET UP!" yelled the scientist on watch.

46   Andy ran to the front door. Clouds obscured the top of the volcano and pelting rain blurred Andy's view. But great black ash clouds—massive, rolling clouds of superheated ash—raged down six miles (10 kilometers) on each side of the volcano.

47   Pyroclastic flows!

48   Moments later, rain and wind from a typhoon[8] that had hit the island completely hid the erupting volcano.

49   Andy rushed to the seismograph.

50   The earthquakes died down, way down, and stayed down.

8 typhoon: a dangerous, powerful tropical storm occurring in the western Pacific or Indian Oceans

51 "This is bad," Andy muttered.

52 The pressure under the volcano was building.

53 "Should we evacuate?" the scientists asked each other.

54 The decision was quick. Someone yelled: "EVACUATE THE BASE!"

55 Everyone started moving all at once, grabbing things, yelling. Officers, MPs, and scientists piled into cars and sped away.

56 From a big field, they watched the dark volcano. They waited.

57 The volcanologists wanted to see their instruments. They wanted to find out what this volcano was up to so they could extend the evacuation zone if needed, or learn something that would help at another crisis. But that would mean risking their own lives.

58 They decided they'd been too hasty evacuating themselves. They drove back to the observatory on the base, along with the base commanders.

59 It was raining. Not just water and ash, but egg-size chunks of pumice[9]. The scientists hurried into the building and crowded around the seismographs.

60 The earthquakes were so intense that the seismograph needles just banged from the top to the bottom of the drum, *TUNK, TUNK, TUNK, TUNK,* making **alarming** blocks of solid ink. Pinatubo blasted ash higher and higher. The scientists watched, aghast, as monitoring stations blinked out one by one on the far side of the volcano— destroyed. Then a station went down on their side.

9 pumice: light, glassy lava

alarming   Something that is alarming makes you worry that something bad may happen.

Threatened by Mount Pinatubo, Clark Air Base was evacuated on June 10. The light-colored peak in the center is the summit of Pinatubo.

The June 12, 1991, eruption of Mount Pinatubo, viewed from Clark Air Base.

> "I had maybe twenty seconds to run to the back of the building. Maybe that would be enough protection."

61 That was only twelve miles (20 kilometers) from where they were standing.

62 Was a searing pyroclastic flow heading their way?

63 Flows moved at up to one hundred miles (160 kilometers) an hour. Did the scientists have only precious moments before they themselves fell **victim** to an eruption and raging, searing pyroclastic flows?

64 This time the scientists knew they had no time to evacuate. They raced for the back of the building, the farthest they could get from the erupting monster.

65 They waited, panting, sweating.

66 Andy could stand it no longer. He went back to the front door. All he saw was black—complete black—from the rain, the dark clouds, the ash fall. The sound was terrifying—like a wall of rock a mile high racing down at breakneck speeds.

67 *I could die,* Andy thought. *All my friends could die.*

68 He watched and he watched, his eyes glued to a row of lights on an airstrip that pointed toward the volcano. "I figured that as long as I could see the lights, the pyroclastic flow hadn't reached us. If the lights went out, I had maybe twenty seconds to run to the back of the building. Maybe that would be enough protection."

69 Then the air and sky seemed to lighten, just a shade. The pyroclastic flow hadn't reached the base. Andy and his friends checked the instruments. Everything was flatlining—all the monitoring stations had been destroyed—except for one. A station on the base.

---

victim   If you fall victim to something, you suffer or die because of it.

70   The volcanologists quickly grabbed what they could, piled into trucks, and tore off. That is, until they merged with hordes of evacuating Filipinos. "It was a huge, slow-moving traffic jam of everybody with a water buffalo strolling out of town," says Andy. "We were going crazy with the delay, but at least we were headed away from the volcano."

71   But Andy, the other volcanologists, and the villagers managed to escape with their lives.

72   The eruption of Mount Pinatubo was the second largest eruption in the twentieth century. A few hundred people died, most in buildings that later collapsed under the weight of rain-soaked ash. But more than 20,000 lives were saved. "We got it right," Andy said. "We questioned ourselves and doubted ourselves as things unfolded, but we got it right."

This ash-covered news box on Clark Air Base tells the story of the headline.

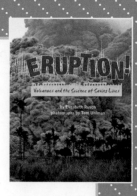

Respond to the Text

Collaborative Discussion

Look back at what you wrote on page 182. Tell a partner two things you learned from the text. Then work with a group to discuss the questions below. Support your answers with facts and details from *Eruption!* During the discussion, explain how your ideas connect to those of others in your group.

1 Review pages 186–194. Does the author include in the text? What do those quotes help you understand?

Listening Tip

Listen to the ideas and details each speaker shares. What new information can you add?

2 Reread page 188. What additional information does the sidebar "Looking for Lumps" provide? Why does the author present it separately from the main text?

Speaking Tip

Think about how other speakers' ideas are related to your own. Ask questions to be sure you understand their comments.

3 What details explain why the decision to evacuate was difficult to make?

Write a News Report

PROMPT

In *Eruption!,* you learned how scientists closely monitored Mount Pinatubo during its eruption. They knew that their observations could help save lives.

Imagine you've been assigned to cover this story for an online newspaper. The date is June 14. Write a news report telling what is happening to the volcano, in the correct sequence. Ask *who, what, when, where, why,* and *how* to gather information from the text to be sure you've recorded all the information readers will want to know. Include a scientific word related to the eruption, and explain the meaning of the word to your readers. Don't forget to use some of the Critical Vocabulary words in your writing.

PLAN

Make notes from the text about the eruption events that happened on June 14. Keep track of the order of events and include a scientific word and its meaning.

WRITE

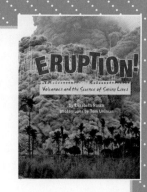

Now write your news report about the eruption of Mount Pinatubo.

Make sure your news report
☐ introduces the topic.
☐ uses evidence from the text.
☐ tells about the events in order.
☐ includes a scientific word and its explanation.

Prepare to View

GENRE STUDY **Informational videos** present information about a topic, person, or event in visual and audio form.

- A narrator explains what is happening on the screen.
- Experts may be interviewed to help explain key points.
- Words that are specific to science or social studies topics may be included.
- First-person accounts are sometimes featured to help viewers better understand an event or experience.

SET A PURPOSE **As you watch**, think about the kinds of events that occur during and after a large earthquake. What do you already know? What do you want to learn? Write your ideas below.

CRITICAL VOCABULARY

prior

magnitude

literally

maintenance

Between the Glacier and the Sea:
The Alaska Earthquake

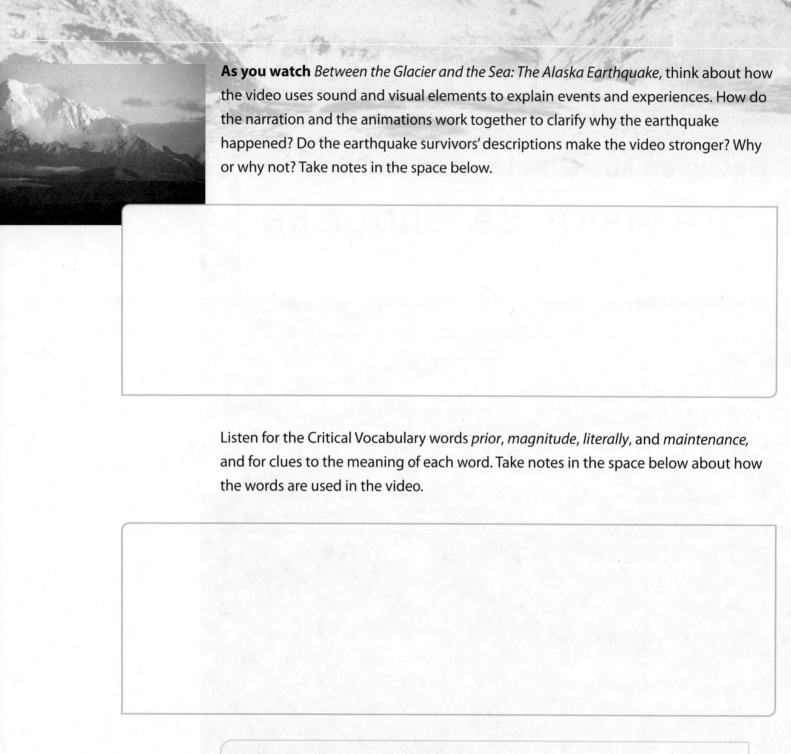

As you watch *Between the Glacier and the Sea: The Alaska Earthquake*, think about how the video uses sound and visual elements to explain events and experiences. How do the narration and the animations work together to clarify why the earthquake happened? Do the earthquake survivors' descriptions make the video stronger? Why or why not? Take notes in the space below.

Listen for the Critical Vocabulary words *prior*, *magnitude*, *literally*, and *maintenance*, and for clues to the meaning of each word. Take notes in the space below about how the words are used in the video.

prior Prior means coming before, in time or order.

magnitude Magnitude refers to the size of something.

literally If you say something literally happened, that means it actually happened, and you aren't exaggerating or using a metaphor.

maintenance The maintenance of something is the act of caring for it and repairing it when needed.

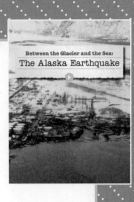

Between the Glacier and the Sea:
The Alaska Earthquake

Collaborative Discussion

Look back at your response on page 198 and talk with a partner about what you learned from the video. Then work with a group to discuss the questions below. Take notes about details and examples in *Between the Glacier and the Sea: The Alaska Earthquake* to support your responses. During the discussion, listen actively to each speaker and build on each other's ideas.

1 What was remarkable about the 1964 Alaska earthquake?

2 Why is hearing the story about the oil fires from one of the survivors important? What impact does it have on you as a viewer?

3 What has the information in the video taught you about the earthquake survivors?

Listening Tip

Watch the facial expressions and gestures each speaker uses to explain his or her thoughts.

Speaking Tip

Use your notes to help you state your ideas clearly.

Write a Video Promo

PROMPT

Between the Glacier and the Sea: The Alaska Earthquake uses narration and visuals to help viewers understand the events, experiences, and feelings surrounding the largest earthquake in North American history.

Imagine you're someone who writes content to promote videos. Write a paragraph that summarizes and promotes *Between the Glacier and the Sea: The Alaska Earthquake.* Use key details from the narration and visuals to grab the interest of viewers and encourage them to watch the video. In your summary, emphasize the effects of the strong audio, visual, and narrative techniques on viewers. Don't forget to use some of the Critical Vocabulary words in your writing.

PLAN

Make notes about the key details in the video and the audio, visual, and narrative techniques used to make those details come to life.

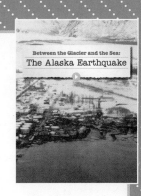

Between the Glacier and the Sea:
The Alaska Earthquake

WRITE

Now write your video promotion.

Make sure your video promo

☐ summarizes the key details from the video.

☐ emphasizes the audio, video, and narrative techniques used in the video.

☐ is written to grab the interest of viewers.

**Notice &
Note**
Numbers and
Statistics

Prepare to Read

GENRE STUDY **Informational texts** tell about a topic, event, or place.

- Informational texts may organize ideas under subheadings. They contain main ideas and supporting details, including facts, examples, and sometimes quotations.

- Informational texts may contain science or social studies words specific to the topic.

- Visuals, such as diagrams and maps, and text features, such as sidebars, may tell more about the topic.

SET A PURPOSE **Think about** the title and genre of this text. What do you know about earthquakes and tsunamis? What do you want to learn? Write your ideas below.

Build Background:
The Pacific Ring of Fire

**CRITICAL
VOCABULARY**

parallel

lateral

destruction

triggered

thrust

radiate

modified

QUAKING EARTH, Racing Waves

by Rachel Young

1   **In July 2004** the village school on Tello Island, Indonesia, had a visitor with a startling story to tell. As the students in their red-and-white uniforms sat quietly listening, geologist Kerry Sieh explained that under the ocean, 60 miles from their island, was a ticking time bomb.

2   For hundreds of years, the Sunda Megathrust Fault had been storing energy that would be released in massive undersea earthquakes. The powerful quakes would likely cause tsunamis, fast-moving waves that could wipe out the entire seaside village.

3   The students and their teachers were surprised by Sieh's warnings. They'd never felt giant earthquakes or seen tsunami waves. How did he know that the earth was going to shake?

4   Sieh explained that, for more than a decade, scientists from the California Institute of Technology had been studying a section of the fault just to the south. They'd figured out that major earthquakes shook the region about every 200 years. The last big quake was in the early 1800s, which meant another could come at any time. Though Sieh couldn't say exactly when it would happen, he was almost certain there would be at least one major earthquake in the students' lifetimes.

5   But no one could have known that the next big quake would hit just a few months later.

RISING CORALS

6   Scientists know a lot about earthquakes after they happen, but they can't predict what hour, day, year, or even decade an earthquake will hit. So how did Kerry Sieh know to warn the Tello islanders that an earthquake might happen soon? He read the corals.

7   In the Indian Ocean, big corals called *Porites* grow from the sea floor to the water's surface, then outward. The ocean floor sinks slowly between

Porites coral

earthquakes, dragging the coral down, then rises quickly during a quake, raising the coral up again. Over hundreds of years, all this up and down causes the coral to grow outward in doughnut-shaped rings. Sieh discovered that by looking at the growth patterns of *Porites* coral heads near the fault, he could pinpoint the dates of past earthquakes, and maybe find a pattern that would help predict future quakes.

8   Using underwater chainsaws, Sieh and other scientists sliced off slabs of coral heads that were hundreds of years old. Sure enough, they found that, on a section of the fault just to the north of the Mentawai Islands and just to the south of Tello, earthquakes occurred in pairs about every 200 years. One pair of quakes hit in the 1300s, another in the 1500s, and a third in 1797 and 1833—almost 200 years ago. According to the corals, it was time for another big quake.

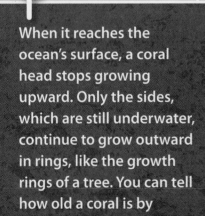

When it reaches the ocean's surface, a coral head stops growing upward. Only the sides, which are still underwater, continue to grow outward in rings, like the growth rings of a tree. You can tell how old a coral is by counting the rings.

Between earthquakes, the ocean floor is slowly sinking. And the coral, which is attached to the ocean floor, is sinking, too. The coral head drops below the water line, and the sides grow up to the water's surface.

During an earthquake, part of the ocean floor springs up, and some coral heads are lifted half out of the water. The section of coral above the sea dies, while the part still under the sea keeps growing. From above, the coral looks like a little doughnut inside a series of bigger ones.

SINKING ISLANDS

9   The corals weren't the only evidence of underground rumblings in Indonesia. The Sunda Megathrust Fault at the bottom of the Indian Ocean marks the collision between two of the plates that make up the earth's surface, one oceanic, the other continental. Between earthquakes, the plates are stuck together. As the oceanic plate slips slowly downward, it squeezes the continental plate sideways about half an inch a year, and drags it down a few inches a year as well. The islands on top of the continental plate are dragged down too, as much as half an inch a year. The more years between earthquakes, the more the islands sink— and the more stress builds up at the fault.

10   The islanders could tell that the water line was shifting. "They can see their boardwalks and harbors sinking," Sieh said. Trees that once grew tall on shore were now underwater, and wells that once gave freshwater were full of salty seawater instead. But no one thought that this had anything to do with earthquakes or tsunamis.

11   Evidence from Global Positioning System, or GPS, stations they'd set up to measure island sinking also had convinced the scientists that a big quake could rock the area at any time. "As we came to realize what we were learning, and how much at risk people were," said Sieh, "we couldn't keep quiet."

12   In July 2004, Sieh visited five islands and gave presentations at schools, churches, mosques, and village squares. Sieh and his colleagues planned to return the following year to visit more islands and teach more people about their research. Then, six months later, a quake struck.

A geographer prepares a GPS station in Indonesia to collect data.

What Makes the Earth Quake?

Next time you're outside, jump up and down. Stomp your feet a few times. The ground seems solid, right? Well, not entirely.

The part of the earth you're standing on, called the lithosphere, is rock-solid. But the lithosphere is very thin—if the earth were the size of an apple, the lithosphere would be about as thick as the apple's skin. If you dug a hole through the earth, you'd find that as you went deeper, what's inside becomes hotter and more gooey. The solid lithosphere is broken up into close-fitting plates that drift on top of the molten rock underneath. We don't feel the plates moving because they're usually drifting only a few centimeters a year—about as fast (or slow) as your fingernails grow.

Earth's plates don't all move **parallel** to each other and in the same direction. At the boundary where two plates meet, called a fault, they bump and push into each other. They're wedged together most of the time, but stress builds up as the plates bump and grind together. Finally the plates break free along a section of the fault, releasing pent-up energy in an earthquake. The force makes objects move up and down and in a **lateral** motion, and it can cause great **destruction**.

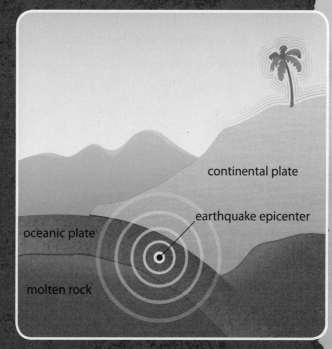

continental plate

earthquake epicenter

oceanic plate

molten rock

There are several different types of faults. The Sunda Fault offshore from the Batu and Mentawai islands is called a megathrust, where the underwater oceanic plate dives under the continental plate.

---

parallel If two or more things are parallel to each other, they move in the same direction.
lateral If something moves in a lateral way, it moves side to side.
destruction Destruction is the act of destroying or ruining something.

DECEMBER 26, 2004

13 The ground shook so violently that people were knocked off their feet. Dishes fell from shelves, roofs collapsed, trees toppled. Two minutes after it began, the shaking stopped. It had been the biggest earthquake anywhere on the planet in 40 years.

14 Like a twig you bend and bend until it breaks, pressure that had been building along the Sunda Megathrust Fault for hundreds of years had finally given way. Along a section of the fault longer than the state of California, the oceanic and the continental plates suddenly, violently separated, which triggered earth-shaking waves. But the worst was still to come.

No Ordinary Waves

Most waves are formed by wind that blows across the ocean's surface, pulling water with it. But a tsunami is started by a disturbance, such as an undersea earthquake, that shifts water at the ocean floor. Water is thrust up from the bottom of the sea all the way to the ocean's surface, and waves begin to radiate out in all directions. As a tsunami wave hits the shallow water near land, it slows down but grows taller. Water at the shore is sucked into the giant wave, exposing fish, shells, and corals that were underwater moments ago. Then, suddenly, a towering wall of water crashes onto the beach.

triggered If you triggered an action or event, you did something to start it.
thrust To thrust is to push something with great force.
radiate To radiate is to spread out in waves or rays.

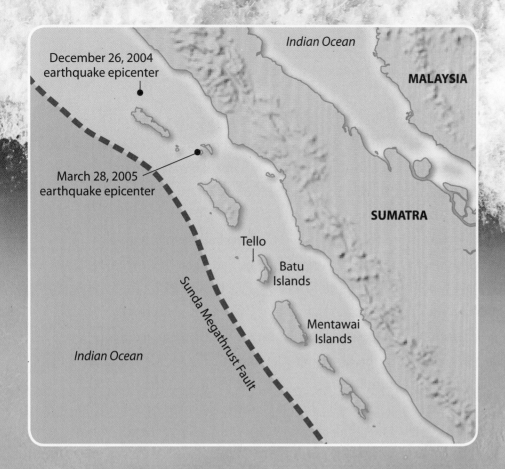

December 26, 2004
earthquake epicenter

Indian Ocean

MALAYSIA

March 28, 2005
earthquake epicenter

SUMATRA

Tello

Batu
Islands

Mentawai
Islands

Sunda Megathrust Fault

Indian Ocean

15   The continental plate sprang up as much as 20 feet, pushing up the
water above it. Tsunami waves rippled out in all directions, gaining power
as they raced across the open ocean as fast as jet airplanes. The first wave,
100 feet tall in some places, hit the Indonesian island of Sumatra
15 minutes after the earthquake. Waves swamped the coast of Thailand
75 minutes later, then India and Sri Lanka, and even Africa, 3,000 miles
from the quake's center.

16   The deadly waves kept flooding beaches for hours. Hundreds of
thousands of people were killed, and millions were left homeless.

17   Kerry Sieh was at home in California when he heard the news.
Immediately, Sieh thought of his friends on the islands he'd visited.
Had they escaped the quaking ground and giant waves? Had their homes
and villages been destroyed? Communication by phone or email was
impossible. On January 1, he flew back to Indonesia, uncertain
of what he'd find.

SAFE FOR NOW

18 People in Tello were lucky. Their island was more than 200 miles from the epicenter of the quake, the most powerful point. On Tello during the quake, the earth shook, but not violently. Later, a small tsunami, three to six feet high, swept through the village, flooding houses. People were shaken and scared, but unharmed.

19 As he traveled to the other islands he'd visited in July, Sieh was relieved to hear the same story. Few homes had been destroyed, and no lives were lost. But danger still lurked. An earthquake on one section of a fault can increase stress along the rest of the fault. And the thousands of miles of the Sunda Megathrust Fault that hadn't ruptured in December were still ripe for another quake.

20 Sure enough, another earthquake shook an area to the south on March 28. This quake was 10 times less powerful than the one in December, yet it was still the second-biggest quake to rock the world in 40 years.

21 Again, Sieh's friends escaped harm. But the quakes were proof that what the scientists had said was true, and they convinced some islanders to take action. Today, on the island of Simuk, many people have left

Destruction after the 2004 earthquake and tsunami in Indonesia

212

their homes near the shore and have rebuilt their town at the island's highest point, the hill where Sieh erected his GPS station. Their modified town is better prepared for tsunamis.

22   The quakes also provided Sieh with a lot of work to do. On Sumatra, the rising continental plate pushed up vast stretches of beach that had been underwater. "We saw thousands of dead corals," Sieh said. He looked at data from the GPS stations to find out exactly how the nearby islands moved during the quakes.

modified A modified version of something is a revised, or changed, version.

Destruction after the 2004 earthquake and tsunami in Indonesia

23   As they traveled the islands by boat and helicopter, Sieh and his colleagues explained why earthquakes and tsunamis happen and what people can do to prepare. They can build their houses out of lightweight wood or bamboo rather than heavy concrete, which would cause more damage if it toppled during a quake. They can move their villages away from the beach, or build pathways to higher ground.

24   Sieh doesn't know exactly when or where it will hit, but he's certain another big quake is coming along the section of the fault south of Tello. Until it does, he'll try to understand as much as he can about why and how the earth moves, and he'll teach the people who live nearby about the danger that lurks under the waves.

Students cover their heads during an earthquake drill in Indonesia.

An official talks to students during an earthquake and tsunami drill in Indonesia.

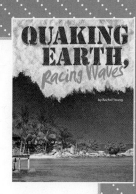

Collaborative Discussion

Look back at what you wrote on page 204. Tell a partner two things you learned during reading. Then work with a group to discuss the questions below. Include details from *Quaking Earth, Racing Waves* to support your answers. Be sure to follow your class's rules for an orderly discussion.

1 Revisit pages 206–207 of the selection. What did Sieh and the other scientists learn from "reading the corals"?

2 Reread page 209. What causes an earthquake? Why isn't it possible for us to feel the usual plate movements that take place on the Earth's surface?

3 What is the difference between a tsunami and a normal ocean wave?

Write a Presentation

PROMPT

In *Quaking Earth, Racing Waves,* you read about a scientist who predicted an earthquake based on evidence he had observed. He and other scientists also gave presentations to people who lived in the danger zone. They told the people why earthquakes and tsunamis happen and what can be done to prepare.

Imagine that you are a scientist and must write a presentation explaining why earthquakes and tsunamis happen. Begin with an opening sentence that introduces your listeners to your topic. Use your understanding of the key information in the text to focus and support your central ideas. Don't forget to use some of the Critical Vocabulary words in your writing.

PLAN

Take notes from the text about what causes earthquakes and tsunamis. Include important details that support the central ideas.

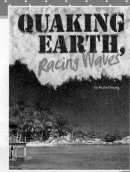

WRITE

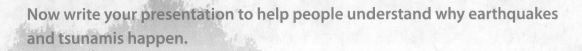

Now write your presentation to help people understand why earthquakes and tsunamis happen.

✓ Make sure your presentation

- ☐ introduces the topic and explains who you are.
- ☐ uses evidence from the text to focus your central ideas.
- ☐ uses details from the text to support your central ideas.
- ☐ concludes by inviting the audience to ask questions.

Notice & Note
Numbers and Statistics

Prepare to Read

GENRE STUDY **Informational texts** give facts and examples about a topic.

- Informational texts are often organized using headings that help readers identify main ideas.
- Science texts include words that are specific to the topic.
- Informational texts often include visuals, such as charts and maps, and sidebar features, which tell more about the topic.

SET A PURPOSE **Think about** the title and genre of this text. What do you know about hurricanes? What do you want to learn? Write your ideas below.

CRITICAL VOCABULARY

surge

eventually

regions

mobile

anchored

foundations

category

track

Meet the Authors:
Alvin and Virginia Silverstein
and Laura Silverstein Nunn

HURRICANES

THE SCIENCE BEHIND KILLER STORMS

**by Alvin and Virginia Silverstein
and Laura Silverstein Nunn**

1 **YOU WILL NOT HEAR ABOUT HURRICANE DISASTERS** in Kansas or the Sahara Desert. Hurricanes not only need heat to form, but they also need moisture—lots of it. The warm ocean waters of the tropics are perfect for the birth of a hurricane.

2 Meteorologists (weather scientists) use the term tropical cyclone to describe any storm over the tropical oceans that spins in a circle around a center of low pressure. Tropical cyclones are known by different names, depending on where they form. If these storms develop in the North Atlantic Ocean, the northeastern Pacific Ocean, the Gulf of Mexico, or the Caribbean Sea, they are called hurricanes.

3 In the northwestern Pacific Ocean, near Japan and the Philippines, hurricanes are known as typhoons. Near Australia and in the Indian Ocean, they are called cyclones.

A Hurricane's Life Cycle

4 A hurricane goes through a series of four stages as it grows: tropical disturbance, tropical depression, tropical storm, and hurricane. Not all storms reach the higher stages.

5 **Tropical disturbance:** Tropical disturbances form over warm, tropical oceans, with water surface temperatures at least 80 degrees Fahrenheit. The warm surface water evaporates, sending water vapor into the air. As the moist air rises, it cools. Some of the water vapor condenses into water droplets, forming clouds. Clouds pile up high into the atmosphere, and thunderstorms develop.

6 **Tropical depression:** As the warm, moist air above the ocean rises, it creates an area of low air pressure. Cool heavier air from the surrounding area sinks, replacing the rising air. A cluster of thunderstorms joins to form a single large weather system. Soon a whirlpool of hot, moist air is spiraling around a low-pressure center. As the swirling winds turn, they gather more energy from the warm water below. The wind speed rises. If the winds reach 38 miles per hour, the growing storm is ready to enter the next stage.

High waves crashed ashore in Shizuoka, Japan, on September 6, 2007, as Typhoon Fitow advanced toward Japan's main island of Honshu. These waves were part of Fitow's storm surge.

What Does "Hurricane" Mean?

The term *hurricane* comes from "Huracan," the god of evil, named by an ancient Central American Indian group. Spanish colonists later changed the spelling to "hurricane."

surge A surge is a sudden powerful movement forward or upward.

7   **Tropical storm:** The storm continues to grow stronger, and the winds blow faster. The strong winds draw up more heat and water vapor from the ocean surface, feeding the storm. Some of the water vapor condenses, producing heavy rain. Thunderstorms release heat, giving the storm even more power. Viewed from an airplane flying above the storm, the clouds have a distinct circular shape. If the wind speed reaches 74 miles per hour, the storm has reached the last stage—a hurricane.

8   **Hurricane:** The swirling winds of a hurricane surround the eye—an area of warm low-pressure air at the center. This is a calm area that may be from 6 to 40 miles across.

9   In the eye of the storm it may be sunny with only light winds. To someone on the ground, it seems like the storm is over. But it is not.

10   The strongest winds blow around the edge of the eye, called the eyewall. Bands of thick clouds, called rainbands, swirl outward around the eyewall. As the storm moves, the area that was below the eye suddenly gets stormy again. The rainbands can produce more than 2 inches of rain per hour.

11   As it develops, a hurricane moves across the ocean. It usually travels northwest at a speed of 10 to 20 miles per hour. It may eventually reach a coast and move inland. As soon as the hurricane passes over land, however, its wind speed drops. Remember that the warm ocean waters supply a hurricane with energy. The air over land areas is cooler and drier, so the hurricane gets weaker. Soon it may become just a tropical storm, and eventually it dies out.

12   Sometimes a hurricane may change course and move back out over the ocean. Picking up energy, it may later hit the coast again in a different spot with greater force. This is what happened with Katrina, which first hit Florida, then moved over the Gulf of Mexico to hit the Gulf Coast even harder. A hurricane can last an average of three to fourteen days, and travel as many as 4,000 miles.

> **eventually**   To state that something will happen eventually means that it will happen at some time, usually after a series of other events.

Why Do Hurricanes Swirl Around in a Circle?

Winds start blowing in a straight direction. But they curve because the Earth moves as it spins on its axis. This is known as Coriolis effect. The faster the winds blow, the more they curve. In a hurricane, winds blow so fast, they form spirals. In the Northern Hemisphere, the winds in a hurricane blow counterclockwise. In the Southern Hemisphere, they move clockwise.

Where Do Hurricanes Start?

The winds that blow over the tropical oceans are typically "easterlies"—winds that blow from east to west. Thunderstorms that develop in low-pressure areas disturb this wind flow, producing a wavelike movement. Meteorologists call it an easterly wave, or a tropical wave. About 80 percent of hurricanes in the Atlantic Ocean start in easterly waves over western Africa.

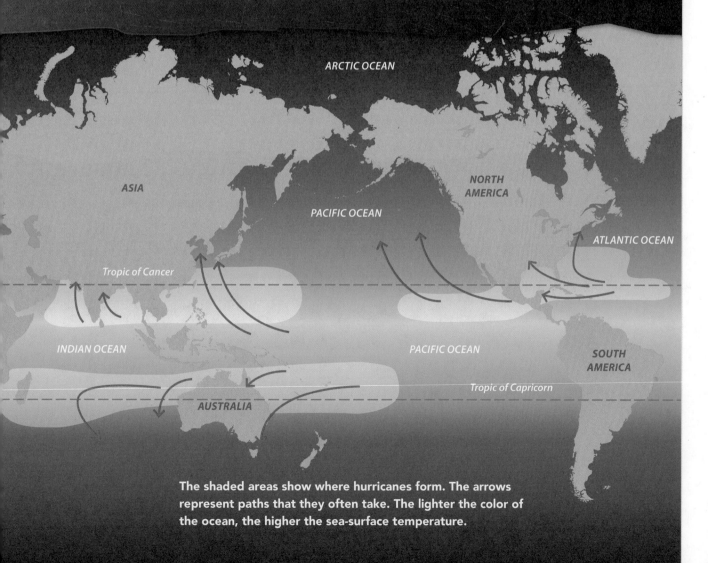

The shaded areas show where hurricanes form. The arrows represent paths that they often take. The lighter the color of the ocean, the higher the sea-surface temperature.

Naming Hurricanes

13 Every year, meteorologists use a special alphabetical list of names for hurricanes. Different lists are used for hurricanes in the Atlantic and Pacific regions. The names are common first names in the languages of the regions where the storms strike.

14   Hurricane names are retired (no longer used) if a named storm causes a tremendous amount of damage or the loss of many lives. "Katrina," for example, will never be used again.

> **regions** Regions are areas.

Are Big Hurricanes More Powerful Than Small Ones?
Not always. Hurricane Andrew, which hit southern Florida in 1992, was the second-most destructive hurricane in U.S. history. But it was fairly small, measuring only 60 miles across, compared to the average hurricane, which covers an area 300 miles wide.

When Is Hurricane Season?
Hurricanes usually form at a certain time of the year, known as the hurricane season. Since hurricanes need warm, moist air to form, they usually develop during the summer and autumn months. The Atlantic hurricane season is from June 1 to November 30. The hurricane season for the northeast Pacific is May 15 to November 30.

This satellite image of Hurricane Katrina shows the storm centered over Louisiana on August 29, 2005.

This towering mass of white clouds is part of Hurricane Katrina's eyewall, the area around the central eye. The strongest winds are found in the eyewall. The picture was taken on August 28, 2005, from a hurricane-hunter airplane.

A historic home was damaged September 24, 2005, by a tree downed by Hurricane Rita at Barksdale Air Force Base in Louisiana.

WHEN A HURRICANE HITS

15 **EVERY YEAR, EIGHTY TO ONE HUNDRED** tropical storms develop around the world. About forty to sixty of them get strong enough to become hurricanes, typhoons, or cyclones. And only a few of those ever reach places where people live.

16 More hurricanes hit some regions than others. In the northwest Pacific Ocean, for example, an average of twenty-eight tropical storms occur each year; nineteen of them become typhoons. In the Atlantic Ocean, however, an average of only ten tropical storms develop every year, and six of them become hurricanes. Over a three-year period, the United States coast gets hit an average of five times by hurricanes, and two of them are major hurricanes. When a hurricane hits land—no matter where—the effects can be disastrous.

Whipping Winds

17 Hurricane winds are extremely powerful. Out at sea, the winds can blow up to 200 miles per hour. Although a hurricane loses energy when it moves over land, the winds still cause a lot of damage. Strong gusts of wind rip huge trees out of the ground. They toss cars and people through the air. The wind can even turn small objects, such as a road sign or a lawn chair, into deadly flying missiles.

18 Hurricanes are especially destructive when they hit an area where many people live. Hurricane Andrew, for example, had winds of 165 miles per hour when it reached the coast of southern Florida in 1992. It passed through an area south of Miami that was filled with homes and businesses. Many of the buildings there were mobile homes, which do not weigh as much as houses. They also are not well anchored to the ground. In some communities, more than 90 percent of mobile homes were completely destroyed.

---

mobile   Something that is mobile is able to move or be moved easily.

anchored   Something that is anchored is firmly attached to something else or weighed down so it won't move easily.

In August 1992, Hurricane Andrew caused massive destruction in southern Florida. Hundreds of thousands of homes and businesses were damaged or destroyed.

Storm Surges

19   Even though a hurricane's winds are dangerous, people are more likely to die from a storm surge. The winds of the storm push ocean waters toward the shore, forming a huge wave. The low air pressure also lifts the water, raising the level even higher. These forces combine with the normal ocean tides, forming a huge wall of water. Many hurricanes have produced storm surges more than 20 feet high.

20   The surging water smashes into buildings and washes out roads. The storm surge may also wash away beaches and remove the soil around the foundations of houses.

> **foundations** Foundations are the base pieces houses and buildings are built upon.

It's a Fact!

Hurricane Camille, which hit the Mississippi and Alabama coasts in August 1969, had the most powerful hurricane winds over land in United States history. They blew more than 190 miles per hour.

Heavy Rains

21 Hurricanes can cause serious flooding even without a storm surge. Their rainbands can dump 10 to 15 inches of rain in a twenty-four hour period. Bigger storms bring heavier rains—up to 20 inches or more. Such huge amounts of rainfall in a short amount of time can flood entire communities.

22 Heavy rains can also cause mudslides. Rain mixes with the soil on mountains and hillsides and forms mud. The mud flows downhill. Rocks break free, adding to the mixture. As the mudslide rushes down the mountain, it rips out trees and carries away houses. Down below, it buries everything in mud. Hurricane Mitch killed more than ten thousand people in 1998 due to mudslides caused by heavy rains.

When Hurricane Floyd came toward land in September 1999, its storm surge collapsed this pier at Daytona Beach, Florida.

WARNING
NO
WATER
ACTIVITY
PERMITTED
BETWEEN THIS
SIGN AND PIER

229

Tornadoes

23 Hurricanes can also bring tornadoes. These are small but very powerful storms. The winds of a tornado, or "twister," rapidly swirl around in a tall cloud that is funnel-shaped. Some hurricanes do not produce any tornadoes; others spawn, or form, many of them. Hurricane Katrina, for example, produced sixty-two tornadoes. The tornadoes that come with hurricanes are not usually as powerful as those that form during thunderstorms in the Midwestern states.

What's the Damage?

24 Scientists use the Saffir-Simpson Hurricane Scale to rank the strength of the hurricane. The scale rates a hurricane from Category 1 (least powerful) to Category 5 (most destructive). The rating is based on average wind speed. Each category also indicates the level of storm surge and how much damage scientists think the hurricane will do.

25 Hurricanes in categories 3, 4, and 5 are considered major hurricanes. They can cause widespread damage to property, severe inland flooding, and significant loss of life. Hurricanes can change categories as they gain or lose strength. That is what happened with Hurricane Katrina. Over the Gulf of Mexico, Katrina had become a Category 5, but it was down to Category 3 by the time it reached the Louisiana-Mississippi border as it moved inland.

> **category** A category is a group of things that are similar to each other in some way.

What Is the Difference Between Hurricanes and Tornadoes?

Hurricanes and tornadoes are both cyclones—powerful windstorms that spin in a circle. But they have major differences:

- Hurricanes form over the ocean. Most tornadoes form over land.
- Hurricanes are huge, often hundreds of miles wide. Tornadoes are usually much smaller, only 4,000 to 5,000 feet wide.
- Hurricanes last for up to two weeks. Tornadoes last for up to three hours.
- Hurricane winds are not as powerful as tornado winds. Tornado winds typically blow 200 to 300 miles per hour.

Are Hurricanes Getting Worse?

26 Some studies have shown that the number of category 4 and 5 hurricanes has increased worldwide since the 1980s. Many scientists believe this increase in severe storms is due to global-warming. They think our planet has been getting warmer. Since a warmer planet means warmer oceans, storms have become more powerful. Other scientists have a different idea as to why strong hurricanes have been recorded. They think that scientists have just gotten better at detecting and tracking hurricanes. Because technology has become so advanced, scientists can track hurricanes better and warn people in advance.

> **track**   To track something is to watch it and see where it moves and how it changes.

Saffir-Simpson Hurricane Scale

CATEGORY	WIND SPEED	STORM SURGE	DAMAGES
1	74–95 mph	4–5 ft	• Some flooding • Little or no damage to building structures
2	96–110 mph	6–8 ft	• Flooding of coastal roads • Some trees blown down • Damage to roof shingles, doors, and windows
3	111–130 mph	9–12 ft	• Damage to house structures • Mobile homes destroyed • Severe flooding
4	131–155 mph	13–18 ft	• Severe flooding inland • Some roofs ripped off • Major structural damage to lower floors of buildings
5	>155 mph	>18 ft	• Severe flooding farther inland • All trees and shrubs blown down • Mobile homes destroyed • Serious damage to building and house structures

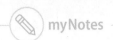

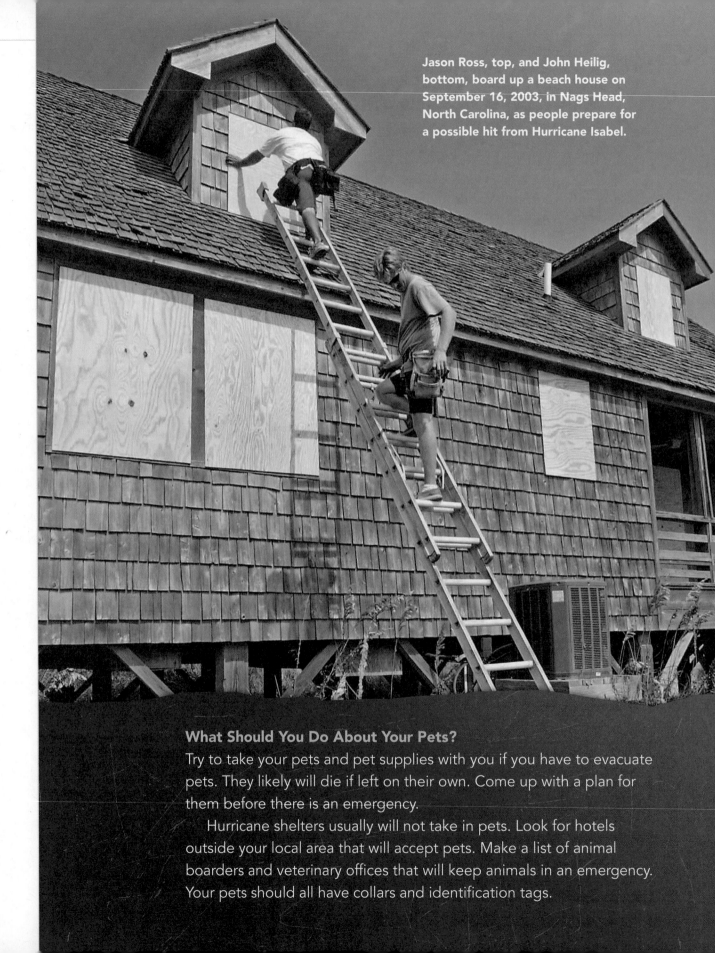

Jason Ross, top, and John Heilig, bottom, board up a beach house on September 16, 2003, in Nags Head, North Carolina, as people prepare for a possible hit from Hurricane Isabel.

What Should You Do About Your Pets?

Try to take your pets and pet supplies with you if you have to evacuate pets. They likely will die if left on their own. Come up with a plan for them before there is an emergency.

Hurricane shelters usually will not take in pets. Look for hotels outside your local area that will accept pets. Make a list of animal boarders and veterinary offices that will keep animals in an emergency. Your pets should all have collars and identification tags.

STAYING SAFE

27 **AN ESTIMATED 35 MILLION PEOPLE,** or 12 percent of the people in the United States, live in the southern coastal regions most threatened by Atlantic hurricanes. As the coastal population continues to grow, the damages due to hurricanes also increase.

28 Scientists may not be able to prevent a hurricane from invading where people live. However, there are a number of things people can do to survive when a hurricane hits.

Emergency Plan

29 In case a hurricane hits, you and your family should have an emergency plan. There are probably special hurricane shelters nearby. Find out where they are and the fastest way to get to them.

30 At home, keep a disaster supply kit handy. You will need items to keep you safe in case the power goes out or your neighborhood is flooded. Emergency supplies can get you through a few days stuck in your home or a shelter until regular services are working again. The kit should include:

• Flashlight and batteries
• Battery-operated radio
• First aid kit
• Emergency food and water
• Special items for babies, the elderly, and pets
• Protective clothing, such as rain gear
• Blankets

31 Listen for hurricane warnings on the radio or TV, and follow the instructions. The National Hurricane Center also posts hurricane warnings on its Web site. If the local officials say you should evacuate, leave as quickly as you can.

If a Hurricane Is Coming

32   If a hurricane warning is issued for your area, damage to you and your home can be reduced if your family does the following:

- Nail boards over your home's windows.
- Pick up toys, bikes, and other objects outside the house. Put them where they will not blow around and cause damage.
- Prevent flooding by placing sandbags around your house.
- Trim bushes and tree limbs hanging over the house.
- Inside the house, put strips of duct tape crisscross on windows to keep broken glass from flying around.
- Fill bathtubs, pails, and bottles with water for drinking and washing. The water supply may be cut off or polluted.

33   Unless there is an evacuation, stay inside your home. Do not leave even if it seems like the storm is over. Remember, it could be the eye of the storm. A hurricane is not over until the second half of the storm has passed.

34   Hurricanes are terrifying disasters, but learning about them can help you be prepared. Knowing where to go and what to do if a hurricane strikes can make a huge difference in keeping you and your family safe.

Vehicles leave New Orleans ahead of Hurricane Katrina on August 28, 2005. Road signs (inset) often inform people of evacuation routes.

Collaborative Discussion

Look back at what you wrote on page 218. Talk with a partner about what you learned from the text. Then work with a group to discuss the questions below. Find information in *Hurricanes* to support your answers. Look for ways to connect your ideas to those of others during your discussion.

1 Reread pages 220–222. What conditions need to be present in order for a hurricane to form?

2 Review pages 227–230. What dangerous elements can hurricanes produce? Why is each one a problem?

3 What do the maps and photos in the selection help you understand about hurricanes?

Listening Tip

Listen closely to each speaker's ideas and think about how they are related.

Speaking Tip

Use words and phrases such as *another reason* or *also* to link your ideas to what other speakers say.

Write a Weather Report

PROMPT

In *Hurricanes*, you learned about how hurricanes form, the types of damage they can cause, and ways people can prepare for these storms. Information such as this is vital for people who live in areas where hurricanes strike.

Imagine that you are a meteorologist for a local TV station, and a Category 2 hurricane is approaching your area. Use evidence from the text to write a weather report telling viewers what kind of effects they can expect the Category 2 storm to cause. Then, explain what viewers should do to stay safe. Be sure to organize the information so that it's easy for viewers to understand. Use a scientific word from the text, and be sure to explain what the word means. Don't forget to use some of the Critical Vocabulary words in your writing.

PLAN

Create two columns of notes, one about expected damage and other effects of the Category 2 hurricane and one about ways to prepare and stay safe. Base your notes on evidence you read in the text.

WRITE

Now write your weather report to inform your viewers about the approaching hurricane.

Make sure your weather report

- ☐ introduces the topic.
- ☐ includes evidence from the text such as the hurricane's strength, possible damage and other effects, and ways to stay safe.
- ☐ uses and explains a scientific word.
- ☐ organizes the information in a way that is easy for the viewers to understand.
- ☐ includes a conclusion.

(?) Essential Question

How can learning about natural disasters make us safer?

Write an Editorial

PROMPT Think back on what you learned about staying safe in natural disasters.

Is your school or community ready for a natural disaster? What more could be done to prepare? Choose one natural disaster that you learned about in the module. Write an editorial for your school paper stating what you think needs to be done to ensure the community stays safe. Support your opinion with evidence from the texts and video.

I will write an editorial about _____.

✓ Make sure your editorial

☐ has an introduction that clearly states your opinion.
☐ explains why the issue is important to your readers.
☐ supports your opinion with reasons in a logical order.
☐ has reasons supported by facts and details from the texts.
☐ uses words and phrases that link the opinion, reasons, and evidence.
☐ has a conclusion that restates the opinion and gives readers specific actions to take.

Decide which natural disaster you will write about. Then think about the position you will take on how to be prepared. Look back at your notes and revisit the texts and video for evidence.

Use the chart below to plan your editorial. Write your topic and a sentence that states your opinion. Then write your reasons and the evidence that supports each one. Use Critical Vocabulary Words where appropriate.

My Topic: _____

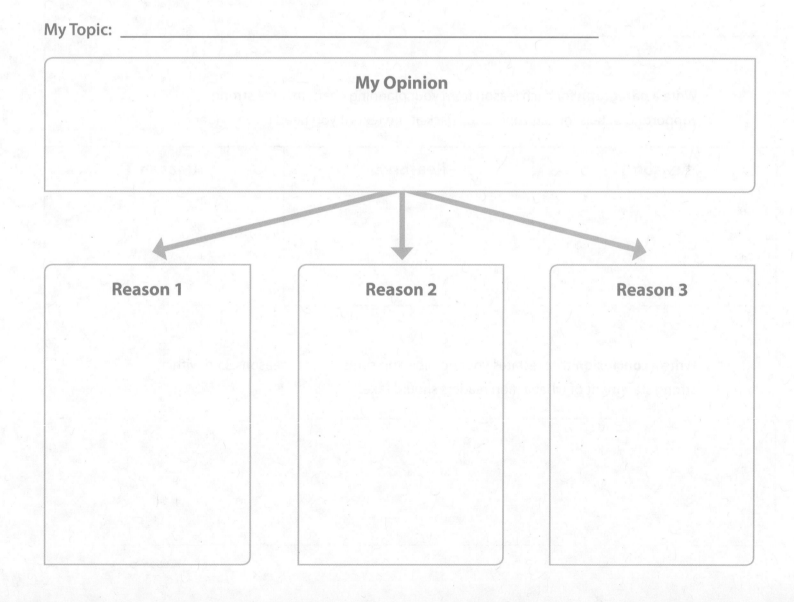

My Opinion

Reason 1

Reason 2

Reason 3

DRAFT ·· Write your editorial.

Write an **introduction** that states your opinion. Explain why the topic is important.

Write a **paragraph** for each reason from your planning chart. Include strong
supporting details for each one. Look back at the texts if you need more evidence.

Reason 1	Reason 2	Reason 3

Write a **conclusion** that restates your opinion and sums up your reasons. End with a
strong statement of what action readers should take.

REVISE AND EDIT ·· Review your draft.

Now it's time to revise and edit your draft. This is a chance to review your editorial and make improvements. Work with a partner or small group. Share suggestions about how to improve each other's work. Use these questions to help you evaluate and improve your editorial.

✓ PURPOSE/ FOCUS	ORGANIZATION	EVIDENCE	LANGUAGE/ VOCABULARY	CONVENTIONS
☐ Does my introduction clearly state my opinion and why it's important? ☐ Does each reason clearly support my opinion?	☐ Are the reasons presented in a logical order? ☐ Does the conclusion restate my opinion and leave readers with an action to take?	☐ Is each of my reasons supported by strong evidence from the texts?	☐ Did I use linking words and phrases to connect the opinion, reasons, and evidence? ☐ Did I use strong action verbs?	☐ Have I spelled all words correctly? ☐ Did I use a variety of sentence types?

PUBLISH ·· Share your work.

Create a Finished Copy. Make a final copy of your editorial. Include an infographic or other visual for additional support. Consider these options for sharing your editorial:

1. Include your editorial in a safety brochure. Print copies and make the brochure available in the school or class library.

2. Give a speech to your class or another student group. Use expression and gestures to help show the importance of your opinion and reasons.

3. Post your editorial on a school or class website. Invite comments from your readers or other suggestions for how to prepare for a natural disaster.

WILD WEST

"On every side, and at every hour of the day, we came up against the relentless limitations of pioneer life."

—Anna Howard Shaw

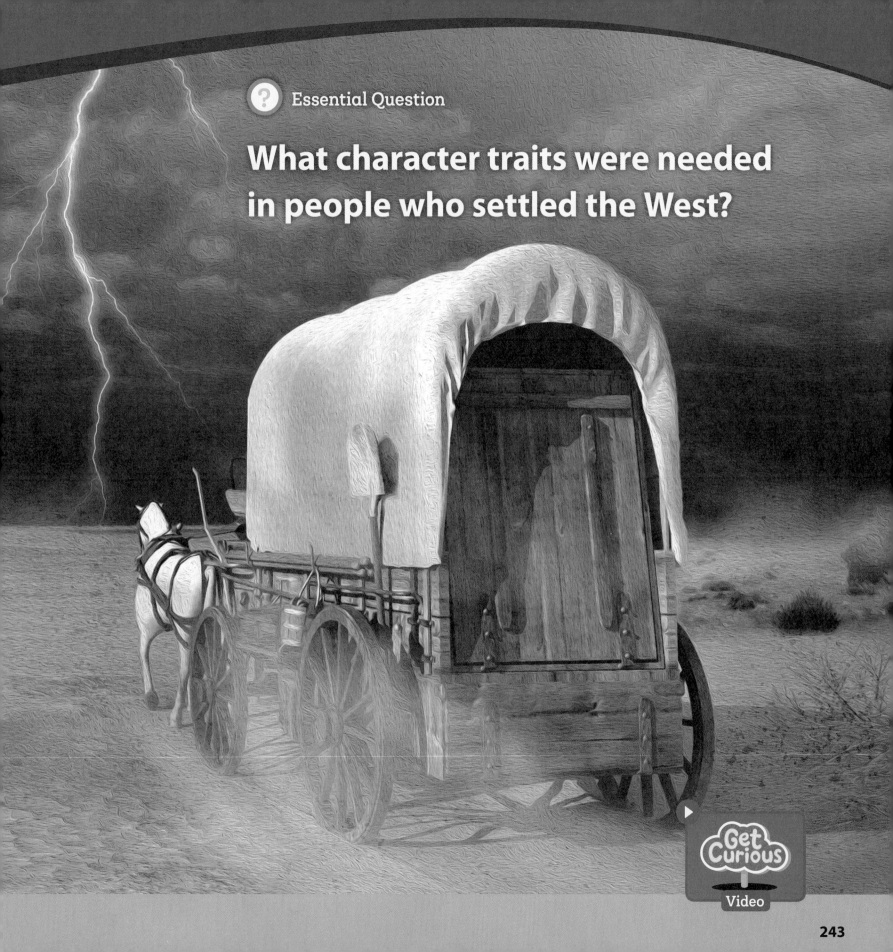

What character traits were needed in people who settled the West?

Get Curious

Video

Words About Settling the West

The words in the chart will help you talk and write about the selections in this module. Which words about settling the West have you seen before? Which words are new to you?

Add to the Vocabulary Network on page 245 by writing synonyms, antonyms, and related words and phrases for each word about settling the West.

After you read each selection in this module, come back to the Vocabulary Network and keep building it. Add more boxes if you need to.

WORD	MEANING	CONTEXT SENTENCE
native (adjective)	A person, animal, or plant that is described as native to a place was born in that place.	Sunflowers are native to the northern regions in the United States.
epic (adjective)	An epic event is very large and impressive, and sometimes heroic.	Thousands of workers faced great danger during the epic construction of the Egyptian pyramids.
midland (noun)	The middle of a country is sometimes called the midland.	Many pioneers began their journey west at Independence, Missouri, in America's midland.
victory (noun)	When you achieve a victory, you overcome a challenge or win against a competitor.	Reaching the end of the long and difficult tournament was a victory for the winning soccer team.

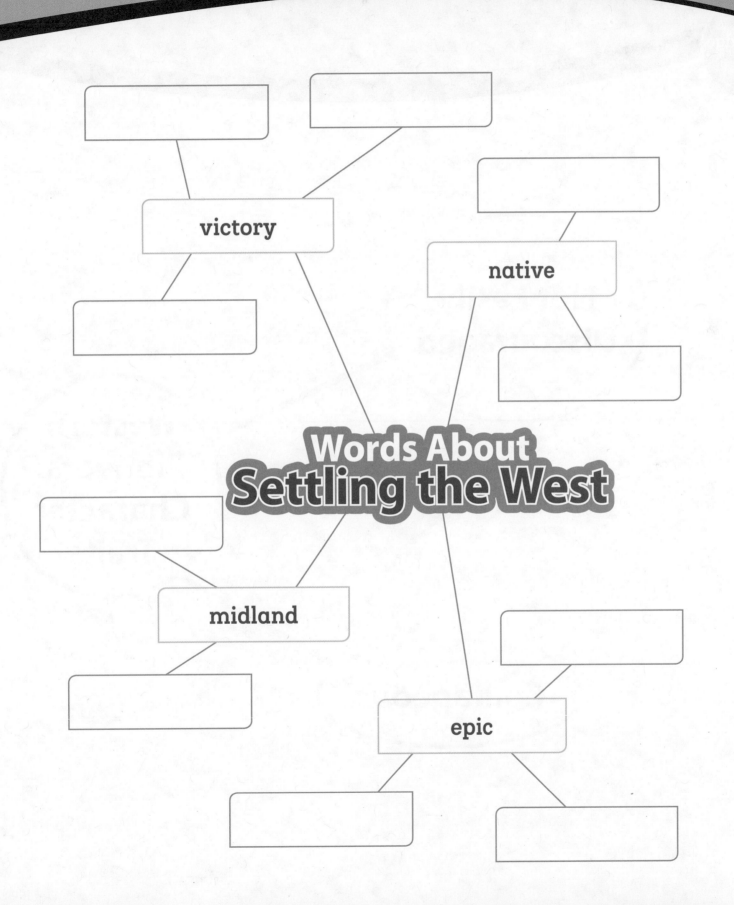

victory

native

Words About
Settling the West

midland

epic

Not Easily Discouraged

Western Pioneers: Character Traits

Courageous

Hard-Working

Looking for a Better Life

Short Read

Why Go West?

Lots of people make a checklist before they travel so they won't forget anything important. During the 1800s, thousands of people might have used a checklist like this one. They left their homes and migrated to undeveloped western sections of the United States. What made them do it?

✓ Leave almost everyone.
✓ Leave almost everything.
✓ Take a chance on something new.
✓ Head west.

The Chance to Own Land

Some saw the chance to become landowners. President Thomas Jefferson bought the Louisiana Territory from France in 1803. Known as the Louisiana Purchase, the new lands doubled the size of the United States. Free or inexpensive land was there for the taking, and it wasn't long before thousands of people, from inside and outside

THE LOUISIANA TERRITORY

the United States, looked to the American west and saw opportunity.

However, the growth of the United States wasn't a victory for everyone. During this period, Native Americans lost their homelands as settlers and pioneers moved west. Many tribes were forced to live elsewhere, and some native cultures were nearly wiped out.

The Chance for a Fresh Start

5   Some people made the journey west in hopes of starting anew. They believed the long, dangerous trip was worthwhile if it led to a better life. Many had faced hard times, with growing families and few ways to make enough money to support them. Hopeful news from friends and relatives who had already gone west encouraged more and more families to relocate, too.

A covered wagon train

6   Many settlers followed the popular Oregon Trail, with some taking it all the way to its end in the Pacific Northwest. They loaded up covered wagons for their epic journey across the midland plains and over mountains. Determination kept these travelers going through challenges and setbacks.

The Chance to Strike It Rich

7   For some, the motivation was pure gold. In 1848, James W. Marshall discovered gold at Sutter's Mill in what is now northern California. The news quickly spread, and the California Gold Rush was on! By 1852, more than 300,000 people had moved to California to seek their fortunes.

Notice & Note
3 Big Questions

Prepare to Read

GENRE STUDY **Informational texts** give facts and examples about a topic, event, or time period.

- Informational texts contain a central, or main, idea supported by details, including facts and quotations. The ideas might be organized under headings or by cause and effect.
- Words specific to the topic or subject area may be included.
- Informational texts may also include visuals and text features such as sidebars, which enhance or support the main text.

SET A PURPOSE **Think about** the title and genre of this text. What do you know about the Wild West? What do you want to learn? Write your ideas below.

CRITICAL VOCABULARY

knowledge

posts

hardships

patriotic

slogans

handy

typical

consisted

**Meet the Author and Illustrator:
Anita Yasuda and Emmanuel Cerisier**

EXPLORE THE Wild West!

by Anita Yasuda   illustrated by Emmanuel Cerisier

WHERE WAS THE
WILD WEST?

1. The "Wild West" was more than just a place. It was more than the western lands beyond the Mississippi River. It was a time of pioneers, cowboys, and Native Americans. It was a time of cowgirls and pioneer women, stagecoaches, saloons, outlaws and lawmen, buffalo hunting, and bank robbers.

2. What we think of as the time of the Wild West started in the early 1800s. By the mid-1800s, when gold was discovered in California, everyone was talking about the Wild West. This period of time lasted until the frontier was closed in 1890.

Missouri River

Key

—— Oregon Trail

—— California Trail

—— Santa Fe Trail

 Great Plains

3　The original American frontier was the Mississippi River. But the frontier pushed west towards the Pacific Ocean as tens of thousands of people moved westward. Stories of plenty of good farmland for everyone made the West sound amazing. Many pioneers went to Oregon and other places because the land was free. When gold was discovered more and more people moved there hoping to strike it rich.

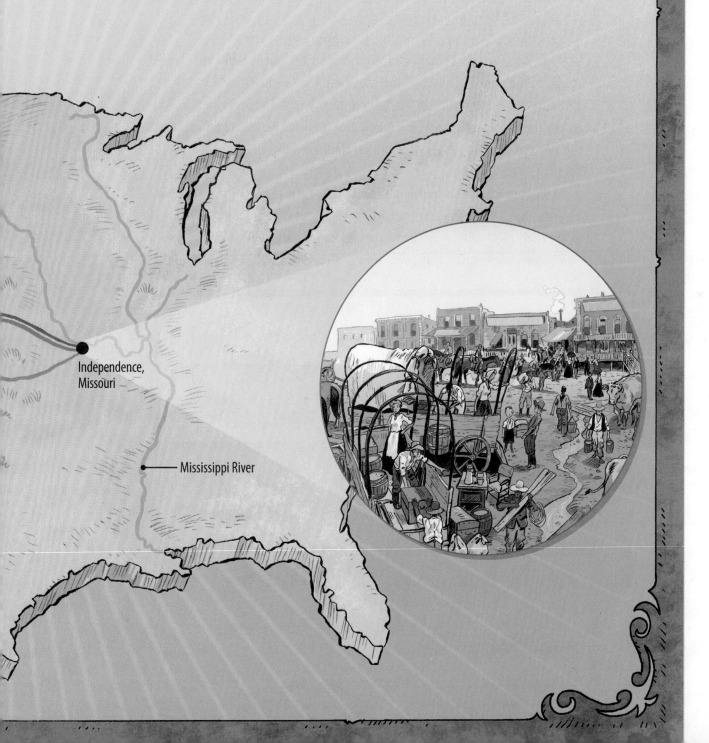

Independence, Missouri

Mississippi River

myNotes

HOW AMERICA GREW

4   How did America get new land for people to explore and settle? In 1803, the United States doubled its size with a single purchase of land—the Louisiana Purchase. The leader of France, Napoleon Bonaparte, sold the Louisiana Territory to President Thomas Jefferson. This area included parts or all of the present-day states of Louisiana, Missouri, Arkansas, Texas, Iowa, Minnesota, Kansas, Nebraska, Colorado, North Dakota, South Dakota, Montana, Wyoming, Oklahoma, and New Mexico.

5   Now that America reached far to the west, President Jefferson needed a map of the area. He sent two men, named Meriwether Lewis and William Clark, to do the job. He hoped they would discover a water route across the continent. Lewis and Clark and their 50-person team explored the West from 1804 to 1806, becoming the first new Americans to see the Pacific Ocean.

6   A French Canadian trapper and his Native American wife, Sacagawea (sak-uh-guh-WEE-uh), translated for Lewis and Clark. This allowed them to speak to the Native Americans they met along the way. When Native American people saw Sacagawea, they believed the group was peaceful.

Then and Now

THEN: The American government paid France $15 million for the Louisiana Territory.

NOW: Today, this land deal would cost billions of dollars.

7   Lewis and Clark kept detailed journals of the plants and animals they discovered. They wrote about the Native Americans they met. Along the way, they sent boxes of seeds, bones, animal skins—and even a live prairie dog—back to President Jefferson.

8   After Lewis and Clark's successful two-year expedition, many explorers, scientists, map makers, and missionaries headed west on the Oregon Trail. Fur traders, often called mountain men, went west along the Oregon Trail too. These men trapped beaver and other small animals. They also traded many goods with Native Americans, such as rifles and steel knives for more beaver pelts. Mountain men used their knowledge of the land to guide soldiers and explorers.

knowledge   If you have knowledge, you have information or understanding about something.

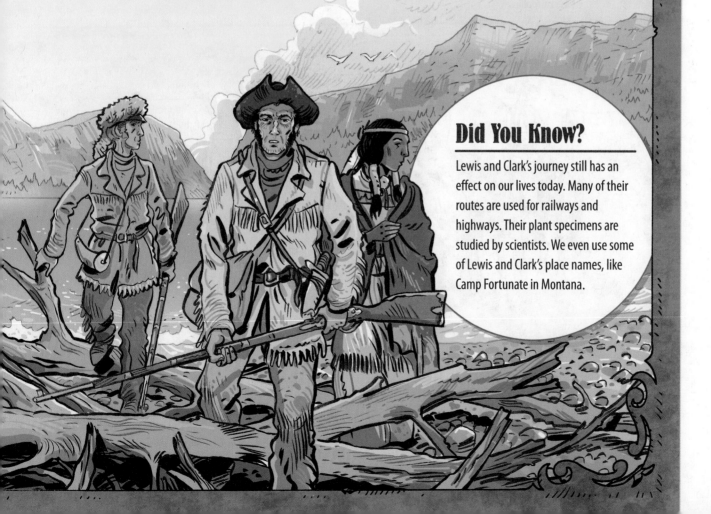

Did You Know?

Lewis and Clark's journey still has an effect on our lives today. Many of their routes are used for railways and highways. Their plant specimens are studied by scientists. We even use some of Lewis and Clark's place names, like Camp Fortunate in Montana.

Presenting . . . James Beckwourth

Born in 1798, James Beckwourth was a famous African American mountain man. He worked as a fur trapper, guide, and translator. He lived among the Crow Indians, where he learned to speak their language. Around 1850, Beckwourth discovered a trail through the Sierra Nevada Mountains that was good enough for wagons. Many settlers and gold miners travelling to California used his route. The Beckwourth Pass is named for him.

9   The trails and posts used by these explorers and mountain men guided the pioneers who came to settle the land west of the Mississippi River. Men, women, and children heading west walked, pushed handcarts, and rode on horses and in wagons. Few knew how hard and long the journey would be.

posts   Posts were forts or stopping places along the trail where people could buy supplies.

Frontier Quick Quote

"... those who will come after us will extend ... and fill up the canvas we begin." —THOMAS JEFFERSON, 1805

MOVING WEST

10 Do you think you could walk all day, every day, for weeks and weeks? That's exactly what kids who walked west with their parents had to do. Depending on where people started and how far west they went, the entire journey could be a few hundred miles or as long as 2,000 miles (3,200 kilometers). It could take five months to get to their new home. No wonder they often went through many pairs of shoes!

11   Newspaper advertisements made the West sound amazing. They encouraged many people in the eastern United States to move. Often these reports did not give a complete picture of the daily hardships of western life.

> **hardships** Hardships are difficulties or suffering caused by not having enough of something.

12   People went west for many reasons—not just for gold. Some pioneers dreamed of owning their own farm or opening businesses. The Mormons went in search of religious freedom. Others moved west for patriotic reasons. They believed that it was good for America to settle all of its land.

13   At this time, Great Britain still controlled parts of what is now the United States. In 1846, the United States and Great Britain agreed that all of Oregon would belong to the United States. Right away, thousands of people travelled west on the Oregon Trail.

THE FRONTIER WAGON

14   Pioneer families moved west by wagon. A pioneer wagon was light and small. It had to be, to make it through narrow mountain passes. The wagon had a waterproof canvas cover. Because its cover reminded people of a ship's sails, they nicknamed the wagon a prairie schooner. (A schooner is a type of ship that has sails.) Some wagon covers had names or slogans such as "Oregon or Bust" painted on the side.

patriotic   People who act in a patriotic way toward a country show that they love that country.
slogans   Slogans are short phrases that are catchy and easy to remember.

Did You Know?

You can see miles of wagon ruts along the Oregon Trail in places like Guernsey, Wyoming. The wagon wheels created trenches in solid rock, some up to 6 feet deep (2 meters)!

GET PACKING!

15 Most pioneers used oxen to pull their wagons. At the end of the journey, oxen could be used to plow fields. They were strong enough to pull 2,000 pounds (907 kilograms)!

16 A wagon carried everything a pioneer needed to begin a new life. Pioneers usually took equipment to repair the wagon, farm tools, seeds for planting, and personal items such as shoes and blankets. They also brought food such as flour, bacon, coffee, and rice. There were no grocery stores if they forgot something! Trading posts along the way sold some food and other items, but everything was expensive and often sold out.

17 Families often packed too much. Then they had to lighten their loads along the trail so the oxen wouldn't get worn out with too much weight. Without oxen, pioneers would have to carry their belongings! Furniture, like trunks and beds, was the first thing to be left behind. One pioneer woman left her apron and three pieces of bacon! Eventually there was so much garbage along the trails that people didn't need a guide or a map to find their way.

18 Unless someone was sick or the weather was bad, people walked beside their wagons. This was mainly to save the space in the wagon for food and to make the load lighter for the oxen. Also, the wagons were bouncy and uncomfortable. The good thing about the bouncing was that pioneers used the motion to churn butter!

Then and Now

THEN: Pioneer families spent $500–$1,000 on supplies for their long, western journey.

NOW: People pay about $400 to fly from the East Coast to the West Coast. They get there in six hours.

WAGON TRAIN

19 Many pioneers began their journey in the frontier town of Independence, Missouri, where they formed wagon trains. Pioneers believed a large group would keep them safe. There would also be many skills in a group that might come in handy on the journey.

handy Something that is handy is very useful.

Did You Know?

On a good day, a wagon covered about 25 miles (40 kilometers). But on days of difficult river crossings and mountain paths, the wagon might travel only 1 mile in the entire day.

Independence Rock

Independence Rock represented the halfway point on the trail. Children and their parents looked forward to carving their names and leaving messages on Independence Rock. It was significant because people needed to reach it by July 4 or risk getting caught in mountain storms farther west. This giant rock rose 128 feet high (39 meters) and to some looked like a beached whale. If you ever visit Independence Rock in Wyoming, you can see the names of many pioneers and the dates they were there.

20   A wagon train could be as long as a hundred wagons or more! A captain led the wagon train. The captain could be the oldest man or the man who owned the most wagons. He decided when the group started, stopped for breaks, and how the group would cross a river. A scout, usually a mountain man, helped the captain. He rode ahead of the wagon train to select tent sites and make sure they were going in the right direction.

TRAIL DANGERS

21 Pioneers faced many dangers along the trail. Rain washed out roads. Buffalo could frighten cattle, which would make them run and crush the wagons. Leaving too late in the season could trap pioneers in snow on the way.

22   River crossings were always risky. If the river was shallow enough, they could wade across the currents and rocks with their oxen. Sometimes they turned wagons into boats by taking the wheels off and emptying them. Other times, families built rafts big enough to hold a wagon by cutting down trees and tying them together. At large rivers, former traders and Native Americans ran toll bridges and ferries where families could pay to have their belongings floated across.

23   Many pioneers were afraid that Native Americans would harm them. They had heard stories of kidnappings or attacks. Fighting did happen, especially after the mid-1800s. But many Native Americans wanted to trade with the pioneers. And many shared their knowledge with the pioneers, such as the best places to cross rivers and where to look for food.

24   Disease was the biggest danger on the trail. Many pioneers died of smallpox and mumps. Cholera, which comes from drinking polluted water, caused the most deaths on the trail.

THE DAILY SCHEDULE

25   After an early breakfast of cornmeal mush, johnnycakes, or cold biscuits, as well as coffee and bacon, the wagons headed out. Each day a different family led the way. Wagon trains took a break called a "nooning" about midday. While the oxen rested, pioneers enjoyed a cold meal of beans or bacon. Children gathered buffalo chips or cow manure to use for fuel on the evening campfire.

26   At mid-afternoon the train would set out again and travel until early evening. Scouts went ahead of the train to find a pasture for the oxen and a large flat area for the wagons. When the wagons arrived they were set up in a circle. The circle made a corral to keep the oxen inside to graze. Tents were set up and campfires built.

Mexican-American War

Many Americans believed it was their right to settle the land all the way to the Pacific Ocean, even if Mexicans or Native Americans lived there. This led to the Mexican-American War in 1846. The Republic of Texas became a state in 1845, but Mexico believed that Texas belonged to it. Mexico went to war to get it back. When Mexico lost, it had to give its territories to America for $15 million dollars. That territory includes the present-day states of California, Nevada, and Utah, and parts of New Mexico, Arizona, Colorado, and Wyoming.

TRAIL FOOD

27   Women learned to bake bread on the trail using Dutch ovens over campfires. Cooking was usually done in the evening and leftovers were eaten for breakfast and lunch.

28   A typical pioneer diet consisted of bacon, ham, rice, dried fruit, bread, coffee, and tea. They also ate wild game like antelope, rabbits, and birds. Some families brought a milking cow with them to provide fresh milk. Pioneers also traded with Native Americans for meat and vegetables. Everyone ate a hard bread called hardtack. Hardtack didn't spoil on the long trip because it had no butter or lard. Pioneers often dipped their hardtack into a hot drink to soften it before trying to bite into it.

> **typical**   If something is typical, it is usual or normal.
> **consisted**   If something consisted of certain items, it was made up of those things.

The Pony Express

It was hard for pioneers to communicate with their families back East. They left letters at trading posts and even under rocks along the trail, hoping that wagons going east would take them. In April 1860, the Pony Express began delivering mail from St. Joseph, Missouri, to Sacramento, California, in only 10 days! Riders changed horses every 10 miles (16 kilometers) and after 70 miles (112 kilometers), a new rider took over.

29 Finding fresh water on the trail was not easy. Rain barrels on wagons collected water, but they never had enough. Pioneers had no choice but to drink from creeks and rivers just like their cattle. One woman wrote of sucking on a rag soaked in vinegar when there was no water. Another wrote about straining pond water through the end of a wagon cover!

30 *In spite of all of these hardships, the pioneers managed to make the journey and settle new towns throughout the West. Their strength, innovations, and adventurous spirits helped shape the United States we know today.*

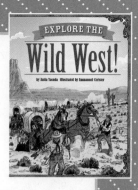

Collaborative Discussion

Look back at what you wrote on page 250. Tell a partner two things you learned from the text. Then work with a group to discuss the questions below. Strengthen your answers with examples and quotations from *Explore the Wild West!* In your discussion, ask questions and add comments that build on the ideas of others.

1 Review pages 254–255. What information did Lewis and Clark gather on their expedition?

2 Reread pages 257–261. What kinds of hardships did people experience as they traveled west?

3 What reasons did people have for moving to the West? Do you think the trip was worthwhile for them? Why or why not?

Listening Tip

Listen carefully to each speaker's ideas. What questions do you have? What ideas of your own are like those of other speakers?

Speaking Tip

Ask questions such as "Can you explain what you mean by that?" to encourage other speakers to tell more about their ideas.

Write a How-to Guide

PROMPT

In *Explore the Wild West!*, you learned about the experiences of families who traveled westward by wagon train in the 1800s. Families making this journey experienced many hardships and had to be prepared for many difficult days of travel.

Create a how-to guide for westward-bound pioneers. Start with an introduction. Then add a paragraph on one of the following: preparing for the trip, including a list of important items to pack, or life on the trail, including possible dangers. End with a conclusion that summarizes the important points you've made. Use specific evidence from the text to give detailed information to your readers. Be sure that each paragraph of your writing includes a central, or main, idea. Don't forget to use some of the Critical Vocabulary words in your writing.

PLAN

Make notes, based on details from the text, that support your central idea of trip preparation or life on the trail.

WRITE

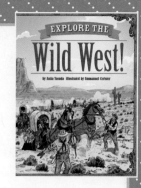

Now write your how-to guide for westward-bound pioneers.

Make sure your how-to guide

- ☐ introduces the topic.
- ☐ includes evidence from the text.
- ☐ organizes information into three paragraphs.
- ☐ includes a conclusion that summarizes the important central ideas.

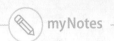

Notice & Note
3 Big Questions

Prepare to Read

GENRE STUDY **Magazine articles** give information about a topic, person, or event.

- Magazine articles may present ideas in chronological order, to help readers understand what happened and when.

- Articles related to social studies may include words that are specific to the topic.

- Magazine articles include text features, such as captions and sidebars, which give additional information about the topic.

SET A PURPOSE **Think about** the title and genre of the text. What do you know about working on railroads? What do you want to learn? Write your ideas below.

CRITICAL VOCABULARY

celestial

complaint

employed

sacrifice

**Build Background:
The Transcontinental Railroad**

THE CELESTIALS'
RAILROAD

BY BRUCE WATSON

1   *Two decades after pioneers began migrating to the "wild west," the U.S. government in 1861 agreed to the construction of a transcontinental railroad system that would link California with the rail network of the eastern United States.*

2   On the Utah prairie where a thousand workers had gathered for the ceremony, four Chinese men carried an iron rail toward the track. It was the last link in the railroad that within moments would span the continent. The date was May 10, 1869. The Union Pacific locomotive stood to one side and the Central Pacific to the other.

3   Because they called China the Celestial Kingdom, the Chinese workers were known as "Celestials." Few of their fellow railroad workers bothered to learn their names. No one knows their names today. But it was on the backs of the Chinese workers that the first transcontinental railroad was built.

4   For the Chinese, the work began as an experiment. Many Chinese men had come to America during the first California gold rush. When they did not strike it rich in the goldfields, they sought other work—but faced discrimination instead.

celestial   Something that is celestial is heavenly.

Construction workers stand on flatcars being pushed by a locomotive across a railroad trestle at Promontory Point in Utah.

5   Then in 1863, Central Pacific and Union Pacific railroad tycoons agreed to build a coast-to-coast link. The Union Pacific would head west from Omaha, Nebraska, while the Central Pacific would extend east from Sacramento, California. The two companies mapped the routes, raised the money, and hired the workers.

6   Within a year, the Union Pacific was well into Nebraska, but the Central Pacific had bogged down at the edge of the Sierra Nevada mountains. In California, most men were busy searching for gold or silver. To complete his contract, railroad magnate Charles Crocker needed help. Over the protests of his workers, Crocker turned to the Chinese.

7   In February 1865, 50 Chinese men were transported by flatcar to the rail's end in the Sierra foothills. While other workers jeered and threatened to strike, the Chinese calmly set up camp, boiled rice provided by the company, and went to sleep. Up at dawn, with picks and shovels in hand, they worked 12 hours straight without complaint. By sundown, Crocker had telegraphed his office in Sacramento: "Send more Chinese." Within a few months, 3,000 Chinese were pushing the Central Pacific eastward. By the end of 1865, more than 6,000 Chinese were working on the railroad.

> **complaint**   A complaint is an expression of dissatisfaction or pain.

Snow didn't stop work on the railroad. Here, Chinese laborers dig a train out of a drift near Ogden, Utah.

Wearing wide-brimmed hats, Chinese laborers work on the Secrettown Trestle in the Sierra Nevada mountains.

8   As the Central Pacific soared toward Donner Summit at the top of the Sierras, the Chinese took jobs no one else would touch. They hung from ropes draped over the edges of cliffs and tapped holes into the sides of mountains. After inserting dynamite, they jerked the ropes and were yanked upward. If they were lucky, they cleared the explosion and lived to tap more holes. If not, they fell into the gorge below.

9   Chinese workers blasted tunnels with nitroglycerin when other workers would not touch the explosive liquid. They graded hillsides. They chopped trees. They carried dirt in wheelbarrows, filled huge gorges with it, leveled it, and laid railroad ties evenly across it. Other workers then laid the iron rails and hammered them down while the Chinese went ahead to prepare the next mile.

10   Most other workers ate stale meat and drank brackish water. Because the Chinese paid for their own food, they were allowed to choose their food. They chose things that were familiar to them, such as oysters, cuttlefish, vegetables, rice, and tea. Crossing Donner Summit at 7,000 feet, many other workers took sick or quit, but the Chinese kept going.

East portal of summit tunnel of the Central Pacific Railroad, during construction in the Sierra Nevada Mountains, California.

This tea carrier brings refreshment to Chinese workers.

11   Mobs of white workers tormented the Chinese at every camp along the way. But across Nevada and into Utah, the Central Pacific inched toward the Union Pacific. And on April 27, 1869, Central Pacific crews, by then 90 percent Chinese, laid 10 miles of track in a single day—a new record.

12   By the time the two railroads met at Promontory, Utah, the Central Pacific employed 12,000 Chinese workers. Together with the Union Pacific crews, they watched as railroad tycoons drove in their golden spikes. But when the cameras recorded the event, the Chinese workers were left out of the picture.

> **employed**   If you hired people to do a job, you employed them.

Despite all their hard labor, not one Chinese worker was present for this photo taken at the joining of the Union Pacific and Central Pacific railroads.

13   On May 10, 1869, the single word "Done!" was telegraphed across the continent. Finished with their monumental task, the Chinese rode the Central Pacific back across the track they had laid. Some went back to "Chinatown" communities in Sacramento, San Francisco, and other cities. Others went to Canada, where they helped build the Canadian Pacific Railroad, or worked on routes in California. Many spread out across the West, finding work or staking claims in mining towns such as Deadwood, South Dakota, and Tombstone, Arizona. Their labor and sacrifice had connected the east and west coasts of the growing nation.

COME ONE, COME ALL

The Chinese were unique in America's westward expansion because they were one of the few immigrant groups that did not come to settle permanently. Drawn for many of the same reasons as Americans who were looking for a better life or religious freedom, immigrant groups from around the world established small communities throughout the West. Most of the Chinese, however, were men who had left their families behind in China. Their intention was to work hard, save their money, and return to their homeland.

sacrifice   A sacrifice is the act of giving up something valued to get something else.

These locomotives in Utah's Golden Spike National Historic Site are replicas of the engines present at the meeting of the two railroads.

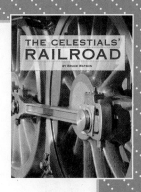

Collaborative Discussion

Look back at what you wrote on page 268 and talk with a partner about what you learned from the text. Then work with a group to discuss the questions below. Strengthen your answers with evidence from *The Celestials' Railroad*. Pay attention as other group members present ideas, to see if those ideas support or change your own thoughts.

1 Review pages 270–271. Why did Charles Crocker decide to hire Chinese workers to complete his section of the railroad?

 **Listening Tip**

As you listen to the discussion, think about what conclusions you can draw. Do any comments change an answer or idea you had?

2 Reread page 272. What jobs did the Chinese workers do to complete the railroad?

 **Speaking Tip**

Briefly summarize comments from earlier speakers and tell your group what you learned from those comments.

3 In what ways were conditions difficult for the Chinese workers?

Write a Television Pitch

PROMPT

In *The Celestials' Railroad* you learned about the Chinese workers who helped to build the transcontinental railroad. Without the dedication of these workers, the railroad may never have become a reality.

Imagine that you want to create a television documentary about the Chinese workers and the challenges they faced. You'll need a description, or "pitch," to persuade television producers that your documentary will be interesting. Begin by introducing the topic. State at least two reasons why you think viewers would be interested in the topic. Use evidence from the text to support the reasons. Don't forget to use some of the Critical Vocabulary words in your writing.

PLAN

Make notes, using evidence from the text, about the reasons why your documentary would be interesting to viewers.

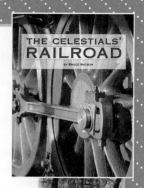

WRITE

Now write the persuasive television pitch for your documentary.

Make sure your television pitch

- ☐ includes a central, or main, idea in the introduction.
- ☐ states why you think your documentary will be interesting.
- ☐ provides at least two reasons for your opinion.
- ☐ uses evidence from the text to support each of the reasons.

Prepare to View

GENRE STUDY **Documentary videos** present facts and information about a topic, place, or event in visual and audio form.

- Narration and images are used to explain key ideas.
- Primary sources and interviews with experts may be featured.
- Documentaries may include words that are specific to a certain time period or experience.

SET A PURPOSE **As you watch**, think about the speaker's main points to help you understand the hardships of living on the prairie. What do you want to learn? Write your ideas below.

CRITICAL VOCABULARY

homestead

primary

domain

residence

ideology

HOMESTEADING

As you watch *Homesteading*, think about how the video uses audio and visual elements to explain events and experiences. How do the narration and footage help you understand the Westward Expansion time period? What does the first-person account teach you about homesteaders? Is it more or less effective than a reenactment would be? Why or why not? Take notes in the space below.

Listen for the Critical Vocabulary words *homestead, ideology, residence, domain,* and *primary*, and for clues to the meaning of each word. Take notes in the space below about how the words are used in the video.

homestead In the late 1800s, a homestead was a piece of land in America's western regions that was claimed, lived on, and settled by a pioneer.

ideology An ideology is a set of beliefs.

residence A residence is a place in which people live.

domain Someone's domain is the land or territory that he or she owns and controls.

primary Something that is primary is the highest in importance.

Collaborative Discussion

Look back at what you wrote on page 278. Tell a partner two things you learned from the video. Then work with a group to discuss the questions below. Offer details and examples from *Homesteading* to support your responses. In your discussion, respond to others by asking questions and making comments that build on their ideas.

1 According to the video, what reasons led people to become homesteaders?

2 Why did President Abraham Lincoln believe that land ownership was important?

3 What was the connection between the Homestead Act and the building of railroads?

Listening Tip

Listen carefully to the responses of others. What questions do you have about their ideas? What comments of your own can you add to expand upon them?

Speaking Tip

Ask questions about another speaker's answer to encourage the speaker to explain or give more details. Add comments of your own to build upon the speaker's ideas.

Write an Interview Script

PROMPT

In *Homesteading*, you heard a first-person account by a homesteader about settling land in the Dakota territory.

Imagine that you could interview this man about his experiences as a homesteader. Write a script showing the questions you would ask and the answers you imagine he might give. Base the questions and answers on details from the video. Use some of the Critical Vocabulary words in your writing.

PLAN

Make notes based on information from the video that will help you create questions and answers for your interview with a homesteader.

WRITE

Now write the script of your interview with a homesteader.

✓ Make sure your interview script

☐	introduces the topic of homesteading and explains who is being interviewed.
☐	uses a question-and-answer script format.
☐	includes details from the video.
☐	ends with a conclusion that summarizes the interview.

Prepare to Read

GENRE STUDY **Historical fiction** is a story that is set in a real
time and place in the past.

- Authors of historical fiction tell the story through the plot—
  the main events of the story. Often, the plot and conflict are
  shaped by the story's setting, or time period and location.

- Historical fiction includes characters that act, think, and speak
  like real people from the past would. It might tell the story of
  fictional characters in a real setting from the past.

- Authors of historical fiction may use sensory details and
  figurative language to develop the setting and characters.

SET A PURPOSE **Think about** the title and genre of this text.
What do you know about pioneers? What do you
want to learn? Write your ideas below.

Meet the Author and Illustrator:
Barbara Greenwood and Heather Collins

CRITICAL VOCABULARY
frolics
stubble
indispensable
dainty
plod
oblivious
proportions
regaled
thresh

A PIONEER SAMPLER

The Daily Life of a Pioneer Family in 1840

by Barbara Greenwood   illustrated by Heather Collins

1 **THE ROBERTSONS** are a pioneer family living on a backwoods farm in 1840. Although the Robertsons are a fictional family, their struggle to clear the forest, to plant, to harvest, and to make a good life for themselves echoes the efforts of our early settlers, who worked hard to build a home, a community, and a country.

2 The Robertsons, like real settlers, live by this motto:

Eat it up,
Wear it out,
Make it do,
Or go without.

Willy   Granny   Sarah   Ma Robertson   Pa Robertson

3   The Robertson children learn early that "many hands make light work" and that it's best to "make hay while the sun shines." But life isn't all chores and making do. Maple-sugar frolics and harvest suppers, husking bees and barn dances, the birth of lambs and the search for a honey tree brighten the days as the seasons pass from winter to spring, from summer to fall.

> **frolics**   Frolics are fun acts, such as dances or parties.

George   **Meg and Tommy**   **Lizzie**

HARVESTING THE CROPS

4 "Stand up properly," Meg said. "You can't carry water all hunched over like that."

5 Willy wiggled his shoulders to make the yoke sit more comfortably, then straightened up. The weight of the buckets made the wood bite into the back of his neck.

6 "It hurts," he complained.

7 "Stop fidgeting." Meg moved the yoke slightly and the pressure eased. "You'll be fine. It's a lot easier than lugging a bucket by hand. And you won't lose nearly so much water. Off you go. The men will be dying of thirst."

8 Carrying water out to the hayfield had always been Meg's or George's job. This year Pa wanted George's help with the harvesting, and Ma had decided that Willy and Sarah were big enough to carry water.

9 Stupid buckets, Willy grumbled to himself as he trudged off, I want to do real work. Like George. That reminded him of George sitting at the grindstone last evening. Making *me* turn the handle while he sharpened the sickle. Thinks he's so important just because Pa's letting him help cut the hay this year.

10 The sun beat down from a blue sky. Pa had been right about the weather. "Listen to those cicadas sing," he'd said the night before. "We'll have good haying weather tomorrow."

11   Willy rested his hands on the bucket handles to keep them from swinging and arched his back against the weight. Across the fields he could see Pa and one of the big Simpson boys who'd been hired on for the summer. They swayed back and forth as they swung the long-handled scythes to cut the hay. George was bent over using the short-handled sickle to trim around a tree stump. Every so often Pa stopped and ran a whetstone over his scythe blade. Willy liked the raspy *zzzzrooop* of the whetstone sharpening the blade.

12   The stubble of cut grass prickled Willy's bare feet as he crossed the field. The soles of his feet were toughened from months of running barefoot, but with the buckets dragging him down, the stubble felt sharp. And he was anxious about tripping over an upthrust stone and spilling the water or, worse still, stepping on a snake. With luck, the snakes would all be gone. Just yesterday he and George had been out with sticks beating the field to scare away snakes and families of skunks and rabbits. "Last thing I want," Pa had said, "is animals exploding out of the grass in front of me when I'm swinging a scythe. Like to cut a foot off."

13   "Ah! Here he is." Pa straightened and stretched. "Time for a rest, boys." Willy lowered the buckets carefully to the uneven ground, shrugged off the yoke, and handed around the gourds he'd brought as water dippers.

14   "Now that you're here," Pa said, "you can stay a while and spread some of that hay. Can't spare anyone from the cutting till we're further along."

15   George smirked, licked a finger, and flicked it across the sharp edge of the sickle as though to say, I'm indispensable. *You* can do the baby work. Willy waited till Pa's back was turned, then stuck out his tongue at George. It wasn't much, but it made him feel a little better. In the afternoon, Ma and the girls came out to help. Finally, at the end of a long, hot day, Pa said, "Well, we've done our best. Let's hope the sun does its best."

stubble   Stubble is the short, stiff stalks of plants that remain in a field after harvesting.
indispensable   Something that is indispensable is necessary.

16   For two days the sun baked and dried the hay. On the third morning, the whole family turned out to rake it into windrows to make loading the sledge easier. Up and down the fields they went, competing with one another to make straight, even rows. "A thing worth doing is worth doing well," Ma always said. Several times during the morning, Willy or Sarah went back to the house to get buckets of cool water to which Granny had added a handful of oatmeal to make a thirst-quenching drink. As Willy trudged out once more with the water buckets, he looked up at the sky. Clouds like balls of carded wool were rolling in. But they were high and white. No danger from rain there.

17   After the noon meal Pa walked the oxen and sledge out to the field. Pitching hay onto the sledge was hard work for Willy. His arms weren't strong enough to throw a forkful to the top of the load. More often than not his stalks slithered off. Finally, Pa, who was up on top building the load, said, "Willy, you take charge of the oxen. Keep moving them forward as we work along this row."

18   The afternoon dragged on. One load was safely back at the barn with another still to come. Ma and Meg were pitching hay now while Sarah carted water. Back at the barn, Pa and George were starting to build the haystack.

19   Hour after hour, Willy inched the oxen along the rows, watching out for stones and roots and stumps. Every now and then, he scanned the sky. The woolly clouds bunched and drifted into fantastic shapes, and Willy's mind drifted with them. A bear and her cub lumbered across the sky, a dainty pony skipped by, then fat fish blowing bubbles, a gray whale. Gray? "Ma, look! Rain clouds."

20   Ma took one quick look at the sky and said, "Get those oxen moving, Willy. We've got to get this load under cover."

dainty   Something that is dainty is delicate.

21   "Heyup," Willy shouted, and the oxen started a steady plod. Low clouds scudded in, darker with each second. Ma and Meg frantically raked windrows into small haycocks. In piles, at least the bottommost stalks would stay dry. Willy concentrated on the sledge. "Gee, Buck, gee, Bright," he shouted to steer the oxen around roots and stumps. As the sky grew darker, he prodded the animals with the goad. "Move, move," he urged them. The oxen blew through their nostrils and plodded steadily ahead. "Never was such a stubborn beast as an ox," his father always said.

22   Willy could see Pa and George beside the barn. They swung their arms in rhythm, oblivious to everything but the orderly layering of the haystack. Then he felt a drop of water.

23   "Pa," he screeched. "Rain, rain!" The sudden noise started Bright off at a trot, with his partner snorting beside him. Pa and George wrenched open the big barn doors, and, just as the clouds burst, the sledge skidded under cover.

24   "Good work, Willy," Pa said as they all crowded into the barn. "You saved that load. You've got a real farmer's eye for weather."

> **plod**   To plod is to move heavily and slowly.
>
> **oblivious**   If someone is oblivious to something, he or she is unaware of it.

25   Willy glowed with pride. For the next few days, as he worked, he pictured over and over his mad dash for the barn until it grew into a story of heroic proportions. When Uncle Jacob Burkholder came over to show Pa how to thatch a waterproof roof for their haystack, Willy regaled him with the whole tale.

26   "Well now, that's quite a feat—moving cattle beasts along like that. Mind you, nothing like a drop of rain to get a man moving." Uncle Jacob laughed as he wove the last of the straw into the roof. "Now I remember when I was a young'un, no older'n you, we saw a dilly of a storm heading up. My brother and I were running around fastening shutters and bolting doors when we heard a tarnation big racket headed our way. Up our lane come a farm rig, horses running like Jehu, all wild-eyed and foaming at the mouth. Wagon bouncing along behind like a pea on a hot skillet. 'Runaway,' my brother shouts. Then we hear the driver screaming, 'Open the doors. Open the doors!' We jumped pretty smart, I can tell you. Swung open those big barn doors, and he drove the whole rig in just seconds before a great crack of thunder. And did those clouds pour rain! I looks in the wagon and sees three hundredweight of flour in linen sacks. A few drops of rain and the whole lot would've caked solid. That man never was any good at reading the weather," Uncle Jacob ended scornfully. "Well, there's your stack roofed in. No fear of rain getting through that."

27   Ma had been busy, too. While she was listening to Uncle Jacob's story she'd bound a handful of hay into the shape of a rooster. "Here, Willy," she said, "scoot up and stick that on top. It'll dress up the stack for us."

28   "Good idea." Uncle Jacob beamed. "And I'll show you how to rig it up as a weather vane so's you'll be warned the next time a storm blows up."

> **proportions** When you talk about the proportions of something, you talk about its size.
> **regaled** If you regaled someone, you entertained them.

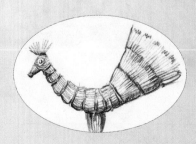

HARVESTING

29 **THE HOT DAYS OF SUMMER** brought hard work for the whole family.

30 The Robertsons had two hayfields. One they had cleared themselves. The other was a beaver meadow. Long before the Robertsons arrived on the land, beavers had dammed the river and flooded several acres. The trees died, the water dried up, and grass grew. Early settlers were delighted to find beaver meadows on their farms because they provided instant fodder (food) for oxen and cows.

31   The hay would feed the animals through the winter, but the people needed wheat. In fact the wheat harvested one year had to last until the next. By the first week of August, the wheat was ready to be cut. The men were out in the fields with their scythes again, and Willy and Sarah were running back and forth with water.

As the men cut the wheat, Mrs. Robertson and Meg followed behind tying the stalks of grain into bundles called sheaves. Ten sheaves propped up against one another formed a stook.

32   Wheat was a precious crop, and the family worked long into the night to get it safely under cover. Mr. Robertson and the hired help packed it carefully into mows (storage lofts) in the barn to keep it safe and dry until they had time to thresh it.

33   Harvesting wasn't all hard work. Sometimes neighbors helped one another bring in the crops. This harvesting bee often finished with a party. The men set up long tables in the fields, and the women brought out food for a harvest supper. To amuse the children, Mr. Burkholder built a maze out of sheaves of grain.

---

thresh   To thresh a plant is to beat it in order to separate its grain or seeds from the rest of the plant.

HARVEST MOON

34　**FARMERS PLANNED TO HARVEST** when the moon was full, so that they had enough light to work until midnight if necessary. In September, the full moon seems to linger in the sky for several nights in a row. This happens because moonrise comes only twenty minutes later each night, instead of the usual fifty minutes. No wonder the September full moon was the harvest moon.

35　Full moons were useful all year round. Many farmers believed that crops planted at certain phases of the moon would grow better. To escape the heat of the day, farmers often did their planting and hoeing in the cool of the night by the light of the moon. In winter, travelers planned long journeys for times when the full moon would give them extra light to get home through the dark forest.

READING THE WEATHER

36   **THANKS TO THE WEATHER FORECASTS,** you can make plans, not just for tomorrow but for the whole week. Pioneers didn't receive reports from meteorologists. They predicted good and bad weather by watching for signals in the world around them. Try the pioneer method of forecasting the weather.

37   Signs of good weather are: birds flying high, smoke rising quickly, cicadas singing loudly, and heavy dew at night. Watch the clouds. The higher they are, the better the weather will be.

38   These signs mean wet weather's coming: smoke curling downward, dark cumulus (or cotton-ball) clouds, overcast cirrus (or long, stringy) clouds. A halo around the sun means rain within ten to twelve hours.

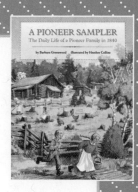

Collaborative Discussion

Look back at what you wrote on page 284. Tell a partner two things you learned during reading. Then work with a group to discuss the questions below. Look for details in *A Pioneer Sampler* to explain and support your answers. Before you begin, decide who will be your group's leader and who will record the ideas you discuss.

1 Review pages 288–289. What details show that cutting hay was hard work?

2 Reread page 291. How can you tell that Willy knows it is important to get the hay to the barn quickly?

3 What parts of the story show that the Robertson family believes that "many hands make light work"?

Listening Tip

Listen to each speaker in the way that you want others to listen when you are speaking.

Speaking Tip

Wait until your group leader invites you to speak. After you share your ideas, ask other members of your group if there are any questions or comments.

Write a Journal Entry

PROMPT

In *A Pioneer Sampler*, you read about the exciting lives of western pioneers in 1840. These pioneers faced and overcame many challenges as they built their new lives.

Imagine that you are Willy Robertson. Write a journal entry from Willy's point of view that describes what happened on the day he saved the hay. What did you see? What did you do? How did you feel about your experiences? Use descriptive, sensory language to make your entry come to life. Be sure your journal entry retells details from the text in sequence and explains the effect of your/Willy's actions. Don't forget to use some of the Critical Vocabulary words in your writing.

PLAN

Make notes, from Willy's point of view, about how you will describe saving the hay. Include text evidence in your notes.

WRITE

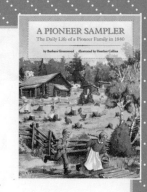

Now write your journal entry describing your experience on the day you saved the hay.

✓	Make sure your journal entry
☐	is written in the voice of Willy, a young pioneer boy.
☐	uses first-person pronouns such as *I, me, my,* and *our*.
☐	uses vivid, sensory language to describe experiences.
☐	uses evidence from the text.
☐	retells events in sequence.

? Essential Question

What character traits were needed in people who settled the West?

Write an Informational Article

PROMPT Think about what you learned about the Western pioneers from this module.

Imagine that a history magazine for young people has invited students to submit articles. Choose one feature or part of the pioneer experience, such as daily life, the journey West, or overcoming challenges. Use evidence from the texts and video to write an article for the magazine.

I will write an article about _____ .

✓ Make sure your informational article

☐ has an introduction that clearly states the topic.

☐ supports important ideas with facts, definitions, and quotes from the texts.

☐ uses headings to group related information in a clear way.

☐ uses precise language and topic-specific vocabulary.

☐ has a conclusion that sums up important points.

PLAN ········ Gather information.

First decide on your topic. Which aspect of the pioneer experience will you focus on? Look back at your notes and revisit the texts and video for ideas.

Use the chart below to plan your article. Write your topic and overall main idea. Then use evidence from the texts to add supporting details for each important point. Use Critical Vocabulary Words where appropriate.

My Topic: ______________________________

Main Idea		
Detail	Detail	Detail

DRAFT ·· Write your article.

Write an **introduction** that clearly states your topic and focus. Give readers a taste of what they will be reading about.

[ ]

Group your important ideas into **sections**. For each section, add supporting details from your planning chart.

Section 1	Section 2	Section 3

Write a **conclusion** that restates your topic and sums up your main points. Help your readers understand the character traits that pioneers needed to survive and succeed.

[ ]

REVISE AND EDIT · Review your draft.

Every good writer reviews his or her draft to find ways to improve it. Work with a partner. Ask your partner to read your article and point out any ideas that aren't clearly explained. Also, use these questions to help you evaluate and improve your article.

PURPOSE/ FOCUS	ORGANIZATION	EVIDENCE	LANGUAGE/ VOCABULARY	CONVENTIONS
☐ Will the introduction get readers interested in my topic? ☐ Does each section focus on one key idea?	☐ Are the ideas presented in an order that makes sense? ☐ Does the conclusion clearly sum up the main points of the article?	☐ Are my main points supported by text evidence? ☐ Where can I add more evidence to strengthen the support?	☐ Did I use precise language and topic-specific vocabulary? ☐ Did I use linking words to connect ideas?	☐ Have I spelled all words correctly? ☐ Did I use commas and other punctuation marks correctly?

PUBLISH · Share your work.

Create a Finished Copy. Use your best cursive handwriting to create a final copy of your article. You can include illustrations or graphic aids such as maps, charts, or diagrams. Consider these options for sharing your article:

1. Combine your article with those of your classmates to create a display on pioneer life for the school library. Include photographs, maps, or objects in your display.

2. With several classmates, conduct a panel discussion on different aspects of the pioneer experience. Invite the audience to comment and ask questions.

3. Make a slideshow presentation. Find historical photographs or illustrations that support or enhance the information in your article. Read your text aloud, or have a friend read it, to narrate the slideshow.

Project Earth

"Only if we understand, can we care. Only if we care, will we help. Only if we help shall all be saved."

—Jane Goodall

How can caring for Earth and its living things improve life now and in the future?

Get Curious

Video

Words About Caring for Earth

The words in the chart will help you talk and write about the selections in this module. Which words about caring for Earth have you seen before? Which words are new to you?

Add to the Vocabulary Network on page 307 by writing synonyms, antonyms, and related words and phrases for each word about caring for Earth.

After you read each selection in this module, come back to the Vocabulary Network and keep building it. Add more boxes if you need to.

WORD	MEANING	CONTEXT SENTENCE
contaminate (verb)	To contaminate something is to add a harmful substance to it.	Some weed killers are harmful chemicals that contaminate soil and water.
benevolent (adjective)	A benevolent person or thing is kind.	Volunteering to plant trees is a benevolent act.
imperil (verb)	To imperil someone or something is to put it in danger.	Military men and women imperil their lives to protect our country.
endangered (adjective)	To be endangered is to be at risk of great harm or death.	Animal species that are endangered might disappear from the planet forever.

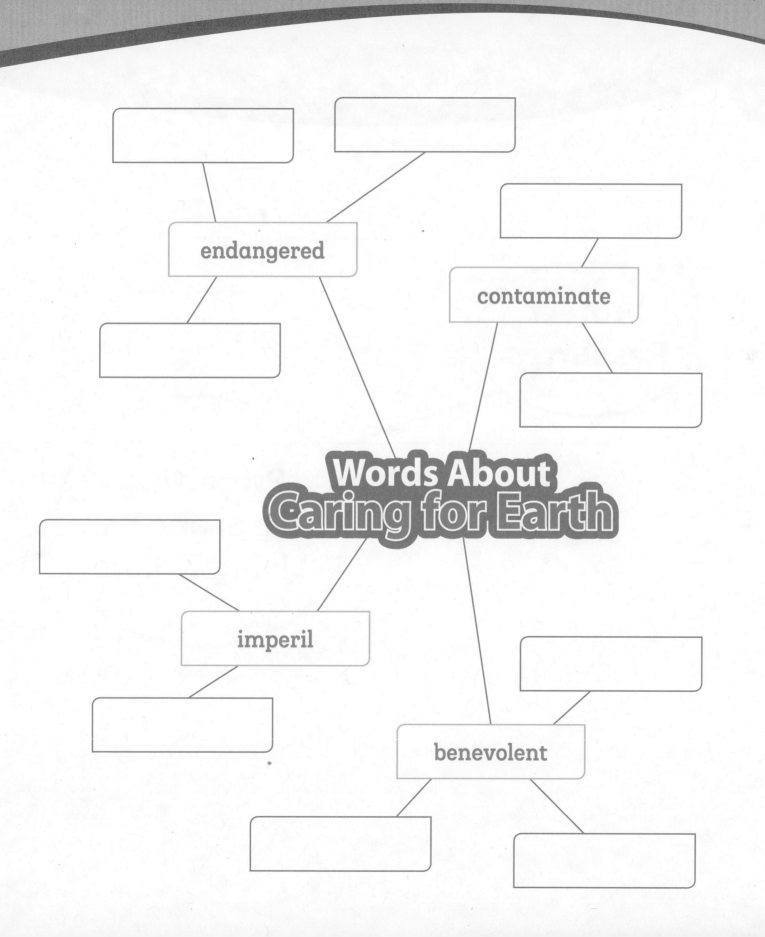

endangered

contaminate

Words About
Caring for Earth

imperil

benevolent

Protect Resources

Protecting Earth and Its Living Things

**Use Fewer
Resources**

Short Read

The Protective Power of Nature Preserves

1 All over the world, humans' actions imperil natural areas and the plants and animals in them. As human populations grow, people put the environment at risk by using up natural resources such as trees, water, and land. As people cut trees and build roads, houses, and businesses, natural landscapes disappear. Plants and animals' homes disappear, too. However, there's a way to protect endangered species and natural areas. It's called a nature preserve.

A Protected Place for Plants and Animals

2 A nature preserve is sometimes called a reserve or a park. It is a place that is protected from harmful human development. Plants are free to thrive as they naturally would, and animals are free to roam. Natural features such as rock formations and bodies of water are protected from damage. Within this carefully managed area, plant and animal populations can hold steady or even grow.

3 Governments or private groups protect nature preserves by limiting or controlling human visitors' actions. Hunting, fishing, hiking, and camping may be allowed in some preserves. In others these activities are prohibited.

How Nature Preserves Are Created

4 Nature preserves have been established in many different countries. The first step toward protecting an area comes when an individual or group recognizes it is at risk. These people work to purchase the land or to convince the land's owners or the government to protect it. One way in which the U.S. government can protect a natural area is by making it a national park.

5 Yellowstone National Park, formed in 1872, was the first nature preserve created as a U.S. national park. Yellowstone includes land that is part of the states of Idaho, Montana, and Wyoming. It is home to bison, wolves, and other species that need protection. It is also home to natural features such as its famous hot springs. The U.S. government protects Yellowstone's plants, animals, and habitats from human destruction.

Why Preserves Are Important to People

6 Nature preserves provide important benefits for people as well as for the plants and animals that live there. A preserve's trees produce oxygen for us to breathe. Wetlands help control floods by storing water. They strain out pollutants that contaminate human water systems, too.

7 Nature preserves also provide scientific and recreational opportunities. In Costa Rica, the Monteverde Cloud Forest Reserve draws scientists to study its incredibly varied plant and animal life. The reserve also brings tourists from all directions. People visit the forest to hike its trails, glide through the treetops on zip-lines, and view more than 500 species of animals. Other preserves provide quieter pleasures. A city preserve might offer the chance to escape car horns and sidewalks for birdsong and dirt paths.

8 In nature preserves, people use natural resources in benevolent rather than harmful ways. By protecting plants, animals, and landscapes, we are protecting nature's balance, which is good for all of us!

The Monteverde Cloud Forest Reserve

Notice & Note
Word Gaps

Prepare to Read

GENRE STUDY **Persuasive texts** give an author's opinion about a topic and try to convince readers to agree with that opinion.

- Persuasive texts may organize ideas by cause and effect. They may also organize ideas by showing problems and solutions.

- Persuasive texts include reasons and evidence, such as facts and examples, to support the author's viewpoint.

- Persuasive texts include strong language and specific techniques, such as appealing to readers' emotions.

SET A PURPOSE Think about the title and genre of this text. What do you know about city farming? What do you want to learn? Write your ideas below.

CRITICAL VOCABULARY
urban
humble
plots
alternative
transform
artificial
yield
influence

Meet the Author:
Hadley Dyer

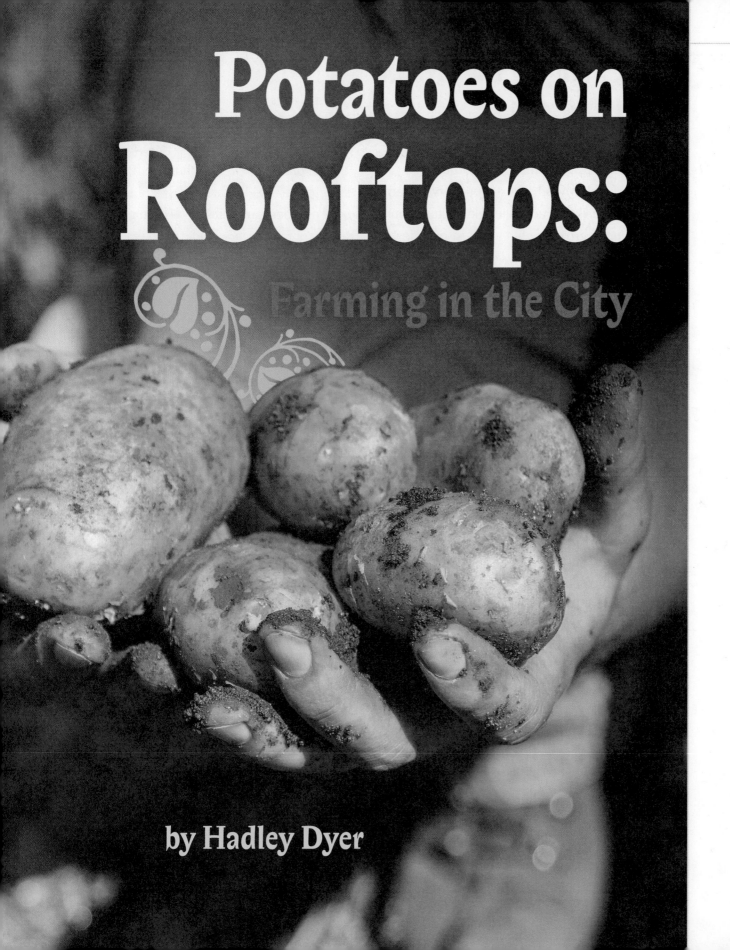

Potatoes on Rooftops:
Farming in the City

by Hadley Dyer

Changing the Urban Landscape

1   Cities are sometimes called "concrete jungles." But imagine an  urban neighborhood so lush and leafy it seems more like an actual jungle. Picture your lunch growing on a vine just outside your classroom window. In some cities, these images are becoming real.

2   About 800 million people grow food in urban areas, from humble herb patches to state-of-the-art farms, and their numbers are going up. These gardeners and farmers are leading the way toward greener, healthier cities. They're changing our urban landscapes while planting the seeds for our future.

> **urban**   Something that is urban is related to a city.
> **humble**   If something is humble, it is simple and not impressive.

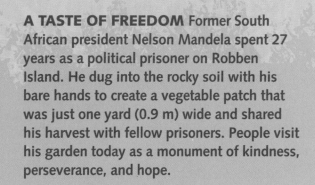

A TASTE OF FREEDOM Former South African president Nelson Mandela spent 27 years as a political prisoner on Robben Island. He dug into the rocky soil with his bare hands to create a vegetable patch that was just one yard (0.9 m) wide and shared his harvest with fellow prisoners. People visit his garden today as a monument of kindness, perseverance, and hope.

If Mandela's humble garden had the power to transform lives, what could we do with the space, tools, and technology available in our cities?

"To plant a seed, watch it grow, to tend it and then harvest it, offered a simple but enduring satisfaction. The sense of being the custodian of this small patch of earth offered a small taste of freedom."

—NELSON MANDELA, FORMER PRESIDENT OF SOUTH AFRICA

Ye Olde Victory Garden

3　During World War I (1914–18), cities around the world began running out of food. Thousands of farmers served in the army instead of tilling their fields. Fertile ground was destroyed by combat and bombs. International waters became very dangerous for ships carrying food.

4　In 1917, a new organization in the United States called the National War Garden Commission decided the solution was to grow food on a small scale closer to home. It encouraged citizens to use all available growing spaces and taught people how to can and preserve food. Soon after, the U.S. Department of Agriculture (USDA) began its own campaign to get people growing. As a result, the number of garden plots rose from 3.5 million in 1917 to more than 5 million in 1918.

> **plots**　Plots are small sections of land that are used for a certain purpose.

"Everyone who creates or cultivates a garden helps . . . This is the time for America to correct her unpardonable fault of wastefulness and extravagance."

—AMERICAN PRESIDENT WOODROW WILSON, 1917

Another Victory for Gardens

5　During World War II (1939–45), the War Food Administration in the United States created the National Victory Garden Program. Its goal was to re-create the huge success of the gardening movement during the previous war. This time, the results were even more astounding. The USDA estimated that more than 20 million plots were planted during the war.

6　By growing fruits and vegetables, people felt they were contributing to the war effort. They were ensuring the country—and its soldiers—had enough to eat, and freeing up resources needed in wartime. For example, metals and other materials normally used in food production could be put to military use instead. Railroad cars carried less food, allowing them to carry more munitions.

Groundwork for Victory

GROW MORE IN '44

In the United States, the Fenway Victory Gardens of Boston and the Dowling Community Garden of Minneapolis are the last remaining victory gardens from the wars.

WAR GARDENS OVER THE TOP

he Seeds of Victory
e the Fruits of Peace

ITE TO NATIONAL WAR GARDEN COMMISSION
WASHINGTON, D.C.

President   Percival S. Ridsdale, Secretary

FILL IT!

HELP HARVEST WAR CROPS

Every Available Inch

7 What was old is new again: Those victory gardeners were ahead of their time! Even in peacetime, there are plenty of reasons to grow our own food in cities. But not everyone has a yard that can be turned into a garden, and some neighborhoods have no green spaces at all. How do you turn a concrete jungle into a source of fresh, healthy food? Fortunately, there's nothing engineers and architects love better than a challenge!

Vertical Gardens

8 When cities are too jam-packed to create wide growing spaces, one alternative is to go up—and up and up! Also known as "living walls," vertical gardens can transform brick, concrete, and siding into artistic and even edible walls.

9 The Urban Farming Food Chain Project in Los Angeles created food-producing wall panels that are mounted on buildings. Those who tend the walls reap the harvest, which is not sold commercially. You can create your own wall panel by recycling shelving units, adding hanging pots to wooden fences, or even hanging old shoe organizers.

> **alternative**   An alternative is a choice or option that can take the place of something.
>
> **transform**   If you transform something, you change it from one thing to another.

This vertical garden is planted with a pleasing variety of spices, flowers, and fruits.

Towering Farms

10 Vertical farms take the concept of growing upward to the next level—skyward! Designers have been imagining high-rise growing spaces that aim to produce as much food as possible without draining all of a city's resources.

11 Creating a vertical farm is more complicated than building a living wall. It's a bigger venture than just converting office towers into farms. For example, if sunlight can't reach all of the plants, solar panels may need to be installed to supply energy for artificial growing lights. Designs also have to include ways to capture, recycle, and pump water throughout the building.

12 Until someone constructs the first vertical farm, we won't know all the challenges of building one. We won't know all the advantages such a farm might bring to a community. But with so many people energized by the innovative plans, it's only a matter of time until we find out.

13 An architect named Gordon Graff designed a 58-story green building, called Sky Farm, for the city of Toronto. It has 8 million square feet (743,000 square meters) of growing space. That's enough to feed 35,000 people per year. Time will tell whether a costly, untested project like this will come to be. But it's the right kind of dreaming.

> **artificial** If something is artificial, it was created by humans rather than nature.

Pictured above are beans and zucchini growing up a city-home trellis. When you can't spread out, you can always stretch up!

"Vertical farms take the concept of growing upward to the next level—skyward!"

Shaping Up

14 Plants need sunlight to grow. In a vertical building, the upper levels can cast a shadow over the lower levels. So designers are experimenting with shapes that will allow light to reach all of the growing spaces.

15   Natalie Jeremijenko, an engineer and artist, created pod-like greenhouses. Although they're called Urban Space Stations, their job here on Earth is to provide growing spaces. Each structure's clear, curved surface absorbs light as the sun moves across the building. The pod also recycles air and water from the building below. Because it doesn't need soil, the station is light enough to be raised off the ground.

Burrowing Underground

16 What lies beneath our city streets? In Tokyo, an underground bank vault was turned into a high-tech farm called Pasona O2. The farm covers 10,000 square feet (1,000 square meters) and grows more than 100 types of produce. It uses a combination of halide, LED, and fluorescent lights, as well as hydroponics—raising crops without soil. With hydroponics, plants are grown in water containing nutrient solutions or materials like gravel or perlite. The word "hydroponics" comes from the Greek words for water (*hydro*) and labor (*ponos*).

17   In addition to growing food, Pasona O2 has a very important goal: to create jobs for youth and older employees who need a second career.

Rooftop vegetable garden at the convention center in Montreal, Canada

Rooftop Gardens

18 Hydroponics can also solve the problem of how to take advantage of all that terrific unused space way up there—on rooftops! Not all rooftops can handle a heavy load of dense soil. But hydroponics can lighten the load by using lighter materials or shallow water beds.

In Tokyo, two telecommunications companies sponsored the planting of sweet potatoes in rooftop gardens. They called this project Green Potato. The wide leaves of the plants were so effective at transpiration that the leaf-covered areas were more than 68 degrees Farenheit (20 degrees Celsius) cooler than the areas not covered by leaves.

19 Rooftops get screamingly hot in the summertime—up to 90 degrees Farenheit (32 degrees Celsius) warmer than the air. But a green roof can actually be *cooler* than the air. That's because plants do a "cool" thing called transpiration. They take water in through their roots and then release it through their leaves. The heat from the air is used to evaporate the water, bringing temperatures down.

20 The idea is clearly catching on. A group called the Rooftop Garden Project has greened roofs all over Montreal and has begun sharing its techniques with people in other countries. They've even taken their skills to Haiti to help establish urban agriculture there in the aftermath of the 2010 earthquake.

21 In Chicago, the Gary Comer Youth Center occupies a building that used to be an abandoned warehouse. It's a huge, reinforced structure topped by a 906-square-yard (800 square meter) rooftop garden. The soil for the garden is 18 inches (46 centimeters) deep and grows an amazing 1,000 pounds (454 kilograms) of organic vegetables per year. The produce is brought home by the volunteer gardeners and is used in the center's cooking classes.

"Hydroponics can also solve the problem of how to take advantage of all that terrific unused space way up there—on rooftops!"

Digging In

22 But what if you're not an engineer or an architect? What if you're just, well, you? The good news is you don't need an underground bank vault or fancy watering system to start your own urban garden. But there are a few things to consider before you dig in.

23 **SPACE** Urban gardens tend to be smaller than rural and suburban gardens. So you may need to choose crops that take up less space. Beans, for example, grow vertically (upward) and do well in containers, which makes them great for narrow spaces. With a big pot and enough sunlight, you can choose a variety that grows more than 5 feet (1.5 meters) tall.

Tall green beans are a good choice for high, narrow spaces.

24 **SUNLIGHT** Some plants, such as tomatoes and zucchini, need lots of sun to produce their fruit, preferably six to eight hours per day. So before you choose what to plant, make sure you know how many hours of sunlight are available. Does your home or a nearby building cast shadows?

25 **TASTE** What do you like to eat? What would you like to try? Arugula, an herb that's used in green salads, is much sweeter if you harvest the leaves when they're young and small. Some varieties of cherries are tart while others are sweet. The more space you have to grow different plants, the more you can experiment.

26 **TIME** Some plants require more care than others. Fruit crops, like peppers, need fertilizer and a lot of water. On the other hand, a container of lettuce is happiest in cooler temperatures, and needs less watering and little or no fertilizer.

Herbs and small plants like strawberries are easily grown in little containers that fit on windowsills.

27 **APPEARANCE** For many gardeners, how their garden looks matters as much as the crops it produces. What kind of space would you like to look at and enjoy spending time in? A carpet of greens? A jungle of tall pea plants?

28 **COST** The start-up cost for a big garden can be a little overwhelming. You may need to buy gardening tools, soil, fertilizer, compost, seeds or seedlings, and containers. It really adds up. But the money your family saves by growing some of your own food instead of buying it can make up for this cost in as little as one harvest. In the meantime, you can save money by borrowing tools and using household items like buckets for containers. Cut costs even more by choosing seeds over seedlings, which are more expensive. You can also share seeds and plant cuttings with other growers. Some types of fruits and vegetables will yield seeds that you can save for the next planting season.

> **yield** To yield means to produce or create something.

29 **PESTS** Cities are full of wildlife, and much of it will be delighted by the buffet on your balcony. Birds may feast on your berries. Raccoons will run off with your harvest. And a compost heap can attract mice and rats. If you've got critters in your neighborhood—and you can bet you do—you'll have to guard your garden against them. One way to do this is by protecting plants with chicken wire.

This masked creature may seem cute but it can be a real pest in your garden!

Pollution Solutions

30 Vegetables may be full of vitamins and other health-giving goodies, but are city-grown veggies safe? What about all those cars coughing on your lettuce?

31 Most airborne pollutants will come off your veggies with a good washing. The more dangerous kinds are lurking underground. Chemicals from nearby industrial sites can turn the earth toxic. One of the most common—and dangerous—contaminants is lead. It can leach into the soil from paint and lead plumbing pipes, among other things.

32 Gardeners who have reason to believe their soil isn't safe can send a soil sample to a lab for testing. Private companies, many city health departments, and some universities also offer this service.

33 If the soil is contaminated, it can often be fixed using lime and organic matter. To be extra safe, concerned gardeners can stick with fruiting crops, such as peppers. That's because the edible part grows above the soil and the parts below the soil don't absorb a lot of chemicals. Or, they can grow plants in containers or raised beds with fresh soil instead.

34 Testing can reveal other things about soil, such as the nutrients it contains, which will influence the type of plants you can grow. If it turns out the soil is safe but of poor quality, you may be able to improve it by adding compost.

> **influence**   If you influence something, you affect it or cause a certain outcome.

You don't have to start big. You can expand your garden each season, one bed or pot at a time.

IS IT A FRUIT OR A VEGETABLE? A botanist—someone who studies plants—would say that if it's fleshy, has seeds, and comes from a flowering plant, it's a fruit. If, however, you eat the root, leaves, or stem, it's a vegetable. So, an eggplant is a fruit and so is a walnut, but carrots, celery, and potatoes are veggies.

Raised beds with wide pathways make gardening easier
for people who have trouble bending and lifting.

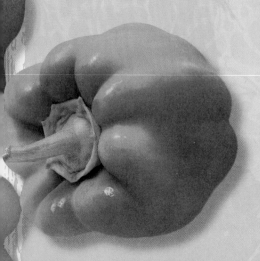

"Vegetables may be full of vitamins
and other health-giving goodies,
but are city-grown veggies safe?"

The Community Garden

35 Another solution for city dwellers with limited space is to share. Community gardens are places in a city where people can get together to grow food and other plants. They add green spaces to neighborhoods and can make a world of difference in a food desert, where fresh produce is hard to come by.

36   No two community gardens are exactly alike. Some are group efforts, where all the work and the harvest are shared and maybe even sold at a farmers' market. Others are divided into separate plots so each person or family can have their own. Most expect members to tend their gardens regularly and do some communal work, such as cleaning out the common areas before winter.

Every dollar that's spent on a community garden plot may yield up to six dollars' worth of veggies.

INGREDIENTS OF A GREAT COMMUNITY GARDEN

TOOLS: Many community gardeners share tools that stay on-site so people don't have to lug their own and can split the cost. The tools are kept in a locked shed, and members have keys.

WATER: A long hose and a rain barrel are handy when rainfall alone isn't enough to give the plants a good soaking.

REST SPOTS: Some community gardens include areas where members can chill out and little kids can play without trampling the plants.

SHARED KNOWLEDGE: One of the best reasons to grow food alongside others is all the information and tips shared among gardening friends.

Good Eats

37 Feeding hungry people is just one good reason to break out your gardening gloves. You'll discover another the first time you bite into a carrot you've grown yourself: taste!

38   Why does home- and locally-grown produce taste so good? The answer takes us back to the 1950s, when food growers started focusing on hybrid varieties of fruits and vegetables. A hybrid is a combination of two or more different types of the same plant. The plants are cross-pollinated to get particular qualities from each. For example, one type of tomato may be able to resist diseases. Another might be big, colorful, or able to stand up to traveling large distances. Factory farms tend to stick to a few types of hybrids that are reliable for mass production.

39   The tomato you grow or buy from a local farmer may be a hybrid variety where taste was made a priority. Or it could be an heirloom variety. Like heirlooms, or antiques, an heirloom plant was grown in an earlier era— usually in the time before hybrids became popular. Heirlooms may not travel as well or produce as much fruit as hybrids, but they can be absolutely delicious. And they all look so different from one another in color, shape, and size! Growing heirlooms is a nice way to feel connected with food growers from the past and to ensure these varieties aren't lost forever.

GOING LOCO Locavores are people who try to source all or most of their food locally by growing or picking it, or by buying from a local farmer. Unfortunately, because smaller farms produce less food than factory farms, their prices are often higher to cover costs.

Is it worth paying more for local food if you can afford to? The locavore movement says "yes." Just like the fruits and vegetables you grow yourself, foods from small, local farms tend to taste better and come in more varieties than the mass-produced kind. Because they don't have to travel as far, local farmers can pick their produce just before they bring it to market. That preserves its nutritional value, freshness, and flavor.

Get Growing

40 Still looking for a reason to get growing? Chances are, farm fashion isn't going to convince you. And mucking around in the garden isn't pretty. You'll get filthy. You'll sweat. People may smell you a mile away (and not because you've got basil in your pocket).

41 The flip side of all that hard labor is that you can get super fit. Studies show that being active throughout the day can burn way more calories than just working out in the gym. All that bending, lifting, and carrying is great strength training. It firms up the major muscle groups in your chest, back, legs, and shoulders. Chores like shoveling are cardiovascular exercise in disguise, working your lungs and heart.

42 Gardening is good for the mind and soul, too. The combination of exercise, time in the sunshine, and fun mucking around in the dirt can help boost your mood and make you feel full of energy.

43 And guess what? Research shows you're more likely to eat fruits and vegetables you've grown yourself. So you'll also be getting better nutrition. Those additional vitamins and minerals in your diet will make your skin glow, your hair shine, and your nails stronger (if somewhat dirtier).

Easy Does It

You can burn up to 300 calories an hour in the garden, about the same as with very brisk walking. Follow these tips to have a safe workout in the vegetable patch:

- Whenever possible, bend at the knees, not your waist, so you don't strain your lower back.
- Build up your stamina slowly, starting with a short session in the garden and gradually increasing the time. If you do too much too soon, you could wind up with an injury or become overly sore.
- Always wear sunscreen to prevent burns and skin damage.
- Stretch, stretch, and stretch some more to help prevent injuries.
- Drink lots of water.

Food for Thought

Horticulture therapy uses plant-related activities to help people work through a whole bunch of physical and mental health issues, from recovering from surgery to reducing depression. Working with plants is soothing and improves motor skills and concentration. And because it requires problem-solving and goal-setting, self-confidence can go up as well.

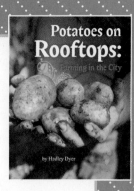

Collaborative Discussion

Look back at what you wrote on page 312. Tell a partner two things you learned from the text. Then work with a group to discuss the questions below. Find examples and details in *Potatoes on Rooftops* to support your answers. Prepare for the discussion by reviewing the text and thinking about its key points.

1 Reread pages 314–315. What language on these pages reveals the author's opinion about urban gardening?

2 Review pages 316–317. How do the posters shown on these pages support the information in the text?

3 Why does the author describe so many different types of gardens in the text? What conclusions can you draw from them about people who grow urban gardens?

Listening Tip

Listen carefully to the responses of others. Think about what details in the text support their ideas. What ideas of your own can you add?

Speaking Tip

Before you make a comment, look back at the text for specific details and examples to support your point.

Write an Advertising Script

PROMPT

In *Potatoes on Rooftops*, you learned about urban gardening and how people can use their available space to make gardening possible, even in the city.

Imagine that your job is to persuade people to start a community garden in your town or city. Write a script for a radio or TV ad that tells would-be gardeners why gardening is good for them and the community. Introduce your topic with a strong "hook" that gets your viewers' or listeners' attention. Then clearly state your opinion, supporting it with reasons and details based on text evidence. Conclude with a memorable statement or slogan. Don't forget to use some of the Critical Vocabulary words in your writing.

PLAN

Make notes about the hook, reasons and evidence, and conclusion for your script.

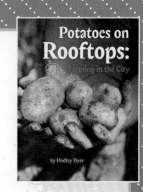

Potatoes on Rooftops: Farming in the City

by Hadley Dyer

WRITE

Now write your advertising script to persuade people to participate in a community garden.

Make sure your advertising script
☐ begins with a strong hook.
☐ clearly states an opinion.
☐ gives reasons and text evidence to support the opinion.
☐ concludes with a memorable statement or slogan.

Notice & Note
Tough Questions

Prepare to Read

GENRE STUDY   A **play** is a story that can be performed for an audience.

- Plays develop characters and reveal the plot through dialogue, or conversation. Authors may use informal language to make the dialogue realistic.

- Plays include stage directions within parentheses to help set the scenes and tell what the characters are doing.

- Many plays include a theme or lesson learned by the main characters.

SET A PURPOSE   **Think about** the title and genre of this text. What do you know about caring for the environment? What do you want to learn? Write your ideas below.

CRITICAL VOCABULARY
reduce
conscious
implying
contradict
cascading
depleted

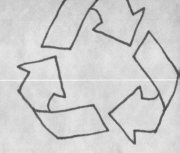

**Meet the Author and Illustrator:
Doreen Beauregard and Tuesday Mourning**

Living Green

by Doreen Beauregard
illustrated by Tuesday Mourning

Characters: Eva, Bo, Grace, Mr. Chen

Setting: Bo's living room

....

1 **Eva:** (*looking at the clock*) Whoa. We've been playing this game for an hour. We haven't made the final version of our "Reduce, Reuse, Recycle" poster for Ms. Garcia's class.

2 **Bo:** (*closing the computer game and settling on the floor in front of a poster board*) No big deal. We know a lot about conservation and sustainable living and stuff. We're very environmentally conscious. This will be easy. Eva, can you get a new piece of poster board from that package?

3 **Grace:** Hmm. Are we really? Environmentally conscious, I mean.

4 **Bo:** Of course we are! Are you implying that we aren't?

5 **Grace:** Well, we've read a lot about environmental topics in school. But has it changed what we do? Do our actions contradict our words?

6 **Eva:** (*frowning*) My family recycles.

7 **Bo:** And I turn off the water while I brush my teeth.

8 **Grace:** Yeah, those are great things to do. But they're just a start. Maybe we need to think about the impact of everything we do. Like that new piece of poster board. Instead of using a new piece, why don't we just turn over the board that we used to make the draft—and make the final version on the other side? No one will even see the original side, because it will be on the wall. Reuse!

9 **Bo:** (*rolling her eyes*) Yeah, okay, but that's so . . .

10 **Grace:** I know, it seems so minor. But all these little things, every day, year after year—they add up. Think about all the energy and resources that go into cutting down the trees, manufacturing the paper, transporting the paper to stores . . .

11 **Bo:** But we're only in fifth grade. It's not like we can change the world.

---

reduce   To reduce something is to decrease the size or amount of it.

conscious   To be conscious of something is to be aware of it.

implying   If you are implying something, you are expressing it without stating it directly.

contradict   To contradict something is to say or do the opposite of it.

12   **Eva:** I used to think that, too. But we won't be kids forever. And we're role models for the little kids. My little sister mimics everything I do. *Everything.*

13   **Bo:** I guess. Maybe we have to change our . . . what does Ms. Garcia call it? Mindset.

14   **Grace:** And maybe our poster should focus on that. You know, some ideas that aren't so obvious.

15   **Bo:** Like . . . (*thinking while idly examining a vine cascading from a nearby plant*) Oh, here's an idea. You know how the water is cold when you first turn on the shower, so you have to let it run a while before you get in? Instead of wasting that water, catch it in a container and use it for watering plants. My mom has *so* many plants and they need a lot of water.

16   **Eva:** Hey, that's good. Reduce! And here's another "reduce" idea. Instead of turning up the heat when you get a little chilly, put on a sweater or a hoodie.

17   **Bo:** Good idea. My brother wears T-shirts all winter, and then turns up the heat because he's cold. Not smart!

> **cascading**   Something that is cascading is falling or flowing in a way similar to a waterfall.

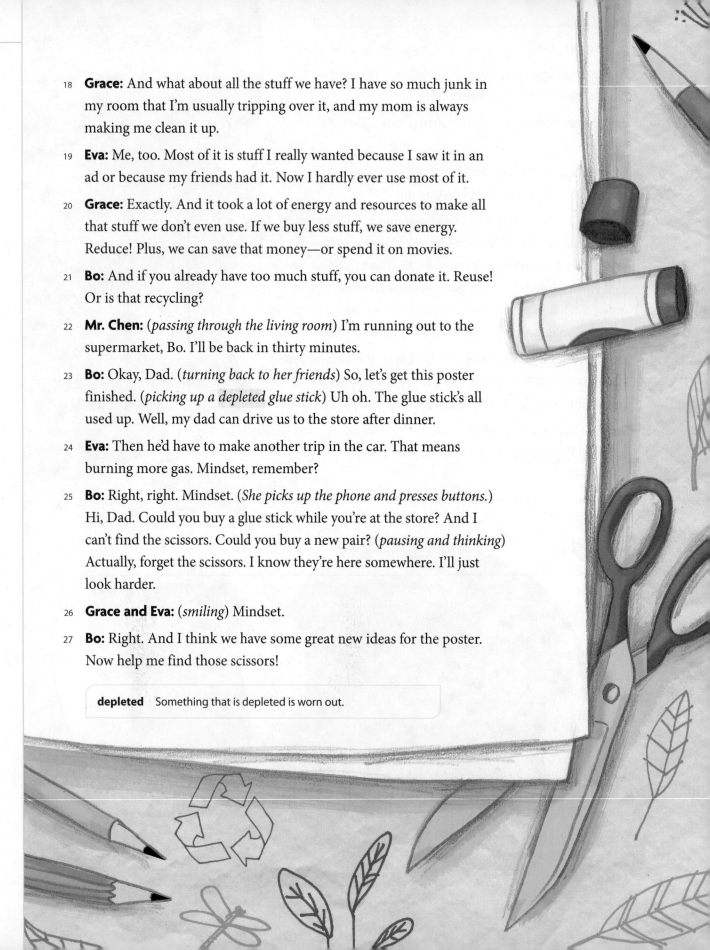

18 **Grace:** And what about all the stuff we have? I have so much junk in my room that I'm usually tripping over it, and my mom is always making me clean it up.

19 **Eva:** Me, too. Most of it is stuff I really wanted because I saw it in an ad or because my friends had it. Now I hardly ever use most of it.

20 **Grace:** Exactly. And it took a lot of energy and resources to make all that stuff we don't even use. If we buy less stuff, we save energy. Reduce! Plus, we can save that money—or spend it on movies.

21 **Bo:** And if you already have too much stuff, you can donate it. Reuse! Or is that recycling?

22 **Mr. Chen:** (*passing through the living room*) I'm running out to the supermarket, Bo. I'll be back in thirty minutes.

23 **Bo:** Okay, Dad. (*turning back to her friends*) So, let's get this poster finished. (*picking up a depleted glue stick*) Uh oh. The glue stick's all used up. Well, my dad can drive us to the store after dinner.

24 **Eva:** Then he'd have to make another trip in the car. That means burning more gas. Mindset, remember?

25 **Bo:** Right, right. Mindset. (*She picks up the phone and presses buttons.*) Hi, Dad. Could you buy a glue stick while you're at the store? And I can't find the scissors. Could you buy a new pair? (*pausing and thinking*) Actually, forget the scissors. I know they're here somewhere. I'll just look harder.

26 **Grace and Eva:** (*smiling*) Mindset.

27 **Bo:** Right. And I think we have some great new ideas for the poster. Now help me find those scissors!

> **depleted** Something that is depleted is worn out.

Collaborative Discussion

Look back at what you wrote on page 332 and talk with a partner about what you learned during reading. Then work with a group to discuss the questions below. Use examples and details from *Living Green* to support your responses. Choose a group leader to keep your discussion moving and a recorder to jot down the group's answers and ideas.

1 Reread page 334. What parts of the dialogue show that Grace has been thinking about how her actions affect the environment?

2 Review page 335. What reasons does Eva give to support the idea that fifth graders "can change the world"?

3 Which ideas or actions show that the girls have a new mindset at the end of the play?

Listening Tip

Be sure to follow your class's rules for discussion by being a good listener. Look at the person who is speaking, to show you are paying attention.

Speaking Tip

When you have finished speaking, ask if anyone has questions or comments about what you have said.

Write a New Scene

PROMPT

In *Living Green* three friends work together on a school project about caring for the environment. In the process they gain a new understanding of how their actions affect the planet.

Write a new scene for the play in which the girls present their poster to the class and explain what they learned about their mindset and behavior. Write the new scene in script format, including character names, dialogue, and stage directions. Think about text evidence as you write what the characters would say and do. Don't forget to use some of the Critical Vocabulary words in your writing.

PLAN

Makes notes for your new play scene, including ideas for dialogue and stage directions.

WRITE

Now write your new play scene for the ending of *Living Green*.

Make sure your new scene
☐ is written in script format.
☐ contains dialogue and stage directions.
☐ is based on details in the text.

Notice & Note
Tough Questions

Prepare to Read

GENRE STUDY **Realistic fiction** tells a story about characters and events that are like those in real life.

- The events in realistic fiction build on each other to keep the plot moving forward.
- Realistic fiction includes characters who act, think, and speak like real people would. It is set in a place that seems real.
- Realistic fiction includes dialogue, or conversation between characters.

SET A PURPOSE **Think about** the title and genre of this story. What do you know about gardening? What do you want to learn? Write your ideas below.

CRITICAL VOCABULARY

spectacle

toddles

packet

retreat

Meet the Author and Illustrator:
Katie Smith Milway and
Sylvie Daigneault

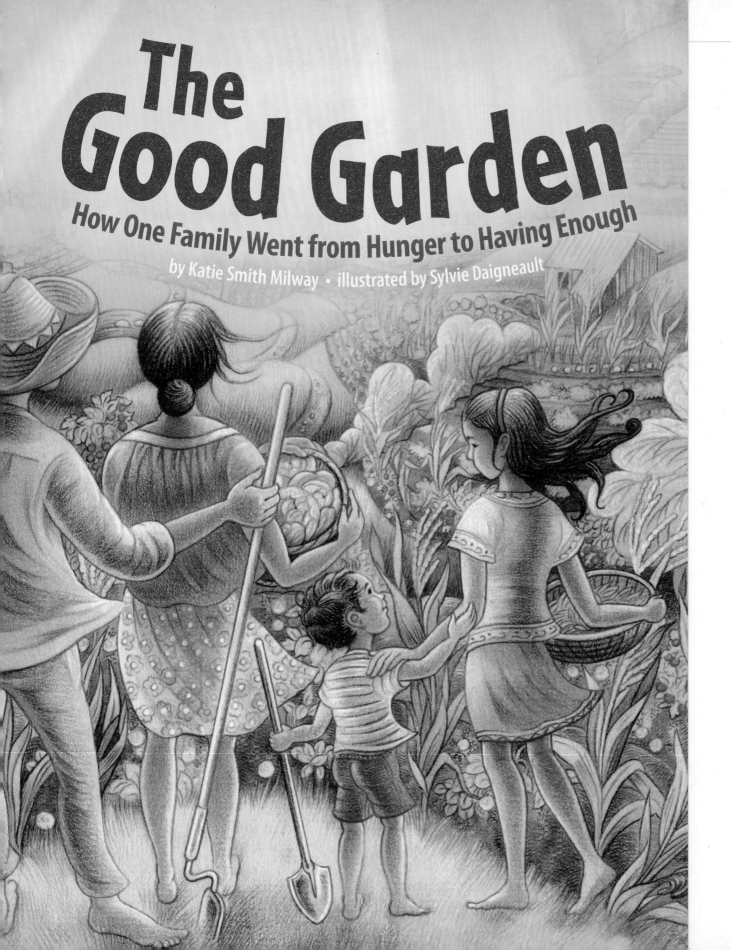

The Good Garden

How One Family Went from Hunger to Having Enough

by Katie Smith Milway • illustrated by Sylvie Daigneault

1   *María Luz Duarte lives with her parents and her baby brother, Pepito, in the hills of Honduras. They grow their own food on a small plot of land. But drought and insects are ruining the crops in their community. They might have to eat the seeds they should save for planting next spring. Then they would have to borrow seeds from the grain buyer, also known as the coyote. The coyote makes money from poor farmers by forcing them to pay back three times the amount of seeds they borrow. Some people lose their farms to the coyote. To avoid this, María's father has gone away in search of work. He's left María with an important responsibility: taking care of the family's crops while he's gone.*

2   The wind pulls at María Luz's hair as she walks to school. The dry season has set in, and there is dust in the air and wispy clouds high above. As she walks, she thinks of her father in the highlands. He has been gone for three months now. Could he be looking at the same clouds?

3   The village school has just one room for all eighty students. It is crowded and dark. María Luz slides onto a bench beside her *amigo* (ah-MEE-goh), Alfredo Gonzales.

4   This year the students have a surprise—a new teacher. His name, he tells them, is Don Pedro Morales. He is not much taller than María Luz, but he has big ideas.

5   The first week Don Pedro teaches his students how to make . . . windows. "This school is good for bats and owls, but not for children," he exclaims, flapping his arms. Soon there is daylight streaming into the classroom, making it easier for María Luz and the others to read and write.

6   After class, Don Pedro picks up a hoe and climbs up the low hill behind the school. María Luz is curious. "Are you making a garden?" she asks. Don Pedro nods. "Well, it will not grow much." She tells him of her garden, and how the land has gone bad.

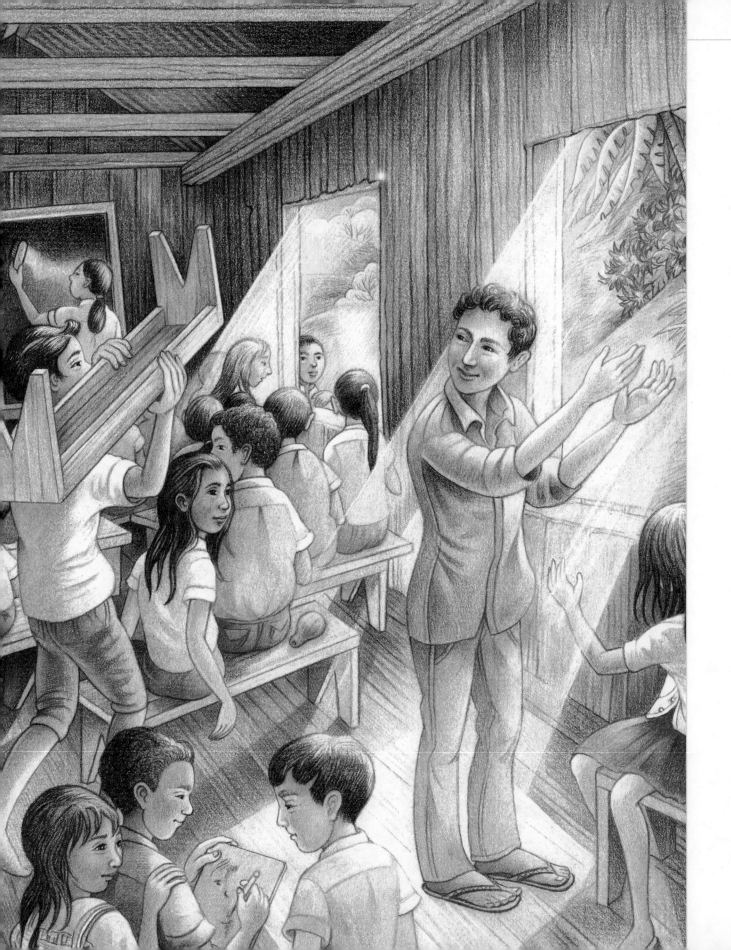

7   Don Pedro stops his hoeing. "Then, there is only one solution, *Señorita* (see-nyor-EE-tah). We must feed the soil and make it good again."

8   Don Pedro heaps up old leaves, corn husks and bean pods. María Luz has watched her father do the same, then burn this waste.

9   But Don Pedro does not burn it—he says he is making food for the soil instead. He covers the pile with a big piece of plastic. With the help of worms and grubs, he explains, the old plants will break down into food for the soil called compost.

10   Don Pedro asks María Luz to stir the compost every day with a stick and make sure it stays damp. He will collect manure from the school's chicken coop and add it to the pile. "Our soil will have a feast," he says.

11   "*Sí, sí,*" laughs Alfredo, who is passing by. "María Luz will make dirt soup!"

12   But María Luz just smiles. She stirs the compost and imagines Papa eating his plantains, *tortillas*, beans and cream. Can a garden have a favorite meal, too?

13   Don Pedro's next gardening project is a big one. María Luz watches as he shovels the soil into giant steps he calls terraces. They rise like a staircase up the hill behind the school.

14   Many people in town come to see the spectacle. Some of them point and shake their heads. But they listen when Don Pedro explains that the terraces make flat surfaces for planting and keep the soil from washing downhill with the rains. On the side of each step, he plants vines and grass to hold the terrace in place.

15   Don Pedro mixes rich compost into the soil, then pokes holes in the terraces and plants his seeds. The *campesinos* nod and whisper but fall silent when the *maestro* (my-EST-roh) plants marigolds in rows beside the seeds. Has he gone *loco*, they wonder? "It may look crazy," laughs Don Pedro, "but the marigolds will keep the insects away."

> **spectacle**   A spectacle is an unusual or interesting sight.

16   Over the next few days, more and more families come by to watch and learn. Some ask Don Pedro how to make terraces. Others ask María Luz how to make compost. Still others admire the marigolds, which Don Pedro calls the smiles of the soil. Everyone is wondering the same thing—could these new ideas help their gardens, too?

17   María Luz begins to try some of Don Pedro's new ways at home. She makes small terraces for her family's winter vegetables. Her steps look rough and uneven, but they will hold the soil.

18   Pepito toddles out to see. He grabs a handful of compost and pats it onto a terrace, just as he has seen his big sister do. Won't Papa be surprised to find two gardeners when he comes home!

19   She remembers all her father has taught her. She pokes holes in the soil and pushes the seeds down deep. She saves one small terrace for something new. Don Pedro has given her a packet of radish seeds. He says they will sprout in just a few weeks and sell for a good price at the market.

> **toddles** When a child toddles, he or she walks with short, unsteady steps.
> **packet** A packet is a small container or envelope.

20 María Luz pictures the coins she will earn and dreams of what she might do with them: Should she take Pepito for his vaccinations or save to buy a burro? Pepito pulls at her to go. She gives his little hand a squeeze and picks up the watering can. "We have fed our soil, Pepito. Now we must give it a drink."

21 The work has made them hungry, but María Luz knows that only a small mound of beans and a little *tortilla* dough remain. Once these are gone, they will have nothing. Unless her father has found work, her radish money may not go to her dreams but to buy food.

22 The air is growing warmer, and the school's little hillside is sprouting. The garden is now part of their classroom. Don Pedro asks his students to count the radish shoots and to measure the distance between onions. He has them divide seeds into equal piles.

23 Every day at home, María Luz checks her vegetables. The tomatoes and chilies are small and green, and the onions are still asleep underground. But her radishes poke their red tops out of the soil into the warm sun. You must grow fat, she tells them. You must!

24 Someone else is also watching María Luz's radishes. One day, as she weeds with Pepito, a long shadow falls across her vegetable rows. "You are growing crops for cash, I see," says the growly voice of Señor (see-NYOR) Lobo, the local *coyote*. "Perhaps you would like me to take them to market for you."

25 María Luz does not raise her eyes. Her hands tremble. She shakes her head but does not speak. She hears the *coyote* snort and watches his shadow retreat. She knows he will be back.

26 Just then Mama calls out, "Come, María Luz, Pepito! Come to the house! We have news!"

27 María Luz and Pepito scramble to the house. Mama has received word from Papa—he *did* find work and will be home soon.

retreat If you retreat, you move back or away from something.

28   A few days later, María Luz is working in their garden when something catches her eye. Her heart skips a beat. A familiar *sombrero* is bobbing up the path to her house. Pa-pa! Pa-pa! María Luz breaks into a run. "*Mi cariño* (mee kah-REE-nyo)," shouts Papa, holding out his arms. At last he has returned.

29   Papa bounces Pepito on his knee and, over strong, hot coffee, tells Mama and María Luz about work in the highlands. Long, backbreaking days on a coffee plantation were worth it, he says. He has earned enough for seeds and fertilizer.

30   María Luz wriggles in her chair. "What is it, María Luz?" asks Papa.

31   "I think you can save your fertilizer money for something else—come see our garden!"

32   Papa looks in wonder at the little terraces, the compost heap, the sprouting vegetables—and the fat radishes. "Where have you learned these things?" he asks.

33   María Luz takes Papa's hand and walks him down the path to the village school. Don Pedro is at work in the school garden. "*Maestro*," calls María Luz. "I want you to meet *mi padre* (PAH-dray)!"

34   "*Mucho gusto*," says Don Pedro pumping Señor Duarte's hand. "Your daughter is my best helper."

35   Papa talks a while with Don Pedro. On the way home, he tells María Luz how proud he is of all she has learned, in school and in the garden. "I should go away more often," he jokes. "But since I am back, I am going to be *your* helper."

Collaborative Discussion

Look back at what you wrote on page 340 and talk with a partner about what you learned during reading. Then work with a group to discuss the questions below. Find details to support your answers in *The Good Garden*. In your discussion, provide positive feedback to other group members and clarify any misunderstandings.

1. Review page 345. Describe the two techniques Don Pedro uses to make his garden flourish.

2. Reread page 346. What has María Luz decided to do in her own garden? What has made her feel hopeful it will work?

3. Which details in the story reveal Maria Luz's character and that her family is important to her?

Listening Tip

Listen politely to the responses of others. What points do you agree with? Is there anything you question or don't understand?

Speaking Tip

Give positive feedback to other speakers. Let them know what you like about their ideas.

Write a Letter

In *The Good Garden*, María Luz must take care of the family's crops while her father is away. Fortunately, she gets some help from her teacher, Don Pedro.

Imagine you are María Luz. Write a letter from María's point of view to a friend in another town. Tell the friend about major events that happened while your father was away, based on text evidence. Tell about the events in an order that makes sense and uses descriptive language. Include a heading, greeting, body, closing, and signature in your letter. Don't forget to use some of the Critical Vocabulary words in your writing.

PLAN ....

Make notes about details from the text that will help you write your letter.

WRITE

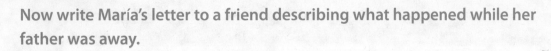

Now write María's letter to a friend describing what happened while her father was away.

✓ Make sure your letter

- ☐ is written from María's point of view and uses first-person pronouns, such as *I, me, we,* and *our.*

- ☐ retells major events from the plot in an order that makes sense.

- ☐ uses strong, descriptive language.

- ☐ includes a heading, greeting, body, closing, and signature.

**Notice &
Note**
Word Gaps

Prepare to Read

GENRE STUDY **Informational texts** give facts about a topic.

- Authors of informational texts may organize ideas by stating a problem and explaining its solution. They may also present ideas in sequential, or chronological, order to help readers know when events happen and how they're connected.

- Informational text authors may include narrative elements to help readers relate to the text's topic, and content-area words that are specific to that topic.

SET A PURPOSE **Think about** the title and genre of this text. What do you know about animal habitats? What do you want to learn? Write your ideas below.

CRITICAL VOCABULARY

flight

toil

merchant

fort

jabbing

captivity

aggressive

**Meet the Authors and Illustrator:
Susan L. Roth and Cindy Trumbore**

Parrots Over Puerto Rico

by Susan L. Roth and Cindy Trumbore
collages by Susan L. Roth

1   **A**bove the treetops of Puerto Rico flies a flock of parrots as green as their
island home. If you look up from the forest, and you are very lucky, you might
catch the bright blue flashes of their flight feathers and hear their harsh call.

2   These are Puerto Rican parrots. They lived on this island for millions of
years, and then they nearly vanished from the earth forever. This is their story.

> **flight**   Flight is the act of flying through the air.

3   Long before people came to Puerto Rico, hundreds of thousands of parrots flew over the island and the smaller islands nearby. *Iguaca! Iguaca!* (ih-GWAH-kah) the parrots called as they looked for deep nesting holes in the tall trees.

4   Down below, waves from the Caribbean Sea and the Atlantic Ocean washed the island's white-sand beaches. Delicate orchids and wide-spreading ferns, tiny tree frogs, kapok trees bursting with seedpods, and big, scaly iguanas covered the land.

5   *Iguaca! Iguaca!* the parrots called as they flew to sierra palm trees to eat
their dark, bitter fruit.

6   Around 5000 BCE, people came to the island in canoes from lands to the
south. These people planted corn, yucca, sweet potatoes, peanuts, and pineapples.
When they looked up, they saw the bright blue flashes of flight feathers.

7   More groups of people came. The Taínos (TIE-EE-nohs) arrived around
800 CE. They hunted the parrots for food and kept them as pets. Taínos gave the
parrots a name, *iguaca*, after their harsh call. They gave the island a name too:
Boriquén (boh-ree-KEN).

8   *Iguaca! Iguaca!* the parrots called when hurricane winds blew down the old trees where they had their nests. After the hurricanes passed, the parrots flew through the treetops to find new nesting holes.

9   Christopher Columbus sailed from Europe to Boriquén in 1493 and claimed the island for Spain. Soon Spanish settlers were planting crops on the island and building houses and schools with wood, bricks, and stone. Each time hurricanes destroyed their homes and schools, the settlers rebuilt them.

10   The Spaniards called the parrots *cotorras* (koh-TOH-rahs), and they gave the island a new name: Puerto Rico (PWAIR-toh-REE-koh), "rich port."

11 In the treetops, the parrots searched for mates. The new pairs of parrots sat on branches, bowing, calling back and forth to each other, and fluffing their wings and tails. Each pair raised one family of chicks every year.

12 Now people from many other parts of the world came to live in Puerto Rico. In 1513, Africans were brought to the island to toil as slaves under the hot sun in fields of sugarcane and other crops.

13 More people came from Spain too, and they married Taínos and Africans. They all called themselves Boricuas (boh-REE-kwahs), people of Boriquén, but they were still ruled by Spain.

---

toil To toil is to work.

14   *Iguaca! Iguaca!* the parrots called when red-tailed hawks chased them in the treetops. The parrots flocked together to protect themselves from the hawks.

15   For centuries, people from other countries in Europe tried to capture Puerto Rico. These countries wanted to control the deep harbor at San Juan (san-HWAN), the capital city, where merchant ships and warships could be launched.

16   The Boricuas protected their island. Starting in 1539, they built a fort that grew and grew until its walls were 18 feet (5.5 meters) thick. For hundreds of years, no country was able to take Puerto Rico away from Spain.

merchant   A merchant ship carries products to sell, usually to a foreign country.
fort   A fort is a strong building usually protected by guards and a wall.

17   *Iguaca! Iguaca!* the parrots called when they found that their nesting holes had been invaded by creatures brought to the island by settlers. Black rats from the settlers' ships climbed the tall trees and ate the parrots' eggs. Honeybees that had escaped from hives swarmed into the parrots' nests.

18   In 1898, the United States declared war on Spain. The war was really about Cuba, another of Spain's colonies, but the fighting spilled over into Puerto Rico. Thousands of American soldiers landed on the island and began battling Spanish troops. Spain lost the war, and lost control of Puerto Rico. The island became a territory of the United States, and in 1917, Puerto Ricans became U.S. citizens.

19   *Iguaca! Iguaca!* the parrots called as the forests where they made their
nests were cut down. The parrots began to disappear from places where
they had flown for millions of years. By 1937, there were only about two
thousand Puerto Rican parrots in the Luquillo (loo-KEE-yoh) Mountains to the
east. A few years later, the parrots were living in just one place, El Yunque
(ell YOON-keh), a tropical rain forest in those mountains.

20   After Puerto Ricans gained American citizenship, many of them moved to
the United States. Those who stayed in rural parts on the island built houses
and farms in the areas where parrots had once lived. Many of the parrots' tall,
old trees were made into charcoal to use for cooking fires. And people still
hunted and trapped the parrots.

21 In the 1950s, birds called pearly-eyed thrashers moved into the rain forest and tried to steal the parrots' nesting holes. Like clever thieves, these birds enter places where other birds are struggling to live and compete with them for nest sites. The parrots fought the thrashers, jabbing at them with their sharp beaks and defending their nests with harsh cries. But the parrots now had too many enemies and too few trees. The flock became smaller and smaller. By 1954, there were only two hundred parrots left.

22 Puerto Ricans elected their first governor, and the island became a U.S. commonwealth—not a state, not an independent nation, but something in between. The people argued: Should their island remain a commonwealth? Should it be a state? Should it be independent of the United States? Everyone had a different idea, but all were proud to say, "*Yo soy Boricua* (yo soy boh-REEK-wah). I am Puerto Rican."

> **jabbing** If you are jabbing something, you are poking it quickly with a great deal of power.

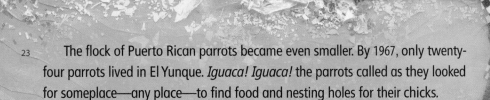

23   The flock of Puerto Rican parrots became even smaller. By 1967, only twenty-four parrots lived in El Yunque. *Iguaca! Iguaca!* the parrots called as they looked for someplace—any place—to find food and nesting holes for their chicks.

24   Puerto Ricans looked up and saw that their iguacas were almost gone. People had nearly caused the parrots to become extinct. Now people started to help the parrots stay alive.

25   In 1968, the governments of the United States and the Commonwealth of Puerto Rico worked together to create the Puerto Rican Parrot Recovery Program. Its goal was to save and protect the parrots. The first part of the plan was to create an aviary, a safe place for parrots to live and raise chicks.

26   Parrots squawked as scientists with long-handled nets gently lifted eggs and chicks from their nesting holes. The scientists always left at least one egg or chick in each nest so some birds could continue living in the wild.

27   In 1973, Luqillo Aviary opened in El Yunque. Incubators in the aviary kept the eggs warm. The Puerto Rican parrots raised in captivity had no experience as parents, so Hispaniolan (his-pah-NYOH-lahn) parrots helped raise the chicks. These parrots come from the nearby island of Hispaniola. They are like cousins of Puerto Rican parrots but are not as rare.

captivity   If something is kept in captivity, it is held in a place and cannot get out.

28   Once hundreds of thousands of Puerto Rican parrots flew over the island. By 1975, only thirteen parrots were left in the rain forest.

29   The worried scientists built special nesting boxes and put them in trees in areas where the parrots were likely to nest. The parrots inspected the nesting boxes and then moved in.

30   These nesting boxes were deep and dark, like the nesting holes Puerto Rican parrots find in the wild. A bird sitting at the top of the box could not see all the way to the bottom. Pearly-eyed thrashers like to see the bottoms of their nests, so the thrashers left the parrots' nesting boxes alone.

31 Wild parrots squawked as scientists gently placed chicks from the aviary in their nests so the chicks could learn how to live in the wild. In 1979, the very first chick raised in the aviary flapped out of a wild nest into the rain forest.

32 The scientists worked hard to keep the parrots healthy—both the captive and the wild birds. One chick was rescued from the wild after its wings were badly damaged by gooey slime inside its nest. The scientists rebuilt the baby parrot's wings using old, discarded parrot feathers, pins, and glue. Then they watched the parrot use its new wings to fly for the first time.

33 By the end of 1979, there were fifteen captive parrots. Most had come from eggs and chicks taken from wild nests to the aviary.

34   Hurricane Hugo roared through the treetops of Puerto Rico in 1989. *Iguaca! Iguaca!* the parrots called as the winds blew down many of their tall trees.

35   The hurricane wiped out crops and wrecked buildings and homes. In the aviary, the scientists worried about all the parrots. What if another bad hurricane blew down more trees? What if the aviary was damaged?

36   *Iguaca! Iguaca!* a group of parrots squawked as scientists moved them from Luquillo Aviary to a new aviary in Río Abajo (REE-oh-ah-BAH-hoh) Forest. This forest is less humid than El Yunque, and many parrots had once lived there. Now there were two safe places for captive parrots to live and raise chicks.

37   Río Abajo Aviary opened in 1993. It had some challenges. Thunderstorms sometimes caused the incubators to lose power. The scientists found generators that kept the power flowing to the incubators.

38   The scientists also tried some new ideas. They kept more aggressive pairs of parrots away from gentler ones, so the gentler birds would not be frightened. They also caged young parrots with adults, so the birds could see how adult parrots behave. The number of parrots in the aviary grew. By 1999, Río Abajo Aviary had fifty-four Puerto Rican parrots. The recovery program was ready for the next part of its plan: releasing adult parrots raised in captivity into the wild.

aggressive   If someone is aggressive, he or she is often angry and ready to attack.

370

39   In 2000, ten captive-bred parrots were released in El Yunque. It was late spring. The wild chicks had already flown from their nests, and the wild adults were still nearby, where the captive-bred parrots could see them and join them. *Iguaca! Iguaca!* the parrots called as they flew with the newcomers and searched for food.

40   The captive-bred parrots had been trained to find food and avoid hawks, but many were caught by hawks anyway. So before the next sixteen parrots were released in 2001, they were given extra training. They heard a hawk's whistle as the cutout shape of a hawk was passed over their cages. They watched a trained hawk attack a Hispaniolan parrot that was wearing a protective leather jacket. In time, the parrots learned to stay still or hide if a hawk was nearby. When these parrots were released, more of them survived in the wild.

41   The scientists were ready to create a second wild flock. In 2006, twenty-two captive-bred parrots were released in Río Abajo Forest. The newly released birds formed pairs, found nesting boxes, and raised their chicks. Dozens of parrots have been released in Río Abajo since then, and they have begun to spread out through the forest.

42   *If you look up from the forest, and you are very lucky, you might catch the bright blue flashes of flight feathers. These are Puerto Rican parrots. They lived on this island for millions of years, and then they nearly vanished from the earth forever. But they are flying over Puerto Rico still, calling,* Iguaca! Iguaca!

Collaborative Discussion

Look back at what you wrote on page 354. Tell a partner two things you learned from the text. Then work with a group to discuss the questions below. Support your answers with details from *Parrots Over Puerto Rico*. In your discussion, explain how your ideas connect to those of others in your group.

1 Revisit pages 358–363. How does the art on these pages help you understand the text?

Listening Tip

Listen quietly and thoughtfully as other speakers share their ideas. Think about how their ideas relate to your own.

2 Review page 365–368. What steps did scientists take to help the parrots once people realized they were endangered?

Speaking Tip

Speak slowly and clearly, giving others time to think about and respond to your ideas.

3 What kinds of challenges did the scientists face when trying to prevent the parrots from becoming extinct?

Write a Website Summary

Parrots Over Puerto Rico describes the plight of parrots living in this region. It also explains scientists' efforts to save endangered parrots through the Puerto Rican Parrot Recovery Program.

Imagine that the Puerto Rican Parrot Recovery Program has set up a webcam to stream live video of the Luquillo Aviary in El Yunque. The webcam allows viewers to watch as eggs hatch and chicks learn to fly. Write a summary for the homepage of the Puerto Rican Parrot Recovery's website. Begin your summary by telling the purpose of the webcam and informing viewers about the program's goals. Then recount the events leading up to the endangerment of the parrots. Explain when and why the program started. Discuss the effects the program has had on the lives of the parrots. Make sure your summary has a clear central idea and inspires readers to watch the video. Don't forget to use some of the Critical Vocabulary words in your writing.

PLAN

Draw a timeline. Using the dates and events in the text, mark the timeline with the information you will use in your summary.

WRITE

Now write your summary for the landing page of the website.

Make sure your website summary

- [ ] introduces viewers to the purpose of the webcam.

- [ ] informs viewers about the program's goals.

- [ ] recounts causes and effects (in order) leading up to the start of the program.

- [ ] recounts details about the effects of program.

Essential Question

How can caring for Earth and its living things improve life now and in the future?

Write an Opinion Essay

PROMPT Think back on what you learned in this module about taking care of Earth and its resources.

Imagine that you've joined a school club called Green Kids. The club invites young people to help the environment in your community. What project can kids in your community do to "go green"? Choose one idea and write an opinion essay for the club's website. State your opinion about why this project is important, and support your opinion with evidence from the texts.

I will write an essay about _____.

Make sure your opinion essay
☐ has an introduction that states your opinion.
☐ presents reasons in an order that makes sense.
☐ uses evidence from the texts to support each reason.
☐ uses linking words and phrases to connect ideas.
☐ has a conclusion that restates your opinion and leaves readers with something to think about.

Think about how to express your opinion clearly and firmly. What reasons support your opinion? Review your notes and the texts for supporting evidence you can use in your writing.

Use the chart below to plan your essay. Write your topic and a sentence that states your opinion. Then write your reasons and the evidence that supports each one. Use Critical Vocabulary words where appropriate.

My Topic: _____

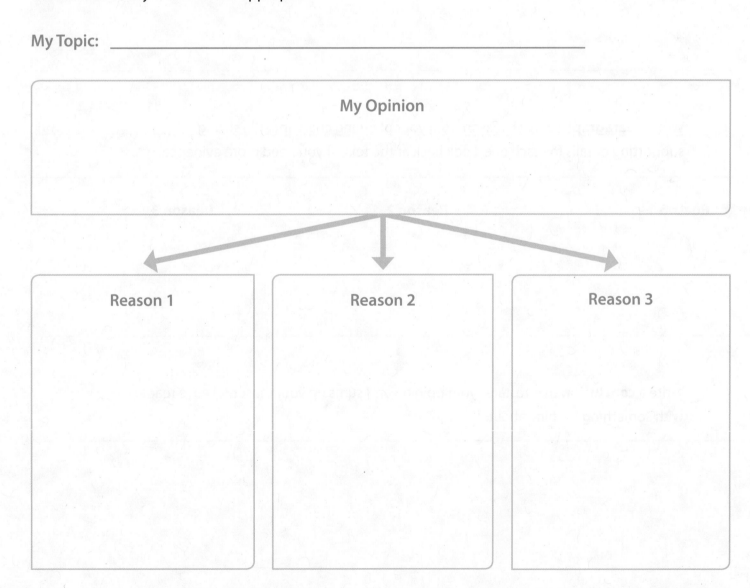

My Opinion

Reason 1

Reason 2

Reason 3

DRAFT .... Write your opinion essay.

Write an **introduction** that clearly states your opinion. Help readers understand why the topic is important.

Write a **paragraph** for each reason from your planning chart. Include strong supporting details for each one. Look back at the texts if you need more evidence.

Reason 1   **Reason 2**   **Reason 3**

Write a **conclusion** that restates your opinion and sums up your reasons. Leave readers with something to think about.

REVISE AND EDIT
.... Review your draft.

Now it's time to review your essay carefully and make improvements. Work with a partner. Share suggestions about how to improve each other's work. Use these questions to help you evaluate and improve your essay.

✓	PURPOSE/ FOCUS	ORGANIZATION	EVIDENCE	LANGUAGE/ VOCABULARY	CONVENTIONS
	☐ Does my introduction clearly state my opinion and engage readers' interest? ☐ Does each reason clearly support my opinion?	☐ Are the reasons presented in an order that makes sense? ☐ Does the conclusion restate my opinion?	☐ Do any of my reasons need additional supporting evidence?	☐ Did I use linking words and phrases to connect the opinion, reasons, and evidence? ☐ Did I use strong persuasive language?	☐ Have I spelled all words correctly? ☐ Did I use commas and other punctuation marks correctly?

PUBLISH
.... Share your work.

Create a Finished Copy. Make a final copy of your opinion essay. Think about including photos, illustrations, or charts that support your position. Consider these options for sharing your essay:

1. Post your essay on a school or class website. Provide concrete suggestions for how other kids can get involved.

2. Make a poster. Include key points from your essay and eye-catching illustrations. Hang the poster in your school or neighborhood.

3. It's never too soon to think about protecting our Earth! Read your essay to a class of younger students. Be prepared to answer their questions.

Glossary

This glossary contains meanings and pronunciations for some of the words in this book. The Full Pronunciation Key shows how to pronounce each consonant and vowel in a special spelling. At the bottom of the glossary pages is a shortened form of the full key.

Full Pronunciation Key

CONSONANT SOUNDS

b	**bib**, ca**bb**age	r	**r**oa**r**, **rh**yme	
ch	**ch**ur**ch**, sti**tch**	s	mi**ss**, **s**au**c**e, **sc**ene, **s**ee	
d	**d**ee**d**, maile**d**, pu**dd**le	sh	di**sh**, **sh**ip, **s**ugar, ti**ss**ue	
f	**f**ast, **f**i**f**e, o**ff**, **ph**rase, rou**gh**	t	**t**igh**t**, stop**p**ed	
g	**g**a**g**, **g**et, fin**g**er	th	ba**th**, **th**in	
h	**h**at, **wh**o	th	ba**the**, **th**is	
hw	**wh**ich, **wh**ere	v	ca**v**e, **v**al**v**e, **v**ine	
j	**j**ud**g**e, **g**em	w	**w**ith, **w**olf	
k	**c**at, **k**ick, s**ch**ool	y	**y**es, **y**olk, on**i**on	
kw	**ch**oir, **qu**ick	z	ro**s**e, si**z**e, **x**ylophone, **z**ebra	
l	**l**id, need**l**e, ta**ll**	zh	gara**g**e, plea**s**ure, vi**s**ion	
m	a**m**, **m**an, du**mb**			
n	**n**o, sudd**en**			
ng	thi**ng**, i**nk**			
p	**p**op, ha**pp**y			

VOWEL SOUNDS

ă	p**a**t, l**au**gh	o͞o	b**oo**t, r**u**de, fr**ui**t, fl**ew**	
ā	**a**pe, **ai**d, p**ay**	ŭ	c**u**t, fl**oo**d, r**ou**gh, s**o**me	
â	**ai**r, c**a**re, w**ea**r	û	c**i**rcle, f**u**r, h**ea**rd, t**e**rm, w**o**rd	
ä	f**a**ther, k**o**ala, y**a**rd			
ĕ	p**e**t, pl**ea**sure, **a**ny	yo͝o	c**u**re, p**u**re	
ē	b**e**, b**ee**, **ea**sy, pian**o**	yo͞o	c**u**be, m**u**sic, f**ew**, c**ue**	
ĭ	**i**f, p**i**t, b**u**sy			
ī	r**i**de, b**y**, p**ie**, h**igh**	ə	**a**go, sil**e**nt, penc**i**l, l**e**mon, circ**u**s	
î	d**ea**r, d**ee**r, f**ie**rce, m**e**re			
ŏ	d**o**t, **o**n			
ō	g**o**, r**o**w, t**oe**, th**ough**			
ô	**a**ll, c**augh**t, p**aw**			
ô	c**o**re, f**o**r, r**oar**			
oi	b**oy**, n**oi**se, **oi**l			
ou	c**ow**, **ou**t			
o͝o	f**u**ll, b**oo**k, w**o**lf			

STRESS MARKS

Primary Stress ´: biology [bī•**ŏl**´•ə•jē]

Secondary Stress ´: biological [bī´•ə•**lŏj**´•ĭ•kəl]

A

acceleration (ăk•sĕl'•ə•rā'•shən) *n.*
Acceleration is the act of moving
faster. The acceleration of the car
around the curve caused it to run off
the road.

· **acceleration**

aggressive (ə•grĕs'•ĭv) *adj.* If
someone is aggressive, he or she is
often angry and ready to attack. The
guard dog took an aggressive posture
when he saw the intruder.

alarming (ə•lärm'•ĭng) *adj.* Something
that is alarming makes you worry that
something bad may happen. The
funnel cloud was an alarming sight.

alternative (ôl•tûr'•nə•tĭv) *n.* An
alternative is a choice or option that
can take the place of something.
Micah chose an apple as a healthier
alternative to cookies.

anchored (ăng'•kərd) *adj.* Something
that is anchored is firmly attached to
something else or weighed down so it
won't move easily. The anchored boat
could not drift out to sea.

artificial (är'•tə•fĭsh'•əl) *adj.* If
something is artificial, it was created
by humans rather than nature.
Scientists have made artificial legs
that function like human legs
for people.

attempted (ə•tĕmp'•tĭd) *v.* If you
attempted something, you tried to do
it. Our dog attempted to dig a large
hole, but I stopped him.

auditorium (ô'•dĭ•tôr'•ē•əm) *n.*
An auditorium is a large room where
an audience gathers for a presentation
or performance. When there is
an assembly, our school uses the
auditorium because it holds the
most people.

Word Origins

auditorium The base word
of *auditorium* comes from the
Latin word *audire*, which
means "to hear."

---

awakening (ə•wā'•kən•ĭng) *v.* If you
are awakening someone, you are
waking him or her from sleep. The
child began awakening at sunrise.

B

benevolent (bə•nĕv'•ə•lənt) *adj.* A
benevolent person or thing is kind.
Volunteering to plant trees is a
benevolent act.

ă r**a**t / ā p**ay** / â c**a**re / ä f**a**ther / ĕ p**e**t / ē b**e** / ĭ p**i**t / ī p**ie** / î f**ie**rce / ŏ p**o**t / ō g**o** / ô p**aw** / ôr f**or** / oi **oi**l / o͝o b**oo**k /

C

captivity (kăp•**tĭv'**•ĭ•tē) *n.* If something is kept in captivity, it is held in a place and cannot get out. The aquarium holds many types of marine life in captivity.

cascading (kăs•**kād'**•ĭng) *v.* Something that is cascading is falling or flowing in a way similar to a waterfall. The water from the stream was cascading down the rocks.

cascading

category (**kăt'**•ə•gôr'•ē) *n.* A category is a group of things that are similar to each other in some way. We place each ball in a different color category.

celestial (sə•**lĕs'**•chəl) *adj.* Something that is celestial is heavenly. On our trip out west, we viewed the star-filled celestial sky.

chugged (chŭgd) *v.* If a machine chugged along, it moved slowly and noisily. The steam train chugged through the mountain passes.

circumstances (**sûr'**•kəm•stăns'•əs) *n.* The way an event happened or the causes of it are its circumstances. Under the circumstances, the picnic was cancelled.

climax (**klī'**•măks') *n.* The climax of a story is its most important event and usually happens near the end. At the exciting climax of the story, the hero ran into a burning building.

complaint (kəm•**plānt'**) *n.* A complaint is an expression of dissatisfaction or pain. His complaint was that the waiter brought him the wrong dinner.

conceived (kən•**sēvd'**) *v.* If you thought of the idea to create something, you conceived it. Cora conceived an idea for a safer bicycle helmet.

conferring (kən•**fûr'**•rĭng) *v.* If you are conferring with someone, you are discussing an idea or trying to make a decision. I saw them conferring about which plan to put into action.

conscious (**kŏn'**•shəs) *adj.* To be conscious of something is to be aware of it. Mario is conscious of how recycling reduces waste.

consequences (**kŏn'**•sĭ•kwĕns'•əs) *n.* Consequences are the outcomes or effects of events. Jay faced the consequences of being late when he found the store had already closed.

consisted (kən•**sĭs'**•tĭd) *v.* If something consisted of certain items, it was made up of those things. The salad consisted of lettuce, carrots, broccoli, celery, tomatoes, and olives.

ōō b**oo**t / ou **ou**t / ŭ c**u**t / û f**u**r / hw **wh**ich / th **th**in / *th* **th**is / zh vi**s**ion / ə **a**go, sil**e**nt, penc**i**l, lem**o**n, circ**u**s

contaminate (kən•**tăm′**•ə•nāt′) *v.* To contaminate something is to add a harmful substance to it. Some weed killers are harmful chemicals that contaminate soil and water.

contempt (kən•**tĕmpt′**) *n.* When you show contempt, you show little or no respect for someone or something. The look on her face shows contempt for her loss.

contents (**kŏn′**•tĕnts′) *n.* The contents of a document are the topics or subjects it includes. The contents of the book were several chapters.

contradict (kŏn′•trə•**dĭkt′**) *v.* To contradict something is to say or do the opposite of it. When we contradict each other about which way to go, we will likely get lost.

contribution (kŏn′•trĭ•**byōō′**•shən) *n.* A person who helps to make something has made a contribution to that work. The jet engine was an important contribution to air travel.

cylinder (**sĭl′**•ən•dər) *n.* A cylinder has circular ends and straight sides. In an engine, a cylinder takes in gas to make other parts move. The mechanic replaced the leaky cylinder with a new one.

D

dainty (**dān′**•tē) *adj.* Something that is dainty is delicate. The bee landed on the dainty petals of the flower.

deficiencies (dĭ•**fĭsh′**•ən•sēz) *n.* If someone has deficiencies, he or she has weaknesses or flaws. The student was tutored in math to correct her deficiencies.

delirious (dĭ•**lîr′**•ē•əs) *adj.* When someone is delirious, he or she is confused due to fever or illness. Her fever was so high she was delirious, and it was difficult for her to think or sleep.

densely (**dĕns**•**lē′**) *adv.* If something is covered densely, the covering is so thick that it is difficult to see through. The ivy densely covered the house making it hard to see the window.

densely

depleted (dĭ•**plē′**•tĭd) *adj.* Something that is depleted is worn out. The artist could not finish her painting with her depleted set of paints.

destruction (dĭ•**strŭk′**•shən) *n.* Destruction is the act of destroying or ruining something. The destruction of buildings is often widespread during an earthquake.

ă rat / ā **pay** / â c**are** / ä f**ather** / ĕ p**et** / ē b**e** / ĭ p**it** / ī p**ie** / î f**ie**rce / ŏ p**ot** / ō g**o** / ô p**aw** / ôr f**or** / oi **oi**l / ŏŏ b**oo**k /

dialogue (dī′•ə•lôg′) *n.* The dialogue is the conversation among characters in a story. The way this character speaks in his dialogue helps me understand more about him.

> **Word Origins**
>
> **dialogue** One meaning of *dialogue* comes from the Greek word *dialegesthai*, which means "to discuss."

distinguished (dǐ•stǐng′•gwǐsht) *adj.* A distinguished group is known and respected for its excellence. The distinguished inventor won an award for excellence in airplane design.

ditty (dǐt′•ē) *n.* A ditty is a song or poem that is short and cheerful. The children sang a little ditty at recess.

domain (dō•mān′) *n.* Someone's domain is the land or territory that he or she owns and controls. This farm has been our family domain for many years.

E

eccentric (ǐk•sěn′•trǐk) *adj.* Someone who is eccentric is odd. The eccentric inventor was always working on odd projects.

elite (ǐ•lēt′) *adj.* Elite members of a group are those who are the best or most skilled. The most elite athletes are invited to compete in the Olympics.

employed (ěm•ploǐd′) *v.* If you hired people to do a job, you employed them. She is employed at a local coffee shop.

employed

endangered (ěn•dān′•jərd) *adj.* To be endangered is to be at risk of great harm or death. Animal species that are endangered might disappear from the planet forever.

epic (ěp′•ǐk) *adj.* An epic event is very large and impressive, and sometimes heroic. Thousands of workers faced great danger during the epic construction of the Egyptian pyramids.

evacuation (ǐ•văk′•yōo•ā′•shən) *n.* An evacuation is the act of moving from a dangerous area to a safer one. The governor ordered an evacuation of their city, so Linda and her mom packed up their car and left.

eventually (ǐ•věn′•chōo•ə•lē) *adv.* To state that something will happen eventually means that it will happen at some time, usually after a series of other events. The horse will eventually reach the finish line.

ōo b**oo**t / ou **ou**t / ŭ c**u**t / û f**u**r / hw **wh**ich / th **th**in / *th* **th**is / zh vi**si**on / ə **a**go, sil**e**nt, penc**i**l, lem**o**n, circ**u**s

evidently (ĕv'·ĭ·dənt·lē) *adv.* If something happened evidently, it happened for an obvious reason. Evidently, Lilah had a very bad fall.

excel (ĭk·sĕl') *v.* To excel at something is to be very good at it. Keep practicing and you will excel.

F

fastenings (făs'·ə·nĭngs) *n.* Fastenings attach objects to other things. Dad repaired the fastenings that attached the door to the frame.

favorable (fā'·vər·ə·bəl) *adj.* Something that is favorable gives a benefit or contributes to success. He always makes a favorable impression because he is so friendly.

flight (flīt) *n.* Flight is the act of flying through the air. We stood at the water's edge and watched the birds in flight.

flop (flŏp) *n.* Something that is a flop is a complete failure. The cake he baked was a flop.

foreword (fôr'·wərd) *n.* The introduction to a book is called its foreword. You should read the book's foreword before you read the rest of the story.

fort (fôrt) *n.* A fort is a strong building usually protected by guards and a wall. We toured an old, stone fort while we were on vacation.

fort

foundations (foun·dā'·shəns) *n.* Foundations are the base pieces houses and buildings are built upon. Workers laid the foundations before the houses could be built.

frolics (frŏl'·ĭkz) *n.* Frolics are fun acts, such as dances or parties. All of us enjoy nice frolics in the meadow on a warm spring day.

G

gadgets (găj'·ĭts) *n.* Gadgets are small, specialized machines or electronic devices. The toolbox at the hardware store had various gadgets.

H

handy (hăn'·dē) *adj.* Something that is handy is very useful. A lasso is a very handy item for a rancher.

hardships (härd'·shĭpz') *n.* Hardships are difficulties or suffering caused by not having enough of something. Some people face hardships like not having enough water.

hazard (hăz'·ərd) *n.* A hazard is a danger. Watch out for the storm surge; it is a major hazard.

ă r**a**t / ā p**ay** / â c**a**re / ä f**a**ther / ĕ p**e**t / ē b**e** / ĭ p**i**t / ī p**ie** / î f**ie**rce / ŏ p**o**t / ō g**o** / ô p**aw** / ôr f**or** / oi **oi**l / o͝o b**oo**k /

hesitate (hĕz′•ĭ•tāt′) *v.* If you hesitate, you wait to speak or act because you're not sure what to say or do. I saw Samantha hesitate before jumping off the diving board.

homestead (hōm′•stĕd′) *n.* In the late 1800s, a homestead was a piece of land in America's western regions that was claimed, lived on, and settled by a pioneer. After many long years of living on this land, the homestead became ours.

humble (hŭm′•bəl) *adj.* If something is humble, it is simple and not impressive. Just beyond the city is a humble cottage.

I

ideology (ī′•dē•ŏl′ə•jē) *n.* An ideology is a set of beliefs. Her ideology about the company did not always match her boss's, but they found a way to work together.

illustrious (ĭ•lŭs′•trē•əs) *adj.* An illustrious person is famous for his or her achievements. The illustrious inventor was known around the world.

imperil (ĭm•pĕr′•əl) *v.* To imperil someone or something is to put it in danger. Military men and women imperil their lives to protect our country.

implying (ĭm•plī′•ĭng) *v.* If you are implying something, you are expressing it without stating it directly. By pausing the story and looking up at us, our teacher was implying that we should stop talking.

impoverished (ĭm•pŏv′•ə•rĭsht) *adj.* To be impoverished is to be poor. Aid workers came from all over the world to bring food and medicine to the impoverished village.

impulse (ĭm′•pŭls′) *n.* An impulse is the desire to do something. Our impulse was to take every puppy in the pound.

incandescent (ĭn′•kən•dĕs′•ənt) *adj.* Something that is incandescent gives off a lot of light. We replaced the burnt out light bulbs with incandescent bulbs.

incandescent

indispensable (ĭn′•dĭ•spĕn′•sə•bəl) *adj.* Something that is indispensable is necessary. The mayor needed to prove that he was indispensable by solving the city's big problems.

ōō b**oo**t / ou **ou**t / ŭ c**u**t / û f**u**r / hw **wh**ich / th **th**in / *th* **th**is / zh vi**s**ion / ə **a**go, sil**e**nt, penc**i**l, lem**o**n, circ**u**s

influence (ĭn'·floo·əns) *v.* If you influence something, you affect it or cause a certain outcome. Store managers influence customers to buy certain products by choosing which items to display.

inspector (ĭn·spĕk'·tər) *n.* An inspector reviews or examines something carefully. An inspector checked the tomatoes to make sure they were clean.

Word Origins

inspector The Latin suffix *-or* means "someone that performs a specific action." The Latin root *inspect* means "to look something over carefully." Thus *inspector* means "someone who examines or inspects something carefully."

irrigate (ĭr'·ĭ·gāt') *v.* To irrigate crops is to supply them with water through a system of pipes, sprinklers, or streams. Farmers in some areas must irrigate their fields in order for crops to grow.

J

jabbing (jă·bĭng') *v.* If you are jabbing something, you are poking it quickly with a great deal of power. My sister began jabbing me to get my attention.

K

knowledge (nŏl'·ĭj) *n.* If you have knowledge, you have information or understanding about something. Our teacher gave us the knowledge we need to succeed in class.

L

lateral (lăt'·ər·əl) *adj.* If something moves in a lateral way, it moves side to side. Only some chess pieces can make a lateral move.

literally (lĭt'·ər·ə·lē) *adv.* If you say something literally happened, that means it actually happened, and you aren't exaggerating or using a metaphor. It literally rained for five days in a row.

locomotives (lō'·kə·mō'·tĭvz) *n.* Locomotives are the engines that make a train go forward. Locomotives pulling freight cars leave the railroad yard every thirty minutes.

locomotives

ă r**a**t / ā **pay** / â c**a**re / ä f**a**ther / ĕ p**e**t / ē b**e** / ĭ p**i**t / ī p**ie** / î f**ie**rce / ŏ p**o**t / ō g**o** / ô p**aw** / ôr f**or** / oi **oi**l / o͝o b**oo**k /

M

magnitude (**măg′•**nĭ•tōōd′) *n.* Magnitude refers to the size of something. The magnitude of the Alaskan earthquake was 9.2.

Word Origins

magnitude The word *magnitude* comes from the Latin word *magnus* meaning "great." Thus the word *magnitude* refers to the greatness in size of something.

---

maintenance (**mān′•**tə•nəns) *n.* The maintenance of something is the act of taking care of it and repairing it when needed. The maintenance needed to keep the school in good condition requires everyone's help.

maneuver (mə•**nōō′•**vər) *v.* To maneuver something is to move it. In the Special Olympics, competitors are able to maneuver their wheelchairs in a variety of ways.

matted (**măt′•**ĭd) *adj.* Something that is matted is a tangled mess. The dog's fur was so matted that we had to shave the dog.

matted

merchant (**mûr′•**chənt) *adj.* A merchant ship carries products to sell, usually to a foreign country. The merchant ship is loaded with cargo at the dock.

midland (**mĭd′•**lənd) *n.* The middle of a country is sometimes called the midland. Many pioneers began their journey west at Independence, Missouri, in America's midland.

mobile (**mō′•**bəl) *adj.* Something that is mobile is able to move or be moved easily. Mobile news vans cover the latest stories as they happen.

modified (**mŏd′•**ə•fīd′) *adj.* A modified version of something is a revised, or changed, version. The plans for the house were modified in case of flooding.

mysterious (mĭ•**stîr′•**ē•əs) *adj.* Something that is mysterious is not fully understood or explainable. Nobody knows what is in the mysterious box.

N

native (**nā′•**tĭv) *adj.* A person, animal, or plant that is described as native to a place, was born in that place. Sunflowers are native to the northern regions in the United States.

ōō b**oo**t / ou **out** / ŭ c**u**t / û f**u**r / hw **wh**ich / th **th**in / *th* **th**is / zh vi**s**ion / ə **a**go, sil**e**nt, penc**i**l, lem**o**n, circ**u**s

notable (nō'•tə•bəl) *adj.* If something is notable, it is worth noticing. The scientist measured a notable increase in the hurricane's strength.

O

objective (əb•jĕk'•tĭv) *n.* An objective is a goal. His objective was to do his best at the race.

oblivious (ə•blĭv'•ē•əs) *adj.* If someone is oblivious to something, he or she is unaware of it. He was oblivious to the person behind him.

P

packet (păk'•ĭt) *n.* A packet is a small container or envelope. Aunt Jane poured the seeds from the packet into the planter.

panic (păn'•ĭk) *n.* Panic is a feeling of strong fear that leaves someone unable to think clearly. When the hero of the movie was in danger, the audience had a feeling of panic.

Word Origins

panic The word *panic* comes from the ancient Greek mythological god, Pan. He was the god of the wild, woods, and shepherds. Pan was noted for causing fear amongst flocks of sheep.

---

parallel (păr'•ə•lĕl') *adj.* If two or more things are parallel to each other, they move in the same direction. The highway was marked with yellow parallel lines.

passionate (păsh'•ə•nĭt) *adj.* To have a passionate feeling is to have strong emotions about it. The researcher is passionate about her work in the hospital laboratory.

patents (păt'•nts) *n.* Patents are legal documents. If you get a patent for an invention, no one else is allowed to make or sell it. Scientists protect their inventions with patents so no one can copy them.

patriotic (pā'•trē•ŏt'•ĭk) *adj.* People who act in a patriotic way toward a country show that they love that country. When people say the Pledge of Allegiance, it shows that they are being patriotic.

phonograph (fō'•nə•grăf') *n.* A phonograph is a machine that plays recorded music or sound. Long ago people played music on a phonograph.

phonograph

ă rat / ā **pay** / â **c**are / ä **fa**ther / ĕ **pe**t / ē be / ĭ **pi**t / ī **pie** / î **fie**rce / ŏ **po**t / ō **go** / ô **paw** / ôr **for** / oi **oil** / o͝o bo͝ok /

photographed (**fō'**·tə·grăfd') *v.* If someone or something was photographed, its photo was recorded on film or as a computer file. Leon photographed important events for our school's yearbook.

plod (plŏd) *v.* To plod is to move heavily and slowly. We watched the horse plod through the snow.

plots (plŏts) *n.* Plots are small sections of land that are used for a certain purpose. Our neighborhood shares small plots of land to grow vegetables.

porthole (**pôrt'**·hōl') *n.* A porthole is a small round window on a ship. I looked out the porthole in my room as the ship approached land.

posts (pōsts) *n.* Posts were forts or stopping places along the trail where people could buy supplies. Pioneers found posts along the major trails where they could buy supplies.

presiding (prĭ·**zī'**·dĭng) *gerund* If you are presiding over an event, you are in charge of it. The judge is presiding over the courtroom.

prestigious (prě·**stē'**·jəs) *adj.* Something prestigious is impressive and important. The most prestigious award in our school is Student of the Year.

primary (**prī'**·měr'·ē) *adj.* Something that is primary is the highest in importance. My uncle's primary home is downtown, but he also has a house on the lake.

prior (**prī'**·ər) *adj.* Prior means coming before, in time or order. Prior to driving, my mother checks to see that I have fastened my seatbelt.

projected (**prŏ'**·jĕk·tĭd') *v.* Something that is projected may appear to be real but is not. The snowboarder in the 3-D movie was projected into the room.

projected

proportions (prə·**pôr'**·shənz) *n.* When you talk about the proportions of something, you talk about its size. The proportions of the furniture fit the size of the dollhouse perfectly.

prose (prōz) *n.* Unlike poetry, prose is "ordinary writing," in the form of sentences and paragraphs. Most stories are written as prose, but some are written as poems.

ōo b**oo**t / ou **ou**t / ŭ c**u**t / û f**u**r / hw **wh**ich / th **th**in / *th* **th**is / zh vi**s**ion / ə **a**go, sil**e**nt, penc**i**l, lem**o**n, circ**u**s

391

prototype (**prō'**·tə·tīp') *n.*
A prototype is a rough model created to test something before creating it in its final form. We built a prototype to show what the real robot would look like.

R

radiate (**rā'**·dē·āt') *v.* To radiate is to spread out in waves or rays. Shock waves radiate from the epicenter of an earthquake just as ripples radiate in a pond.

Word Origins

radiate The word *radiate* comes from the Latin word *radiāt-* meaning "to emit beams" and is derived from the Latin word *radius* meaning "rays." Thus the word *radiate* means " to emit beams or rays" as in the sentence, Heat will radiate from the stove.

---

reasonable (**rē'**·zə·nə·bəl) *adj.* If something is reasonable, it is logical and easy to understand. It is reasonable for this father to think that his son knocked over the planter and spilled dirt on the ground.

reasonable

reduce (rĭ·**dōōs'**) *v.* To reduce something is to decrease the size or amount of it. You can reduce waste when you recycle.

refrain (rĭ·**frān'**) *n.* A refrain is a verse or phrase that is repeated in a song or poem. Her mom sang the verses and Emma sang the refrain.

regaled (**rē'**·gəld) *v.* If you regaled someone, you entertained them. Chen regaled her family with funny stories about her day.

regions (**rē'**·jənz) *n.* Regions are areas. Many regions in the western United States had damage due to wildfires.

reservoir (**rĕz'**·ər·vwär') *n.*
A reservoir is a place where a supply of something is collected. The water behind the dam formed into a reservoir.

residence (**rĕz'**·ĭ·dəns) *n.* A residence is a place in which people live. Our residence is on the west side of town.

restless (**rĕst'**·lĭs) *adj.* If you are restless, you find it hard to relax or stay still. The child was tired after a restless night's sleep.

ă r**a**t / ā p**ay** / â c**a**re / ä f**a**ther / ĕ p**e**t / ē b**e** / ĭ p**i**t / ī p**ie** / î f**ie**rce / ŏ p**o**t / ō g**o** / ô p**aw** / ôr f**or** / oi **oi**l / ōō b**oo**k /

restrain (rĭ·**strān′**) *v.* When you restrain yourself, you stop yourself from doing what you want to do. Our dog was able to restrain herself from taking food off of the table.

retreat (rĭ·**trēt′**) *v.* If you retreat, you move back or away from something. The tortoise will retreat into its shell when it feels threatened.

Word Origins

retreat The prefix *re-* means "again" or "back." Thus *retreat* means "pull back." Many common English words begin with *re-* and have base words from Latin: *require*, *revere*, *restrain*, and *remove*.

revere (rĭ·**vîr′**) *v.* If you revere someone, you think very highly of that person. I revere people whose inventions improve the world.

S

sacrifice (**săk′**·rə·fīs′) *n.* A sacrifice is the act of giving up something valued to get something else. Janice made a sacrifice when she gave up her blankets and other supplies to help the victims after the storm.

scrawled (skrôld) *v.* If you scrawled something, you wrote it quickly and sloppily. He scrawled a note on a piece of paper before he left the house.

seismographs (**sīz′**·mə·grăfs′) *n.* Seismographs are instruments that measure and record details about earthquakes, such as their strength and how long they last. Seismographs tell us that moderate earthquakes often last 10 to 30 seconds.

seized (sēzd) *v.* If you were seized by an idea or feeling, you were suddenly overwhelmed by it. I was seized by fear when I saw the huge snake at the zoo.

slogans (**slō′**·gənz) *n.* Slogans are short phrases that are catchy and easy to remember. We saw several billboards with eye-catching slogans advertising products.

specialized (**spĕsh′**·ə·līzd) *v.* If a company specialized in something, it provided a specific type of product. My father used a company that specialized in making wheelchairs.

spectacle (**spĕk′**·tə·kəl) *n.* A spectacle is an unusual or interesting sight. The fireworks show was an amazing spectacle.

spontaneous (spŏn·**tā′**·nē·əs) *adj.* A spontaneous action is one that happens naturally and isn't planned. She made a spontaneous decision to jump into the lake.

ōō b**oo**t / ou **ou**t / ŭ c**u**t / û f**u**r / hw **wh**ich / th **th**in / *th* **th**is / zh vi**s**ion / ə **a**go, sil**e**nt, penc**i**l, lem**o**n, circ**u**s

sputtered (**spŭt'•**ərd) *v.* If something sputtered, it worked in a rough or uneven way and made popping noises. The engine sputtered as the car drove down the road.

stubble (**stŭb'•**əl) *n.* Stubble is the short, stiff stalks of plants that remain in a field after harvesting. After the tractor moved across the field, all that was left of the corn plants were rows of stubble.

stubble

surge (sûrj) *n.* A surge is a sudden powerful movement forward or upward. A surge of water from the hurricane flooded coastal areas.

T

tendrils (**tĕn'•**drəls) *n.* Tendrils of plants are long, thin sections that often twist around an object or another plant. The plant had long tendrils that wrapped around the other plant.

tendrils

thresh (thrĕsh) *v.* To thresh a plant is to beat it in order to separate its grain or seeds from the rest of the plant. Neighbors often helped one another thresh the wheat.

thrust (thrŭst) *v.* To thrust is to push something with great force. The violent movement of the earthquake thrust the ground up through the pavement.

toddles (**tŏd'•**lz) *v.* When a child toddles, he or she walks with short, unsteady steps. My little sister toddles when she walks.

toil (toĭl) *v.* To toil is to work. The worker had to toil to collect all of the vegetables.

track (trăk) *v.* To track something is to watch it and see where it moves and how it changes. Meteorologists track storms to warn people in their path.

traditional (trə•**dĭsh'•**ə•nəl) *adj.* Something that is traditional has been made or done in a certain way for a very long time. It is traditional to wear red, white, and blue on Independence Day.

transcend (trăn•**sĕnd'**) *v.* If you transcend a boundary, you go above or beyond it. Astronauts must transcend limitations and challenges.

ă **r**at / ā **pay** / â **c**are / ä **fa**ther / ĕ **p**et / ē **be** / ĭ **p**it / ī **pie** / î **fie**rce / ŏ **p**ot / ō **go** / ô **paw** / ôr **for** / oi **oi**l / o͞o **boo**k /

transform (trăns•**fôrm'**) *v.* If you transform something, you change it from one thing to another. Kayla is able to transform a sheet of paper into a paper animal.

tremor (**trĕm'**•ər) *n.* A tremor is a small earthquake or uncontrolled shaking in a body part. The tremor that shook the town was minor and did little damage.

Word Origins

tremor The word *tremor* comes from the Latin word *tremere*, which means "to tremble."

---

triggered (**trĭg'**•ərd) *v.* If you triggered an action or event, you did something to start it. My hand triggered the dominoes falling.

typical (**tĭp'**•ĭ•kəl) *adj.* If something is typical, it is usual or normal. My mom dropped me off at school at the typical time.

U

urban (**ûr'**•bən) *adj.* Something that is urban is related to a city. As our population grows, urban areas expand.

urban

V

victim (**vĭk'**•tĭm) *n.* If you fall victim to something, you suffer or die because of it. Rescuers carried a victim of the storm's devastation.

victory (**vĭk'**•tə•rē) *n.* When you achieve a victory, you overcome a challenge or win against a competitor. Reaching the end of the long and difficult tournament was a victory for the winning soccer team.

W

watchful (**wŏch'**•fəl) *adj.* If you are watchful, you pay attention to everything around you. An owl is a watchful animal.

widespread (**wīd'**•sprĕd') *adj.* If something is widespread, it happens over a large area or among many people. The ash that spewed from the volcano was widespread.

witness (**wĭt'**•nĭs) *n.* A witness is someone who appears in court to say what he or she knows about a crime. The witness saw what happened and promises to tell the whole truth about it.

Y

yield (yēld) *v.* To yield means to produce or create something. The field will yield a larger crop because there has been plenty of rain.

ōō b**oo**t / ou **ou**t / ŭ c**u**t / û f**u**r / hw **wh**ich / th **th**in / *th* **th**is / zh vi**si**on / ə **a**go, sil**e**nt, penc**i**l, lem**o**n, circ**u**s

Index of Titles and Authors

Acknowledgments

Excerpt from *Airborn* by Kenneth Oppel. Text copyright © 2004 by Kenneth Oppel. Reprinted by permission of HarperCollins Publishers and Writer's House, LLC.

Excerpt from *Captain Arsenio: Adventures and (Mis)adventures in Flight* by Pablo Bernasconi. Copyright © 2005 by Pablo Bernasconi. Reprinted by permission of Pablo Bernasconi.

"The Celestials' Railroad" by Bruce Watson from *Cobblestone Magazine,* January 2008. Text copyright © 2008 by Carus Publishing Company. Reprinted by permission of Cricket Media. All Cricket Media material is copyrighted by Carus Publishing d/b/a Cricket Media, and/or various authors and illustrators. Any commercial use or distribution of material without permission is strictly prohibited. Please visit http://www.cricketmedia.com/info/licensing2 for licensing and http://www.cricketmedia.com for subscriptions.

Excerpt from *Eruption! Volcanoes and the Science of Saving Lives* by Elizabeth Rusch, photographs by Tom Uhlman. Text copyright © 2013 by Elizabeth Rusch. Photographs copyright © 2013 by Tom Uhlman. Reprinted by permission of Houghton Mifflin Harcourt Publishing Company.

Excerpts from *Explore the Wild West!* by Anita Yasuda, illustrated by Alex Joon Kim. Copyright © 2012 by Nomad Press, a division of Nomad Communications Inc. Reprinted by permission of Susan Schulman Literary Agency LLC on behalf of Nomad Communications Inc.

Excerpt from "Wheelchair Sports: Hang-Glider to Wheeler-Dealer" from *Faster, Higher, Smarter: Bright Ideas That Transformed Sports* by Simon Shapiro, illustrated by Theo Krynauw. Text copyright © 2016 by Simon Shapiro. Illustrations copyright © 2016 by Theo Krynauw. Reprinted by permission of Annick Press Ltd.

Excerpt from *The Good Garden* by Katie Smith Milway, illustrated by Sylvie Daigneault. Text copyright © 2010 by Katie Smith Milway. Illustrations copyright © by Sylvie Daigneault. Reprinted by permission of Kids Can Press Ltd., Toronto, Canada.

Excerpt from *Hurricanes: The Science Behind Killer Storms* by Dr. Alvin Silverstein, Virginia Silverstein, and Laura Silverstein Nunn. Text copyright © 2010 by Dr. Alvin Silverstein, Virginia Silverstein, and Laura Silverstein Nunn. Reprinted by permission of Enslow Publishing.

Excerpt from *The Inventor's Secret: What Thomas Edison Told Henry Ford* by Suzanne Slade, illustrated by Jennifer Black Reinhardt. Text copyright © 2015 by Suzanne Slade. Illustrations copyright © 2015 by Jennifer Reinhardt. Reprinted by permission of Charlesbridge Publishing, Inc.

Excerpt from *Jane Goodall: 40 Years at Gombe* by Jane Goodall. Text copyright © 2010 by Jane Goodall. Reprinted by permission of Express Permissions on behalf of Stewart, Tabori, & Chang, an imprint of Harry N. Abrams, Inc., New York.

The Miracle of Spring by Helen Hanna. Text copyright © 2013 by Helen Hanna. Reprinted by permission of *Plays, the Drama Magazine for Young People/*Sterling Partners Inc.

"Quaking Earth, Racing Waves" by Rachel Young, art by Jo Lynn Alcorn from *ASK* Magazine, October 2005. Text copyright © 2005 by Carus Publishing Company. Reprinted by permission of Cricket Media. All Cricket Media material is copyrighted by Carus Publishing d/b/a Cricket Media, and/or various authors and illustrators. Any commercial use or distribution of material without permission is strictly prohibited. Please visit http://www.cricketmedia.com/info/licensing2 for licensing and http://www.cricketmedia.com for subscriptions.

Parrots Over Puerto Rico by Susan L. Roth and Cindy Trumbore, illustrated by Susan L. Roth. Text copyright © 2013 by Susan L. Roth and Cindy Trumbore. Illustrations copyright © 2013 by Susan L. Roth. Reprinted by permission of Lee & Low Books Inc.

Excerpt from *A Pioneer Sampler: The Daily Life of a Pioneer Family in 1840* by Barbara Greenwood, illustrated by Heather Collins. Text copyright © 1994 by Barbara Greenwood. Illustrations copyright © 1994 by Heather Collins/Glyphics. Reprinted by permission of Houghton Mifflin Harcourt Publishing Company and Kids Can Press Ltd., Toronto, Canada.

Credits